CE 330 Ramanos

This book is treated as a RESERVE
book — See the POSTED RULES

It MUST be returned to the desk

If loaned OVERNIGHT — it must be
returned by 9:00 a. m. on the day
after it was loaned if the library
is open

AUTOMATIC FINES will be assessed
for violations

**National Transportation
Policy in Transition**

National Transportation Policy in Transition

Herman Mertins, Jr.
Public Administration Program
West Virginia University
Morgantown, West Virginia

Lexington Books
D.C. Heath and Company
Lexington, Massachusetts
Toronto   London

Library of Congress Cataloging in Publication Data

Mertins, Herman.
    National transportation policy in transition.

    Bibliography: p.
    1. Transportation and state- United States.
I. Title.
HE203.M38   380.5'0973   72-3553
ISBN 0-669-84426-8

Published simultaneously in Canada.

Printed in the United States of America.

International Standard Book Number: 0-669-84426-8

Library of Congress Catalog Card Number: 72-3553

To the Senior Mertins

Contents

List of Figures and Tables

PREFACE

This book is designed to provide a framework for evaluating national transportation policy in the United States. But its focus is not only directed toward the historical past; the book intends to reflect concern for future prospects of national transportation policy. It interprets the present as a period of transition in which crucial decisions governing the potential impact of the federal role are being made.

The book emphasizes the importance of maintaining a realistic perspective on both the evolution and future of national transportation policy. To accomplish this goal, its contents have been designed to deal with past efforts to integrate national transportation policy formulation; mechanisms used to implement these efforts; results that have been achieved; and pressures now emerging to develop more comprehensive strategies for the future.

One point of view of the author, based on considerable evidence, is that past attempts to have the federal government assume and perform the role of an "organizing force" for rationalizing transportation policy have been largely unsuccessful. A corollary is that this failure has resulted in an accumulation of knotty policy problems that are intensifying and growing in number in the modern era. Balanced against this sum of discouraging results are a number of hopeful signs, recently emerged and still taking form, indicating that some important shifts from past practices may be in the offing.

Throughout the study, particular attention is given to the federal role in influencing and shaping national transportation development. The imperatives for federal policy leadership are seen as magnifying in the wake of continued urbanization, the rapidly growing need for inter-modal planning, the crises brought about by a growing tide of transportation demand that cannot be accommodated by traditional supply, and the impact of technological change.

The plan of the book is to synthesize and interpret events and issues that appear to have been most significant in evolving transportation policy. The first three chapters are devoted to analyzing the character of the federal role in developing and influencing the use of national transportation resources. Questions examined include: How has the interaction of governmental policy and private-enterprise activities molded the national transportation system? What attempts have been made to restructure policy mechanisms and what do the outcomes portend? How significant are precedent and tradition to the future of national transportation policy? What influences will the blending of transportation and environmental planning have on future policy?

In the fourth chapter, the process that led to the formation of the Department of Transportation is analyzed in terms of its antecedents, conflicts of political power, and the strengths and limitations of the organization that emerged. The role DOT should play in developing national transportation investment standards and criteria is examined closely.

The fifth chapter is a direct outgrowth of the standards-and-criteria question. It evaluates the application of cost-benefit analysis to highway planning and how this approach is being extended into other aspects of transportation planning. Various models, ranging from those traditionally employed to those that offer considerably more potential for future application, are analyzed.

The sixth and seventh chapters are devoted to examining the policy implications of technological change. Here, I give primary attention to the federal role in instigating such change, as well as in discouraging it. For example, the study analyzes federal efforts to create a new mode of transportation — High Speed Ground Transportation — and its abortive attempt to sponsor development of the Supersonic Transport. Also identified and discussed in these chapters are a number of the major barriers to innovation in transportation which either have faced or will face federal policy-makers.

The final chapter highlights a number of the major characteristics of transportation policy formation and identifies critical factors that could change the emphases and directions of future policies. These possibilities are viewed in terms of alternative futures which will depend on the mix of programs that are selected.

For assistance in the preparation of this book, the author is indebted to more people than can be mentioned here. However, I would like to express my appreciation to those individuals who were important in bringing the book into being.

The author is grateful to Bertram M. Gross who suggested that the book be undertaken and who provided encouragement and stimulating challenge, particularly in the early phases of its development; Guthrie S. Birkhead who offered full support throughout its preparation and valuable criticism that improved the quality of the manuscript; Frank N. Marini whose evaluations of the research contributed importantly to its completion in this form; and Peter A. Rumsey who worked with the author in an examination of the transportation sector that preceded this study.

The author is particularly indebted to his wife, Barbara J. Mertins, who not only was a source of continuing encouragement, but also assisted in many phases of the research and review of the manuscript. Finally, special appreciation is due to Carol Sue Cummins and Lucille A. Bottorff who worked so diligently in typing the manuscript in final form.

Introduction

The 1970s portend a number of basic changes in the fundamental thrust of national transportation policy in the United States.

Certainly justification for such a reorientation exists in overwhelming quantity. Even from the limited perspective of the local scene, virtually every individual experiences growing difficulties in securing adequate levels of transportation service in journeying to and from work, to recreation and shopping, on business trips and in a host of other ways. Or, if one wishes, he may raise his sights above local concerns and review the major classes of national tranportation problems emerging in each of the modes. Here again the array of problems is huge — and still growing. Yet the dimensions of the challenge appear in even sharper outline when viewed against the composite background of national population growth, the well-established trend toward higher-density concentration of people and industry, and the steadily growing environmental crisis. Each of these views of the transportation scene reveals a number of the failures and shortcomings of national transportation policy — past and present.

Fortunately the cumulative effects of all these crises have begun to forge new strategies for reorienting policy at the federal level. The beginnings are small but are growing significantly. New federal commitments have been made; a limited number of innovative programs are under way. Moreover, now more than ever, the federal government possesses the capability of exercising the greatest influence over the direction of transportation policy development. The question remains whether it will capitalize on its new perceptions of need and grasp the opportunities at hand.

How does this book differ in its treatment of transportation compared to other works in the field? The answer lies in the nature of the focus. Many books on transportation concern themselves primarily with economics — certainly an important subject. Detailed attention has been devoted to matters of transportation pricing and efficiency, rate policy, subsidies, development of the individual modes and of course, regulation.

The primary focus of this work relates to the political, administrative, and institutional aspects of transportation policy. In this dimension, comprehensive national transportation policy is interpreted as potentially performing a more far-reaching, catalytical function in our society than ever before, thus exerting an enormous influence on all sectors of national life.

By the same token, in my view, it is apparent that if adequate coordination of transportation policy fails to evolve, the full potential of the nation — both human and material — cannot be tapped. Nowhere is this point more evident than when one analyzes the continuing urbanization taking place in the United States, as well as all over the world. Where transportation policies provide a rich network, varied and capable of adjusting to dynamic change, the opportunities for high-quality urban life are enhanced. But where transportation policy fails, and thus access to employment opportunities, social intercourse, cultural advantage's, and markets is restricted, the potentialities for enhanced human advancement, at least in part, must go unrealized.

The effects of transportation policy also heavily influence the scope of national wealth, power, growth and prestige. In fact, at some of the most critical junctures in United States history, the cumulative effects of such policy have played a fundamental role in spatially integrating the nation and in assuring its survival in the face of outside threats.

However, the fact that the United States is the most prosperous country of the world and has survived periods of national emergency hardly gives an indication of the adequacy of past national transportation policy. It reveals little about the degree to which federal policy has been responsible for developing this national capacity. Likewise, it tells us nothing about the nature of the federal role in stimulating development within the transportation sector. Nor does it show whether comprehensive policy formation would be either feasible or desirable in the future.

The examination of federal involvement in national transportation evolution poses a number of fundamental questions. How has the interaction of governmental policy and private-enterprise activities molded the character of national transportation systems? What strategies have been employed at the federal level to rationalize the formation of transportation policy? In what manner does structural change within the federal government affect the development of national transportation policy? Does the Department of Transportation, now well into its first decade of existence, provide a means for integrating transportation policy on a national scale? What are the discernible signals that suggest possibilities of a new orientation of national transportation policy?

The Approach Utilized

This book represents one approach to evaluating national transportation policy. It attempts to synthesize and interpret the events and issues that appear to have played the most influential roles in creating policy — such as it is.

There are a number of things that the book does not attempt. First, to achieve manageability of content, detailed review of a number of subjects has not been undertaken. Thus, labor problems pertinent to national transportation are excluded. Similarly, comprehensive analyses of transportation economics, pricing practices and regulation are not presented. Neither are the complex interrelationships of all forms of public subsidies of transportation explored in great depth.

A basic aim of the book is to identify major turning points of broad policy emphasis and content. Thus, one of its characteristics is reliance on analysis of the crucial "building blocks" of transportation policy. This reflects the view of the author that many present policies are deeply imbedded in the events of the past — but not in the sense of "old history." Rather, the point is that national transportation policy, here and now, is perhaps more affected by tradition and precedent than are many other fields of federal policy.

A selected number of crucial factors affecting policy formation are analyzed in detail. These include the creation of the Department of Transportation, the application of various evaluation techniques to national transportation programs, and the impact of changing technology on federal policy.

Throughout the book, primary attention is placed on interpreting the directions of national transportation policy in terms of policy outputs — specific legislation, Executive Branch actions, plans and studies, the work of the "independent" agencies, influences of private enterprise directly affecting policy, and the like. Where considered particularly pertinent, the processes of policy formulation are related to the specific time periods in which they occurred. Again, this reflects the view that an appreciation of the *changing environment* of federal transportation policy-making is crucial to understanding its specific content.

**National Transportation
Policy in Transition**

The Evolution of National
Transportation
Development
(1780–1939)

1 The Evolution of National Transportation Development (1780 - 1939)

A time perspective is crucial to understanding the form and nature of the transportation sector in the United States. It is apparent that the sequence of historical circumstances played a large and, in some cases, dominant part in tracing the rudimentary outlines of present federal transportation policy. Embryonic developments often cast long shadows, portending not only future progress and growth, but also problems as well.

Historical tradition almost always presents problems for the present. Never are the circumstances which produced the rationale for a particular course of action or development reproduced in their entirety again. As a consequence, established policy often fails the tests imposed by new contexts, changing conditions, and forecasts of future requirements. Yet the "power of the past" in almost all phases of federal involvement in planning for transportation has exerted strong influence on the present. One need but examine the lasting influences of early economic commitments, laws, administrative actions, and political decisions to sense the "layered" quality of present-day transportation development.

A second major aspect of understanding the background of federal transportation policy relates to the catalytical nature of transportation development. The impact of transportation policy, almost without exception, is intertwined with numerous other policy considerations. In its most narrow sense, transportation provides for the movement of people and goods. But in the broader, more encompassing context, transportation performs the role of organizing and maintaining community life — a social role of fundamental importance.

In this regard, Wilfred Owen maintains that the interpretation of transportation as a separate sector of the economy has caused a number of problems. He views it not as a sector but a *link* between sectors. Further, he feels that the idea of improving transport for its own sake is erroneous, and that the only justification for providing transportation lies in serving other objectives as well. Central to his point of view is his criticism of planning and managing transport in isolation.[1]

National leaders in both public and private sectors seldom interpret the provision of transportation as an end in itself. Rather, it is most frequently viewed as a means for accomplishing other objectives. These objectives, of course, change from time to time as both actors and circumstances change. But

3

the single attribute of transportation that appears to endure is its essentiality.

A third crucial bundle of considerations that emphasizes the importance of the evolution of transportation policy formation in the United States — one that accounts for some of its peculiar twists and turns — is its mixed-enterprise characteristic. The transportation facilities of the nation represent a conglomeration of public and private interests. Their development has traced a jagged line separating the two spheres; increasingly, the line has been obliterated by decision-makers crossing it. As a consequence, the nation's transportation modes have never been directed in their growth or management from a single source of power; pluralism in control has been, and remains, the hallmark of planning transportation facilities.

Yet a fourth dimension of the historical perspective involves the tremendous impact of changing technology on national transportation policy formation. Rapid changes have rendered the planning of transportation particularly volatile and risky. Technology has always held the potential of not only changing the relationships drastically among modes, but also of creating new modes and eliminating "established" ones. This attribute would appear to call for the development of extremely flexible federal transportation policies, constant redefinition of the respective roles of public and private enterprise, and long-range efforts to forecast both the needs of, and future developments in, transportation.

So, too, must the human motivations of those who plan for or benefit from transportation development be taken into account. Enormous political, economic, and social stakes are involved in the whole range of transportation policy formation. A multitude of pressures are continually being produced, affecting the *status quo*. These result in a never-ending struggle to maintain it or change it.

A fifth aspect relating the sweep of historical precedents to the present is closely related to the observations just made; that is, to what degree technological problems of providing transportation are bound up with institutional problems of public-private transportation development. It would appear that while efforts to meet initial challenges are more heavily weighted toward technological factors, the typical pattern is for long-range concern to shift in the direction of institutional arrangements.

The analysis which follows highlights the evolving bases of need and pressure that have changed the substance of national transportation policy from rather simple goals and mechanisms of execution to a highly elaborated, complex system in which both objectives and means to accomplish them have become difficult to identify, and almost impossible to measure.

Policies Affecting Early Forms of Transportation

A pattern of piecemeal development of federal transportation policies affecting early forms of transportation was firmly established in Colonial America. In the beginning, it was characterized by non-involvement of the federal government. At this point, virtually the entire population settled either on the Atlantic Coast or on the rivers which flowed to the Atlantic. Watercraft were improvised to ply unimproved rivers and tributaries, and, to a considerable degree, westward settlement continued, not because of transportation accessibility, but rather in spite of its absence. Many early American towns were so completely isolated that they operated on a virtually self-supporting basis, and their attitudes became dominated by self-sufficient farmers.

As the tide of commerce grew, however, it soon became apparent that more access was needed. The problem was money. The obvious need was for improved canals.

Waterways and Shipping Policy

At this early stage, virtually no thought was given to expenditures of federal funds for waterways and shipping purposes. State governments were considered as *the* government, and almost without exception leaped into the yawning "investment gap." Stimulated by the success of the Erie Canal, which opened in 1825, state funds flowed at a reckless pace, contributing substantially to successive financial panics and crises. Although slowed by such events, by the year 1850 more than 4,400 miles of canals were completed.

The principal motivation for these efforts would later reappear in the pressures which arose for direct federal involvement in national transportation development. This was the drive to achieve "cheap" transportation. Paradoxically, such was to be accomplished at almost any price!

But, initial federal involvement in the development of waterways, outwardly at least, reflected a particularistic orientation — the need to remove navigational obstructions on the Mississippi. The problem was presented as interstate in character and the states involved had no agreement among them on how this type of improvement-cost would be borne. As traffic grew, user-pressure intensified on the Congressmen involved — a pressure they in turn directed to the Congress. Nor were they hesitant to express the needs of the situation in national terms. Representatives of midwestern and eastern states, particularly, saw the possibilities of securing similar improvements for their own interstate waterways through bargaining and negotiation.

The resultant legislation — the Rivers and Harbors Act of 1823 — thus laid the cornerstone of "development bartering" for national transportation expenditures. The implications of this "small beginning" became more apparent following the Civil War, when Congress began appropriating funds for rivers and harbors at one-, two-, or three-year intervals.

Development of Land Routes

Perhaps in no sphere of early transportation development was the influence of sectionalism and local self-government more evident than in the development of land routes. Initially, private enterprise made the first attempt to provide some type of roadway system. The motive, of course, was profit, and the means, toll-road construction.

Turnpike companies abounded and, in New England alone, some 180 such companies were chartered by 1810. But the needs for greater amounts of capital and interconnection of these roads forced private enterprise to turn again to the states for assistance. Such was frequently provided in the form of stock subscriptions or direct subsidies. Yet even this governmental action fell short in the eyes of some, and private-enterprise pressure rose again for more of a "national" effort to provide roadways.

The first entry of the federal government into transportation development activity occurred in road building, specifically the Cumberland Road project. Even at this date, the project fostered a sufficient number of side issues to indicate the range and difficulty of the future federal role in transportation planning. Washington, Jefferson, and others, for example, felt that the isolation of the West was a menace to national life. The roadway was thus viewed as a means for "opening up" new territory and uniting the country. Furthermore, construction of the road helped to settle several problems of the federal government and the State of Ohio. The primary one was the disposal of federal lands within the state.

But, development of the roadway also intensified well-established rivalries. Thus, the States of New York and Pennsylvania opposed construction of the road. Philadelphia feared that it would promote Baltimore, while New York thought that it would be too competitive with the Erie Canal.

Early Railroad Development

The planning and development of railroads during the early period represented the first large-scale application of advanced technology to nationwide transportation. In a short time, its spreading influence would have far-reaching effects on governmental expenditures devoted to roads, canals, rivers, and harbors. In the span of a hundred years, the network would grow to over 200,000 miles in length.

By providing direct assistance in the initial stages of development, the states again preceded the federal government. And, as in the planning of canals and roadways, the assumptions were narrowly conceived. Typical state policy was to consider itself a kind of "independent economy," engaged in vigorous competition with other states for the riches of commerce.

This attitude imposed a high price. Up to 1837, the states incurred debts totaling over $40 million in support of railroad development. A number of states had passed legislation which allowed them to control railroad construction as part of "internal improvements." Their method of "planning" was to connect their own cities and develop their own trade with little thought to interstate cooperation. But when faced with near financial disaster, many passed "Free Railroad Laws" in the 1850s to put the railroads on their own. These laws provided the basis for highly independent control by the railroads over their own affairs.[2]

Initial federal participation in railroad expansion confined itself to the fringes of development. But as the pressures of financiers and railroad men upon individual Congressmen and the executive branch mounted, hesitating steps began toward direct participation. In 1838, for example, the railways were all made post-routes, reflecting a tendency to intertwine postal policy and transportation planning – a pattern that would be repeated as technology created new modes of transportation.

As the years passed, pressure for more direct assistance to railroad expansion mounted inexorably. The eventual result was passage by Congress of a land grant act in 1850. It provided the basis upon which the spanning of the continent by several railroad networks eventually would take place. This basic element of transportation policy represented a mixture of motivations, ranging from bases of broad, national concern to selfish, individual pressures aimed solely at achieving profits and advantages. Again, the rationale for its adoption was of mixed character. It involved concerns for achieving a higher level of "efficiency" in transportation; however, more important were the goals of accelerating economic growth, and promoting political and social cohesion.[3]

President Franklin Pierce supported land grants to speed construction and provide "great thoroughfares" between the most important points of commerce. But he questioned whether the nation was investing to excess in the railroad system. Then, too, there were the questions raised by the strict constructionist views of the Democratic majority of Congress who opposed the idea of aid being extended on a national scale. There was also the view that railroad development represented interests foreign to the "common" people, that such interests were inherently undemocratic.

In spite of the cross-currents that the land grant policy produced, it proved to be the federal government's greatest single contribution to the development of the railroad network of the country. Up to 1871, these grants amounted to approximately 131 million acres; before the program was discontinued, another 27 million acres were added.

It was thought initially that the railroads could be operated much in the manner of toll roads, with individual operators providing the motive power and equipment, and the road providing the right-of-way. This quickly proved impractical, and the consequences of short-sighted planning were soon felt.

Indeed, the awakening to the inevitable formation of railroad monopolies came very late.

Aside from the spanning of the country by the Union Pacific-Central Pacific in 1869, little thought was given to any kind of "master plan" for railroad development that could use the incentive of land grants as a lever. Instead, the strategy appeared to be aimed toward increasing transport capacity in any and all directions. In time, the welter of phenomenal expansion, managerial abuses, the flow of increasingly swift sectional cross-currents, and bitter resentment of concentrated financial power in any form led to official inquiries by Congress into the needs for regulation.

Early Pipelines

Early pipelines were developed prior to 1880. As in the case of other modes, its technical progress preceded federal interest in it. Private enterprise was the basic stimulus. As early as 1865, pipelines were built to transport crude oil to refineries near wells. During its first thirty years of existence, this transportation industry was largely confined to Western Pennsylvania and adjacent sections of Ohio, New York, and West Virginia. Pipelines, however, were not viewed as a "problem" requiring federal action, and without such concern, this mode received scant attention.

The Second Time Frame (1880 – 1920)

By the end of the nineteenth century, the railroads had grown to a position of dominance in national transportation. Because of their planning and acquisitions policies, they had begun to form a vast, nationwide network. This was attained without the benefit of a coordinated "national plan." New roads stretched westward, while eastern and southern roads "backfilled," enlarged, and consolidated. So great had been the attention given to railroad development that many cities and towns found themselves with no alternative but to depend upon the services of a single railroad.

But the fruits of success also contained the seeds of trouble for the future of the railroads. The practices of employing varying rates and services to give advantages to particular individuals and corporations, and to improve competitive positions, became widespread. Nor did the close relationship between the periodic national financial crises, railroad speculations, and financial manoeuvres go unnoticed. This period after 1880 represented the disenchantment felt by "grass roots" users of rail service, and those from all walks of life who resented railroad power.

Early Foundations of Regulation Policy

In its early stages, regulation of railroads was attempted by state commissions attempting to enforce charter provisions, or to apply devices previously tried in England. Another powerful force setting the tone for regulation was the Granger Laws of the late 1870s, which finally led to the Supreme Court's consideration of the Granger cases, and its landmark conclusion that the government had the right to regulate the railroads.

The consequences of these actions and reactions could not help but increase pressure steadily for federal action to deal with abuses. Congress struggled with the problem for twelve years, reflecting the tremendous pressures brought to bear by the railroads upon it to do nothing, as well as its own inability to formulate a policy satisfactory to most of the protagonists.

The final impetus virtually forcing action resulted from the Supreme Court's decision in the *Wabash* case, in which it ruled that a state could not control interstate commerce rates.[4] Since, by this time, nearly three-quarters of all railroad traffic was interstate in character, there was no choice for the federal government but to intervene. The alternative would have been the elimination of most railroad regulation altogether.

The Act to Regulate Commerce, 1887

This legislation, its title notwithstanding, was hardly designed to regulate interstate commerce in general. Rather, it was a "rifle shot," aimed specifically at the railroads. It was primarily directed toward assuring a "just and reasonable" rate structure and preventing discriminatory practices.[a] Whenever interstate or foreign commerce involved railroads, in whole or in part, the Act was to be applicable. Exemption from the law of common carriers operating completely by water served to make more emphatic the point that the railroads were indeed the "target."

From a policy point of view, one of the most important provisions of the Act was the establishment of a five-member Interstate Commerce Commission to administer the law. Additional legislation in 1889 required the Commission to report directly to Congress. It thus became the first "independent" regulatory agency.

The Act is, of course, significant in a number of respects. Perhaps most important is the fact that the first major expression of a *national transportation policy* was couched in selectively punitive terms. The transportation genie of

---

[a]The detailed provisions of the Act will not be outlined here. The highlights included provisions to require publication of rates; prohibition of personal discrimination, undue preference or prejudice; a short- and long-haul clause prohibition of pooling.

three decades earlier had grown too large and had come to disregard his "master." If he could not be put back into the lamp, he could at least be controlled and restrained.

A second significant attribute of the Act was its pattern-setting influence. This kind of mechanism provided a convenient model for handling future transportation problems irrespective of very basic differences in the circumstances and conditions involved. Again, the strong pull of precedent, conceived as a foundation for policy formation, would be felt.

A third significant point concerning the Act was its initial failure. Controlling the railroad industry was a massive assignment — too massive to yield clear-cut results in a short time. An era began of "trial and error" regulatory planning, in which Congress used a step-by-step approach to patching here and reinforcing there.

The Control of Monopoly and Consolidation

Intimately intertwined with the evolution of national transportation policy, such as it was during this period, was the problem of controlling monopoly and consolidation; nor were the railroads an inconsequential part of the problem. By the 1880s, in fact, a nationwide movement toward railroad consolidation was well under way.

These combinations had the motive of eliminating competition; the build-up of respective railroad systems was secondary. If competition could be destroyed, system growth would follow soon enough.

Important consolidations took place in all sections of the country. However, these developments occurred in a national context that viewed competition as the major source of protection against excessive rates. Quite naturally, therefore, the accelerating growth of railroad combinations was viewed with alarm.

The private interests that had induced the original regulation of railroads again proved influential. This complex of individual enterprises and industries, as well as agricultural producers and distributors — all major users of railroad services, and almost totally dependent upon them — saw monopoly as a threat to maintaining low rates. In their view, competition among the suppliers of transportation had to be maintained if they were to survive.

Once again a battle raged in Congress and ultimately the Sherman Anti-Trust Act of 1890 was passed. Although other trusts were involved, the primary "villain" was the railroads. In some quarters, the legislation was seen as a move to close the gaps left by strict court interpretation of the Interstate Commerce Act and the hamstrung Commission created by it.[5]

As a consequence of the Act, a number of railroad consolidations came to an end. Thereafter, railroad mergers in particular would be looked upon with suspicion. In this phase of its development, national transportation policy directed itself toward enforcing railroad competition as an end in itself.

Emerging Policy for Pipelines

As indicated previously, pipelines comprised a mode developed not on an independent competitive basis, but as a part of the oil-refining business. In some respects, therefore, pipelines were subject to even more monopoly abuses than the railroads.

At the turn of the century, the Standard Oil Company planned to serve its own interests superbly. With thousands of miles of pipeline under its control, it smothered all competition. Standard opposed all efforts of other firms to enter its "territory." And the railroads often seemed to act in league with it by refusing permission to companies wishing to cross railroad rights-of-way.

The thrust of national transportation policy at this time was to react to excesses of private enterprise. Following the pattern set in regulating the railroads, the Hepburn Act of 1906 brought pipeline transportation of oil under the control of the ICC.

Although the pattern of regulation applied to pipelines had much in common with that applied to the railroads, it was much less extensive. Notably lacking were a "Commodities Clause," control over new construction, abandonments security issues, and, regulation of consolidations and acquisitions of control.

Waterways and Ocean Shipping Policy

Waterways and ocean shipping policy in this period also developed from small beginninngs.

From the start, navigational projects developed strictly on an *ad hoc* basis. Individual Congressmen cooperated with private waterway and industrial interests, and "bargained" with one another to obtain appropriations for rivers and harbors in their own districts.

The early survey and study work undertaken by the Corps of Engineers was followed in 1902 by establishment of the Board for Rivers and Harbors. It was to review projects from an engineering and economic viewpoint. But its early efforts appeared to accomplish little more than to screen out most of the outlandish projects and provide the remainder with "pseudo-technical" packaging.

Congress continued its development of piecemeal national transportation policy with passage of the Shipping Act of 1916. Under that Act, the United States Shipping Board was created, and given jurisdiction over water common carriers operating in interstate or foreign commerce, and on the Great Lakes. But the tone and intent of this legislation were decidedly different from those controls applied to railroads and pipelines. Thus, the Act provided a vehicle for prohibiting "cutthroat" competition, deferred rebates, use of "fighting ships," and retaliatory practices.

The carriers made the case convincingly that theirs was a "sick" industry. And the nation's oceangoing shipping capacity in World War I tended to prove the point – all too sadly. As a consequence, the Board was assigned a developmental function – that of creating a naval auxiliary and reserve fleets, and a merchant marine. Thus, federal policy took another twist on its tortuous journey with the establishment of an agency to perform functions which involved *both* regulation and promotion.

Highway Development Policies

At the turn of the century, the "highways" of the country were perhaps the least developed of all the modes of transportation. The reason was the basic lack of demand for their services.

A number of events, however, heightened the pressure to reorient policy. Foremost among these influences was the beginning of urbanization on a substantial scale. Secondly, the technological development of the automobile, although still in its infancy, began to be felt. In 1895, four passenger cars were registered in the United States. By 1900, 8,000 were on the roads (such as they were). The number grew to over 458,000 by 1910.

The response of the federal government was to establish the Office of Road Inquiry within the Department of Agriculture in 1893. At that point, the pressure for roads was rural in origin. The primary client was the farmer.

Even though these were significant influences, the major impetus for inducing federal participation in improving roads was supplied by the "Good Roads Movement." Almost religious in its fervor, the movement was made up of diverse interests: academics, business, bicycle interests, auto interests, even railroads (looking for feeders to procure merchandise for their lines).

Each year from 1890 to 1916 swelled the number of groups supporting good highways. "Good roads" trains toured the country; "good roads" conventions were organized. Farmers, originally hostile to the high costs of roadway development, were won over by the argument that their land values would rise. In 1907, the National Grange became active in the campaign. Thus, over this period of time, states opposing such national participation because of the investment they themselves had made in roads were simply overwhelmed by "national" pressure.

The final result of these pressures was passage of the Federal Aid Highway Act of 1916. As in the case of legislation affecting other modes, it established a pattern for policy formation that has survived to the present day. Funds provided under the act were to be supplemented by the states on a 50-50 basis. Each state was to establish a highway department, which would develop management- and construction-standards acceptable to the federal government.

The potential impact of improved roads on the competitive standing of other modes hardly received consideration, except in a mild sense. Similarly, the effect of the financing mechanism on future federal budgets received scant attention. In this way, a long-dormant mode of transportation began to reassert itself in a manner that few planners – public or private – would anticipate.

The Third Time Frame (1920-1939)

Following World War I, the railroads still dominated national transportation. They were responsible for 84 percent of intercity freight and 85 percent of all the passenger miles traveled by public carriers. Intercity auto and air travel was negligible. It was little wonder, therefore, that the national transportation problem and the railroad problem were viewed by many as identical.

The Transportation Act of 1920

The stated purpose of the Transportation Act of 1920 was to promote an adequate transportation system for the country. But, realistically, it resulted from railroad pressure to modify the punitive nature of previous legislation.

In essence, the Act broadened the control of the ICC over the nation's railroads and at the same time relaxed some of the stringent regulations that, up to that time, had blocked cooperation among railroads. In the first case, the new policy introduced the concept of a "fair rate of return" as the rule of rate-making. The ICC was given permission to prescribe minimum, as well as exact rates. Also included was a "Recapture Clause," designed to assist "weak" railroads at the expense of "strong" roads, and control over the issuance or purchase of securities by railroads.

The Act directed the ICC to prepare and adopt a plan for nationwide railroad consolidation, although only consolidations in harmony with the plan could be approved. Pooling arrangements under "just and reasonable" conditions and the joint use of railroad terminals were also authorized.

Finally, almost as an aside, the Act directed the ICC to work for the preservation of water transportation as a matter of national policy.

A Time of Upheaval

The Transportation Act was not designed to deal with a period of change and upheaval. Indeed, the "new" transportation policy was conceived solely on the basis of past experience. It assumed that that experience could be extrapolated into the future, while failing to anticipate either the technological or social forces which were fundamentally restructuring the transportation modes of the country.

Railroad dominance of transportation steadily diminished. Its place was taken by a group of highly flexible carriers, which vied for both passenger and freight traffic. To make matters worse for the railroads, adjustment to these changes was muddled by the impact of the Great Depression. As the federal government struggled with its enormous challenges, most aspects of significant transportation policy were found to be intimately entangled.

Congress attempted to encourage cooperation among railroads in 1933 with the passage of the Emergency Transportation Act. It repealed the "Recapture Clause," liberalized the interpretation of "just and reasonable rates," and established an Office of Federal Coordinator of Transportation.

This legislation was the product of "crisis planning," and had little positive effect. Railroad prosperity could not be legislated. Once again, the impact of structural changes induced by private enterprise and intensified competition caused by the Depression were to thwart the achievement of the objective set by government.

The Growing Influence of Highway Policy

It appears ironic that Congress should have passed the Federal Highway Act of 1921 — legislation which would have enormous influence on the character of national transportation — within a year of its passage of the Transportation Act of 1920, which was designed to place the railroads on a firmer footing. Yet, consideration of the highway legislation took place with virtually no regard for its effect on the railroads. Of course it should be noted that, even in the more "enlightened" periods to follow, the interrelationships of modes received scant attention during the consideration of specific transportation legislation.

The 1921 Act provided a firm basis for development of a national system of interstate highways. Each state, in any year, could receive aid for mileage not to exceed seven percent of its existing system of improved highways. As in 1916, the legislation made funds available on a matching basis.

The pressures that produced this legislation welled up from a broad, although different, base than in 1916; state and local governments, the traditional providers of highway facilities, found their resources inadequate for the mammoth construction work to be done. Then, too, there was the problem of providing a coordinated system of interstate roads. Clearly, the need for such linkages made it almost mandatory for central planning to be carried on at the national level.

Foremost among the private pressures for such action were the farm producers and distributors who saw great advantage in the possibility of private trucking as an ideal alternative to rail service. Others, too, saw the possibilities of over-the-road common carrier service.

Perhaps the greatest influence on national policy was the individual citizen's growing "love affair" with the automobile — a trend upon which auto manufacturers capitalized in building congressional and administration support for a road program of national proportions. Even at this time the industry was building vehicles at a much faster rate than existing roads could accommodate. In 1920, there were over 8.1 million passenger cars and over 1.1 million motor trucks; by 1930, this number had mushroomed to almost 23 million passenger cars and over 3.5 million trucks.

Just as the federal government was virtually forced to "back into" assuming responsibility for interstate rail regulation, so it did for motor truck transportation. Again, the Supreme Court played a decisive role in setting this course when it ruled that states could not control interstate truck transportation.

The Motor Carrier Act of 1935

The Motor Carrier Act of 1935 was passed in large measure because there was widespread concern that truckers were on the verge of destroying themselves as an industry. There was also the feeling that undermining of motor carriers would demoralize and impair the nation's transportation system during the course of destroying itself.

All motor carriers engaged in interstate and foreign commerce became subject to the Act. Again, federal policy followed precedent in establishing controls. Thus, federal policy applicable to another transportation industry came long after *private* planning decisions had significantly shaped its character and development.

The ICC assumed control over such matters as the regulation of rates, control over consolidation, safety, financial reporting, and the issuance of "certificates of public convenience and necessity." This latter control of entry was considered by some observers to be crucial, because in effect it was a "competition-limiting" device. As such, it served to increase the ICC role as a market-allocator, designed to accomplish "fair-sharing" of traffic. The Act provided for "grandfather" rights to be extended to carriers in *bona fide* operation as of June 1, 1935. This covered a staggering total of 89,000 carriers.

In retrospect, federal regulatory policies affecting other modes of transportation might have appeared relatively straightforward, compared to the problem of controlling motor carriers. That industry was highly diversified, and grossly different in its operation and economic characteristics from either rail or water carriers. Control could not be achieved through the exercise of one simple system of regulation.

The challenge to maintaining a consistent federal transportation regulatory policy was also complicated by the fact that federal, state, and local governments provided the rights-of-way for motor carriers. This factor, as much as any other, contributed to the bitter squabbles that were to take place on the question of modal parity.

Finally, there was the serious dilemma of how regulatory policies designed for the nation's railroads, which maintained an essentially monopolistic character, could be transferred and applied to the motor carrier industry, which displayed highly competitive and fragmented attributes. On what basis would policy be formulated to establish relationships among the water, rail, and truck modes?

Domestic Waterways and Ocean Shipping Policies

After 1900 came a growing interest in waterways as a "ready substitute" for railroad transportation. As a result, expenditures for improvements continued slowly but steadily during the period of 1920-1940.

After 1930, Congress intensified its concentration on the regulation of water transportation. As a result, the Shipping Board lost its independent status and was incorporated in the Department of Commerce. The pattern of control appeared to resemble the strategy that had followed passage of the Interstate Commerce Act, and its subsequent adjustment to the unforeseen problems of railroad regulation. In 1936, the United States Maritime Commission was created to administer the Shipping Act.

The Merchant Marine Act of 1936 signaled another sharp change in the metamorphic course of regulation. It represented a further example of "crisis legislation" – justification for which had slowly built up in the drifting, "year at a time," milieu of federal transportation policy formation.

Private shipbuilders and ship operators had been in a state of decline since the post-World War I buildup and exerted increasing pressure to intensify the subsidy program. Within the federal government itself, there was increasing concern, particularly in view of an ominous world situation, over the nation's relative position in merchant marine capacity. This centered upon both trade and national defense.

The legislation which resulted provided for a long range shipbuilding program, subsidized by the federal government. With this action, the overriding character of waterways and ocean shipping policy moved toward a greater emphasis on development and promotion.

Early Federal Aviation Policy

At the outset, federal aviation policy was primarily concerned with use of its capabilities for the delivery of mail. Greatest initial interest in it centered about the Post Office Department. Here, as was the case of early federal interest taken in the development of road and rail transportation and ocean shipping, the national planning priority assigned to the delivery of mail proved crucial.

In 1916, Congress made a small appropriation to the Post Office Department for experimental air service and, in 1918, air mail service began between

Washington and New York, with planes provided by the War Department. This, in part, indicated some of the influence of military experience during World War I.

From this small beginning, other more important legislation began to flow. The sources of pressure for its passage, however, differed from that experienced by other modes. For in this case, primary advocacy and sponsorship stemmed from the Post Office and War Departments, as well as from the infant aviation industry.

Some of these influences came to the fore in the Kelly Act of 1925, which authorized the award to private carriers of contracts for carriage of mail. Nor was the increasing tendency of federal policy to promote modal development, with the exception of rail, ignored in the provisions of the Act. Thus, while carriers were assured of an income for carrying mail, they were also required to provide facilities for transporting passengers.

It soon became apparent that the control and coordination of safety and navigation practices in aviation were virtually non-existent. And this situation worsened as the number of aircraft in service grew. In this case, however, it did not require a court decision to convince Congress that the problem was one of *national* scope.

These concerns led to the passage of the Air Commerce Act of 1926. The provisions of this Act provided the basis for future expenditures of great magnitude. Again, the pattern of reacting to the problem in its existing dimensions was repeated. Under this Act, the federal government assumed responsibility for the maintenance of civil airways and aids to navigation, as well as the regulation of safety matters for private and commercial operators.

But federal transportation policy, even as it applied to a mode for which government could plan from its very beginning, lost none of its piecemeal character. This was demonstrated again by the Air Mail Act of 1935 – another example of "crisis legislation." It was concerned primarily with the air safety of commercial carriers. Paradoxically, most of its strict provisions were, in fact, the result of tragedies which, for the most part, involved Army flyers.

Just how hastily this legislation was constructed is indicated by its provisions, which split federal aviation functions among three separate agencies. The ICC was still considered the governmental expert on rate administration and so was given authority to set "fair and reasonable" rates for the carrying of mail. But the Post Office Department retained the power to award mail contracts under competitive bidding. The third agency, the Bureau of Air Commerce of the Department of Commerce, was given the important tasks of administering air safety and navigation, aircraft registration, "air worthiness" certifications, pilot examinations and ratings, ratings of airlines, and the like.

The Civil Aeronautics Act of 1938

The "stopgap" nature of this last legislation was emphasized by the passage within three years of legislation of much broader, more comprehensive scope – the Civil Aeronautics Act of 1938.

This Act established a Civil Aeronautics Authority, composed of five members, to function as an independent regulatory commission comparable to the ICC. Within the Authority, however, two agencies responsible to the President were established – the Administrator, and the Air Safety Board. So deep was the concern for aviation accidents, which stood in sharp contrast to concern for accidents in the other modes of transportation, that the Board was set up on an independent basis to investigate them and to make recommendations for their prevention.

This legislation provided the foundation stone for modern regulation of air carriers. But it also went much further. Specifically, it provided for the explicit differentiation of the air mode from the other modes of transportation. In this sense, the Act was an anti-integrative force in the development of federal transportation policy. While it was under consideration, it was recommended that the ICC *not* be given jurisdiction over air carriers, on the grounds that cases would need to be handled "promptly," and that invalid analogies with other forms of transportation might be drawn. The underlying rationale was that aviation should be considered within its own "policy compartment."

In spite of all the claims made for the uniqueness of aviation, it is revealing to note how closely the provisions for its economic regulation paralleled those applied to other modes by the ICC. Included was the control of rates and fares, abandonments, consolidations, mergers and acquisitions, interlocking directorships and pooling, reports and accounting procedures.

Also of major significance was the agency's control of "certificates of public convenience and necessity." This paved the way for carefully controlled competition among the airlines. Again, it reflected an increasing federal policy concern for the carriers themselves – not necessarily the service they performed. Once more, the "grandfather clause" found favor. This "blanketing in" resulted in the granting of certificates to airlines that were in existence in 1934. These were thought to have a "presumptive right" to certification.

Finally, it should be noted that the Act included a statement of "national transportation policy" for aviation. In effect, the policy stated that the development of air transportation should be encouraged and that its regulation was not intended to hinder its development. Thus, if Congress was "for" any mode of transportation, it was aviation!

Summary

In the first hundred years of building the transportation network of the country, participation by the federal government was fragmentary but nevertheless indispensable. The land grant program that benefited the railroads proved to be a most significant aspect of federal involvement. The assistance given in river and harbor improvements, and in turnpike development, also was important in that it established precedents that would be followed in later federal programs.

Early transportation development decisions were made largely on an *ad hoc* basis with virtually no attention given to potential interrelationships. In good part, this was explained by the dominance of private enterprise and vehement sectionalism that pervaded the development of the early forms of transportation. In retrospect, the role of state governments in assisting transportation development proved highly significant but financially disastrous.

One of the primary goals of early federal support for transportation development was the desire to open up new territories for exploitation. This goal was coupled with a strong commitment to achieve "cheap" transportation to serve these areas. At the same time, there was widespread recognition of the roles that railroads, roads, and canals could play in unifying the country and in reducing sectional isolationism.

Outside of programs designed to achieve these goals, an explicit federal transportation policy did not exist. The overriding drive was to encourage development of all facilities of transportation. Growth in capacity — whatever its form — was considered desirable; the potential problems of modal interrelationships received little attention.

During the period from 1880 to about 1920, the transportation resources of the nation grew enormously. But the role of the federal government took a somewhat different course. The primary emphasis of national transportation policy shifted to almost singular concern with regulation of the railroads. This largely represented a reaction to abuse and to what were considered "violations of the public trust." The imperative for action was a widespread fear of high cost transportation, dominated by an uncontrolled group of railroad managements. As a consequence, a long series of stumbling, trial-and-error steps was initiated to bring the industry under control.

The railroad problem also became confused with, and aggravated by, national reactions to monopolies and trusts. This gave further rise to the idea, increasingly supported by the federal government, that there ought to be ready substitutes for the individual modes. The strategy adopted was to promote competition, even where basic economic conditions might have justified a "natural monopoly."

For a complex mix of reasons, impetus was also given to the development of a federally-supported merchant marine, as well as for the creation of a national highway system. Both were characterized by a greater emphasis on development and promotion than on regulation. As in the previous period, the concept of what the federal government should undertake in increasing the nation's transportation capabilities was defined on a step-by-step, piecemeal basis.

In the time from 1920 to the beginning of World War II, national transportation policy again shifted, and differentiated, in reaction to the conditions of the time. Railroad regulation was eased somewhat in recognition of the importance of the mode to the well-being of the country. These modifications, of course, would not prove enough to restore the health of the industry, since deeply-rooted structural changes were taking place, affecting both freight and passenger transportation. In many respects, the accumulation of long-established federal policies and practices contributed unwittingly to these changes.

There was a general tendency to apply the experience of railroad regulation to the other modes of transportation, and then to modify these policies in response to pressures and problems as they arose. Thus, increasingly stringent regulation was applied to common carriers. This contributed to the substantial growth of private and contract carriers.

At the same time, there was a steady expansion of federal promotion and development of water, over-the-road, and air transportation. The policy foundations of these actions established important precedents for federal programs and further accentuated the lack of uniformity of federal policies that applied to the modes individually.

Development decisions also grew in their particularistic orientation. Specific policies for individual modes were defined with a minimum of attention to the growing seriousness of inter-modal competition. Each mode was assigned a separate federal administrative mechanism to regulate it, promote it, or do both. In effect, separate "policy components" were constructed for each of the modes and were carefully tended by a growing melange of federal bureaucracies.

On virtually all fronts of federal transportation policy formulation and execution, there was slow reaction to the implications of developing new modes of transportation and the rates of technological change within existing modes. Particularly crucial were the rapid advances made in highway and air transportation. The formulation of federal policy failed to anticipate the magnitude of these changes. Instead, it devoted itself primarily to forging solutions to problems that were already receding into the past.

At the end of this period, the nation's transportation facilities reflected the incremental accumulation of numerous public and private actions. No real framework for approaching transportation needs in terms of comprehensiveness or long-range planning existed. Transportation systems and subsystems existed and flourished. But, in reality they sprang from a "growing together" of short-range responses to immediate problems. There was little conscious federal coordination of transportation policy that could match the scale of emerging needs.

Early Attempts to Integrate National Transportation Policy

2 Early Attempts to Integrate National Transportation Policy

In my view, the concept of integrated policy formation in transportation carries with it a number of connotations.

Foremost among these is the notion that a primary goal, or series of goals, can be formulated and be made operationally feasible. A second implication is that various sets of strategies to achieve goals will be considered. A third emphasizes the need for a blend of policies, each placed in perspective, so as to maximize their overall consistency and minimize internal conflicts. A fourth dimension involves the time element. Policymaking activities, by definition, seek to establish future "rules of the game" – guidelines that govern both the motivation for action and the tangible commitments that lead to action.

If the above are assumed realistically descriptive of the nature of an "ideal" model for integrating policy formation in transportation, several questions arise: Under what conditions, if any, has such policy formation for transportation taken place in the United States? What situations have provided the wellsprings for attempts at the federal level to develop comprehensive transportation plans? And, perhaps of major importance, what forces have been the prime movers in achieving integration, and what does this portend for the future of similar efforts, if such are undertaken?

The discussion which follows necessarily incorporates rather disparate subject matter. This is indicative of several facts. One is that efforts designed to unify national transportation policy in the United States have been limited in number. Another is that the nature of motivations for achieving either whole- or partial-integrations varies enormously with the needs of the time. These range from the early setting of goals for an "undeveloped" country to the lofty objectives established by a detached study of the entire national transportation panorama. Then, too, the *forms* of policy evaluation or change, which are chosen by or forced upon policymakers, also vary considerably. They include special reports and studies, wartime and peacetime emergencies, executive Orders, legislation, bureaucratic innovation, and the like.

This chapter identifies the kinds of situations that have inspired attempts to "pull together" national transportation policy. As will become evident, these developments rarely have followed a predictable sequence. Put another way, transportation policymaking has not proceeded through a series of logical steps from a point of narrow concern to the comprehensive weighing of long-range alternatives. To the contrary, more typical of the process has been short-range concentration upon pressing problems, and sporadic efforts to obtain an overview.

23

This analysis also stresses the role of crisis in forcing consideration of transportation policy on a much broader scale than is evident when "normalcy" holds sway. Nor is the appearance of crisis a phenomenon that appears in a consistent pattern. In fact, crisis seldom wears a particular mask more than once.

My analysis also focuses on the unique, perceptive studies that were made of present transportation problems when they were in their infancy. These findings indicate that proposed solutions to problems have seldom been in short supply. But they also demonstrate that, at least in the period just prior to World War II, national leadership was presented with a considerable number of recommendations when it took the first few, halting steps toward rationalizing national transportation planning. That this did not occur indicates that knowledge alone has not, and probably can never, bring about significant redirection of national transportation policies.

Relation of Early American Tradition to Comprehensive Transportation Planning

The early American tradition of local self-government, and pursuit of sectional and state interests, played an important part in the development of each of the modes of transportation. Thus, it might well be expected that moves to bring about any system of nationwide planning for transportation improvements would encounter resistance and lack of enthusiasm.

Yet, forces with rather different perceptions of national needs existed very early in the nation's history. In particular, several of the early presidents became deeply concerned about overindulgent self-interest, and the possibility that separate social entities within the nation could develop easily. One manifestation of this concern and ferment was the Gallatin Plan.

The Gallatin Plan

In 1808, Albert Gallatin, Secretary of the Treasury, presented the first official proposal of any branch of the federal government dealing with the planning of national transportation improvements. The program he proposed involved development of projects as follows:[1]

1. great canals along the Atlantic seacoast to unite New England with the South;
2. development of links between the Atlantic and western waters;

3. transportation between the Atlantic, St. Lawrence, and the Great Lakes;
4. interior canals and roads.

Nearly all of the states were to be recipients of favors rendered by the federal government. The design of the plan thus combined a master plan to provide for commercial unity as well as a political strategy for making it feasible.

Aside from the question of national unity, Gallatin's Plan dealt with two factors which proved to be crucial to subsequent federal participation in transportation development up to the period of the 1880s. One was the fact that private capital was scarce. If major public works were to depend upon this source for accomplishment, they simply would go unattended. The second factor centered upon the sparse distribution of population within the nation's territory. The lack of concentration of population left huge gaps in portions of the country that transportation facilities had to cross, if a system were to be created.

As previously discussed, this general problem of national transportation development was a primary factor in the evolution of policies governing land grants to the railroads and in development of a national roadway system. Many of its attributes, in fact, appear in new forms in modern-day transportation problems.

Gallatin's Plan failed to be enacted for many of the same reasons that early federal participation in development of individual modes was so stubbornly resisted. Most pivotal were the Constitutional debates on the respective powers of the states and the national government, and the rising tide of sectionalism which, although foreseen, could not be dampened. States that had already invested considerable funds within their own borders for internal improvements were less than enthusiastic about contributing to the cost of improving the accessibility of other areas.

The War of 1812 served to reinforce the recognition of the need for development of transportation because it threw the nation on its own resources. But the perceived need was for *more* transportation facilities, not an integrated network planned on a national scale. The pattern of piecemeal development outlined earlier thus became dominant.

The century following the Gallatin Plan passed almost without a move of major consequence to integrate national transportation policy, or to take stock cross-modally on a national scale. Even the Civil War failed to leave any lasting imprint on public policy or facilities.[2] Nor did the rising tide of pressure for federal regulation of transportation, ranging from the Act to Regulate Commerce of 1887 through the Transportation Act of 1920, reflect an awareness of the relationship between the control of competitive practices among modes and public investment and promotion of modes on a selective basis.

Impact of World War I on Federal
Transportation Policy

The impact of World War I quickly helped to establish the ordering of the various transportation priorities of the nation. In this war, the heaviest transportation burdens fell upon the railroad and shipping modes.

Wartime Railroad Policies

Several factors loom as particularly significant in considering the performance of the nation's railroads in response to the emergency transportation conditions of World War I, and the ultimate efforts of the federal government to cope with them.

In the first place, the railroads represented a highly competitive industry, scrambling for business in all sections of the country. This situation was intensified and exacerbated by federal regulatory policy, purposely designed to foster competition above all else.

Another factor was that a railroad "net" required coordination by the railroads themselves in the routing of freight. No central coordinator existed; cooperation was achieved through cumbersome, step-by-step procedures. Furthermore, the railroad network was the product of numerous private enterprises operating independently. It was hardly ready to meet the instantaneous demands of national security. This kind of responsiveness had never before been required (except on a much smaller scale during the Civil War), and the institutional mechanisms for dealing with such challenges simply did not exist.

In spite of the fact that it lacked the administrative tools, authority, experience, and legal means to integrate railroad operations, the industry established a Railroad War Board in an attempt to achieve wartime unity. This integrating effort failed badly. A number of factors contributed to this failure.

For one, when re-routing on the basis of the *whole system* was attempted, the earnings of some of the railroads were seriously affected.[3] Moreover, the Justice Department refused to waive the provisions of the Sherman Anti-Trust Act of 1890. Nor were the anti-pooling provisions of the Interstate Commerce Act suspended; they remained a barrier to the unification of railroad operations.[4]

Other difficulties also arose. While the railroads experienced great increases in costs, they did so without the benefit of increases in rates. And to add to the mounting transportation crisis, various government departments issued "expedite orders" indiscriminately, thus causing tremendous congestion at juncture points, wharves, and docks.

But, as if to add the "final straw," the War Board found itself with no power to coordinate operations, divert traffic, rearrange facilities, regulate car supply, or clear congestion. So staggering were these problems that the net car shortage approached 150,000 in November of 1917.

At this point of utter chaos, the federal government was faced with the choice of either directing and coordinating the railroads without assuming control over them, or assuming direct control. Joseph B. Eastman indicates that the latter course of action was chosen for two primary reasons, (1) the great strain of the wartime situation called for a supreme authority, and (2) prices in the nation had risen so steeply that a large wage increase was deemed inevitable. It was equally clear that a large increase in rates and fares would be required.[5]

The United States Railroad Administration was created in December, 1917, to deal with these problems. All railroad employees became government employees and each railroad received a guaranteed profit equivalent to its average annual profit for the preceding three years.[6] Interestingly enough, the federal government initially resisted the rate increases that had been part of the justification for its entry into this role and, as a result, accumulated a $1.5 billion deficit before the railroads were returned to private operation. At that point, it left the problem of an "income gap" for the railroads to solve.

Federal operation of the railroads during World War I fails to rank as one of our nation's great transportation "success stories." Its operational debt alone would have been intolerable, if private investors had had to assume it. Nor was the Railroad Administration equipped to handle the complex administrative procedures and problems of the railroads, operating as a system for the first time.

The roles that had to be played proved too diversified and too technically oriented for the Administration to handle well, particularly considering the small amount of "lead time" that ensued between the time a take-over was decided upon and the day on which it actually took place. The responsibilities of the Railroad Administration included those of railroad operator, purchaser of supplies and equipment, common carrier, lessee, source of capital for whatever improvements were needed, and, employer of two million railroad workers. Yet, in spite of these problems, railroad service was improved somewhat, and congestion was reduced at least enough to maintain tolerable levels of men and materials moving to Europe.

As far as its impact on integrated-transportation policymaking was concerned, this venture was confined to a broad operating role, largely within one mode of transportation. Little attention could be directed toward the larger questions of long-term coordination, either for future planning or operation of other modes. Indeed, under the emergency circumstances, it was fortunate that the short-term goal of government take-over was largely accomplished.

Only near the War's end did the possibility of continued government operation receive serious consideration, and, prior to the passage of the Transportation Act of 1920, the government operated the railroads for sixteen peacetime months. This period, however, was characterized more by hesitancy than by bold, decisive steps to lay out a new course for overall modal planning or inter-modal coordination and cooperation.

Wartime Emergency Planning for Shipping

World War I presented the federal government with an ocean shipping emergency of immense proportions – at least equal in importance to that of railroad operation. Prior to this time, the American shipping industry floundered in its attempts to compete with European shipbuilders. Federal policies designed to assist the industry through ocean mail contracts at best proved to be uneven and unfruitful. As a result, the nation faced staggering ocean shipping needs with virtually no shipping capacity.

The consequence of not having an adequate merchant marine capacity forced heavy reliance on foreign tonnage. But rates began to rise fantastically, and soon precipitated a crisis situation which led to passage of the Shipping Act of 1916.

During the war, the entire shipping industry was placed under government control. Ships were diverted from coastal and Great Lakes shipping for service on transoceanic routes, priority uses were established, and a massive shipbuilding effort was initiated.

The latter program was conducted by the Emergency Fleet Corporation of the United States Shipping Board. Unfortunately, most of the ships built under the program were delivered too late to be of the help anticipated for the war effort. But the quantity of ships finally produced totaled 1,693 steel steamers – 11.6 million deadweight tons – at a cost of $2.5 billion.[7] It was clearly a case of "too much and too late."

The overwhelming impact of federal activities in meeting the emergency conditions of the war was to reverberate for the next twenty years. The huge new fleet was eventually sold to private operators, who realized enormous savings in acquiring modern ships with which to compete for world trade. In one swoop, federal policy had made obsolete the limited, wooden merchant marine fleet, and had produced enough ships to depress that industry until the time of World War II. (Between 1922 and 1928, not a single ship was built for the transoceanic dry cargo trades.)

A second major consequence of the expansion policy was to lay the groundwork for making the "new" merchant marine technologically obsolete at the same time. Thus, as competitor nations gradually introduced diesel ships and other improvements, the United States Merchant Marine found itself out of the competition.

A third major effect was creation of the basis for direct federal intervention in merchant marine development and operation, by means of heavy subsidies. This pattern of dependence became fixed and, in fact, has continued to the present day.

Fourth, the wartime condition made it abundantly clear that the merchant marine was vital to national security, and possessed characteristics not common to some of the other modes of transportation. It also became evident that the short-term supply tended to be highly inelastic. This eventually led to a provision in later legislation to allow for government increases in shipbuilding when hositlities loomed. The policy which evolved thus became very precautionary – one based primarily on future logistical requirements, in the event of hostilities.

Fifth, government policy for shipping shared a common attribute with that applied to the railroads. In both cases, an attempt was made to integrate governmental administration within each of the respective modes. In both cases, the functions of operating the modes as complete "subsystems" were undertaken.

Early Transportation Policy Studies

In the period immediately following World War I, the drift of federal policy was to revert to prewar approaches to transportation and to defer examination of the needs for unifying policy. To be sure, the Transportation Act of 1920 reflected a somewhat broader appreciation of the problems of the railroads, but it could hardly have been called a comprehensive approach.

The wartime bureaucracies developed for the purposes of dealing with extraordinary logistical problems faded into the background of efforts by all sectors to return to "normalcy." But these tactics were doomed to failure by the effects of the Great Depression – a deeply rooted crisis that could not be overcome by the simple continuation of federal wartime policies.

Although piecemeal transportation policies continued to be fostered during the decade of 1930-1940, the period witnessed a new mood of reassessment, in terms of federal policy applicable to the individual modes of transportation, as well as in the consistency and equity of policies that applied "across the board." The results, however, reflected more of a desire to become aware of the potential needs for broadly-based national transportation policy than for positive action that would commit the federal government to attempt an "optimal mix" of strategies in order to accomplish broad transportation objectives. Thus, the studies and investigations undertaken during the period clearly fell into the category of "policy explorations."

Studies of the Federal Coordinator
of Transportation

As noted earlier, the Emergency Transportation Act of 1933 created the Office of Federal Coordinator of Transportation. Under the leadership of Joseph B. Eastman, it made many studies and recommendations aimed at the following ends:

1. bringing about more economical operation of the railroads on a nationwide basis, including the elimination of wasteful practices;
2. promoting the reorganization of railroads in financial difficulties in order to reduce fixed charges;
3. ascertaining the means of improving conditions surrounding transportation in all of its forms.[8]

The objectives of national policy thus were interpreted by that Office not only in terms of the old standby problem — the railroads — but also in the light of the current problem, the interrelationships of all of the modes of transportation.

In pursuing the first two objectives, the Coordinator studied merchandise traffic, containers, passenger traffic, marketing, car pooling, terminal facilities, port terminal charges and associated rail problems. At the same time, the possibilities of new approaches and devices were explored. Of these, the proposals to establish a rail clearinghouse to coordinate railroad fiscal matters, and to create a scientific and engineering research agency for the railroads were most significant. All were designed to weld the disparate lines of the country into a full-fledged "system." And while these broad-scaled studies were under way, regional staffs of the Coordinator worked in the field with regional coordinating committees of the railroads to achieve emergency economies, as envisaged in the Act.

In spite of considerable effort and noble intentions, these efforts bore little immediate fruit. Virtually all of the recommendations developed were either ignored or opposed by the railroads. But this result should hardly have been surprising. While federal policy posed the high ideal of national unity in railroad operations, it underestimated the importance of the practical problems faced by railroad managements. In reality, they represented a multiplicity of separate, and often conflicting, private enterprises seeking to protect their individual well-being. They were not public organizations desirous of giving up what they considered competitive advantages for the "common good." From this perspective, federal policy appeared ingenuous.

The work of the Coordinator, upon achieving the third major objective, made a more lasting contribution to an analytical overview of national transportation policy. These studies were the first "across the board" review of the results of an *unintegrated* approach to transportation policy formation. As such, they spelled out in some detail the consequences of piecemeal regulatory and promotional policies.

In brief, the Coordinator found that the transportation sector was experiencing deterioration of the financial position of carriers, accompanied by degeneration in performance. He also concluded that service had become unreliable and irresponsible — a situation aggravated by the existence of unstable and discriminatory rate structures. And reflecting the depressing results of attempted cooperation with the railroads, the Coordinator concluded that competitive practices had grown wasteful and destructive.

Finally, the Coordinator concluded that the weakness of regulatory policy was that it did not cover all forms of transportation, or impose similar standards of control. The suggested remedy was *extension* of regulation. This recommendation, incidentally, stands in sharp contrast to conclusions reached in later studies, in which the most frequent suggestion was to foster greater reliance on the marketplace, i.e., to *lessen* regulation, particularly for the railroads.

Although little immediate action resulted from these studies, they provided a broad perspective and informational base for subsequent evaluations of federal transportation policy. On the negative side, the lack of tangible results presaged future difficulties that would arise in bringing about changes. Again, long tradition, "sunk costs," well-established pressure groups, and the multitude of control points within the federal government itself would loom large. All would exert a tenacious influence over the formation and implementation of national transportation policy.

Activities of the National Transportation Committee

Awareness that the country faced a severe national transportation problem also stimulated the interests of private institutions to reevaluate the status of federal policy, and led to the creation of the National Transportation Committee.[9]

The Committee associated itself at the request of certain business associations, savings banks, insurance companies, fiduciary and philanthropic institutions interested in railroad securities. Their assumption was that no more important task could be undertaken than to attempt to "solve" the railroad problem and put railroads on a "business basis." The study itself was conducted by The Brookings Institution.

Although the study was directed principally toward the railroads, some of the recommendations had much broader implications. In fact, many of the conclusions reached concerning the railroads bore a striking similarity to those reached by the Federal Coordinator of Transportation, and to those arrived at in the 1950s and 1960s.

The dominant tone of this analysis was that the nation's railroads should "pull in their belts" and get themselves on a "business basis." This meant "tighter" management, consolidation, and elimination of parallel lines. In particular, consolidation was considered so vital to the public welfare that the Committee recommended it be imposed, if not accomplished voluntarily.

A corollary point of view, strongly expressed, was that all modes of transportation should meet the tests of *self-support*. And here the question of waterway policy came in for scathing criticism. On a comparative basis, the study group estimated that, up to that point, subsidies to railways (mostly land grants) represented about four percent of the investment of Class I railroads, while the amount of subsidy to waterway interests approached eighty-five percent of investment. They also found that " . . . the costs of waterway projects in this country have usually run from fifty to several hundred percent above the estimates."[10]

As part of the "self-support" proposal, the study raised serious questions about whether highway transportation paid its own way. It proposed the concept of user charge, which would be equivalent to the property taxes that would be imposed upon the real estate used by the highways, if the real estate were privately owned. This proposal undoubtedly oversimplified the problem, but it at least defined an issue of federal policy that had not been seriously considered up to that point – one that has not, in fact, been resolved to this day.

Recommendations for New Approaches. Even though broad policy recommendations outside the rail problem were actually secondary to the purposes of the Committee, several are noteworthy for their perception and grasp of national needs.

The study group viewed the ICC not as a part of the apparatus for solving the national transportation problem, but as *part of the problem*. It criticized its organization for narrowness in approach, and recommended that it be reformed to concentrate more on "protection of the public" and on developing a healthy national system. Nor were the broad needs for national transportation information and advice omitted. The report suggested that the ICC have inquisitorial powers and report to Congress on the state of the nation's whole transport system with its recommendations for betterment.

Alfred E. Smith, in a report supplementing that of the Committee, recommended that the ICC be abolished and that, in its place, a new Department of Transportation or a one-man bureau in the Department of Commerce be created. He believed that the fundamental problem was nationwide consolidation and reorganization. He summarized his view thus: "What we need is a new transportation system, not endless hearings on a system that does not work."[11]

In one of its most farsighted proposals, the study group analyzed the relationship of transportation to the development of cities and towns. It called for comprehensive planning policies which would, first, coordinate the transport facilities of the city and, then, integrate them with the other aspects of city planning. Joint facilities for both passengers and freight were advocated, as was the use of belt lines. Finally, the Committee concluded that coordination of transport facilities in urban areas was the first logical step toward a *national transportation plan*.

In this regard, the report was almost singular in pinpointing urban planning and land-use planning, as the keystones of national planning of transportation. This stood in contrast to federal actions which displayed primary concern with rural access, intercity movement of passengers and freight, and a host of associated issues. Indeed, little federal attention had been given, up to this point, to the city itself and its dependency upon transportation, not only as a means for providing its lifeblood, but also as the chromosomal ingredient shaping its future growth.

Other Studies of Transportation Policy

During the period of the late 1930s, a number of additional evaluations of national transportation policy were made in an attempt to reorient future actions. All proved comparatively inconsequential in achieving tangible results. These included studies by the Committee of Three, the Committee of Six, and the Select Committee to Investigate the Executive Agencies of the Government.

Perhaps their greatest significance was that they indicated increasing concern for coordination of national transportation policy. In combination with the more comprehensive efforts previously discussed, this constituted a slight shift in the focus of transportation policy from almost complete emphasis on transportation modes, within their own "compartments," to a position, although still basically modally oriented, in which coordination and unified consideration of federal policy were, at least, accorded some attention.

Effects of Depression on Transportation Policy

The objectives of national transportation policies, even those of a limited nature, have almost always been related to goals that go beyond the provision of economical, efficient transportation. Various "transportation policies" have been designed to unify the country, provide an adequate postal service, reduce production and distribution costs of depressed areas of the economy, "break" trusts and monopolies, win wars or provide for peacetime national defense, and exploit new areas and territories. The examples that follow indicate the catalytic potentials of transportation, and how partial integrations of transportation policy and non-transportation policy have been attempted.

Transportation policy in the Depression Era illustrates one kind of linkage that can be forged between federal transportation activities and other national objectives. Then, the goal was to lift the nation out of a sagging economic milieu by providing publicly-sponsored employment where little or no private employment existed. One of the primary vehicles for accomplishing this was the Works Progress Administration.

As it developed, roads and streets were particularly well adapted for the WPA work-relief program because their construction required large quantities of unskilled labor, and because a ubiquitous need for highway improvements existed.

The impact of this work proved to be immense. Wilfred Owen estimates, for example, that more than 651,000 miles of highways, streets, and roads were either constructed or improved through this mechanism.[12] In addition to this mileage, the National Resources Planning Board concluded that the following associated work was completed by 1941:

Construction Work by WPA[13]

	New Construction	Reconstruction and Improvements
bridges and viaducts . . . (number)	64,426	39,794
drainage ditch and pipe . . . . (miles)	60,332	75,203
sidewalk . . . . (miles)	17,166	6,195
traffic signs . . . . . (number)	692,000	—

In addition to these projects, considerable relief work involving both airports and water-transportation facilities was undertaken.

This combination of anti-Depression and transportation development policies was characterized much more by expediency than by rational, long-term planning. Integration with the needs of other sectors was achieved, to some degree. But needs for coordinated planning within the field of transportation itself were hardly served at all. In fact, it is clear that this huge concentration of activities in roadway development served to distort the relationships of the highway mode with other modes of transportation.

The consequences of "make-work" proved substantial. In retrospect, it appears that many roads of questionable value were constructed, eventually to become maintenance cost problems at a later point. In addition, the supply of roadways grew so rapidly that existing modes of transportation serving many areas suffered from severe traffic diversions. In particular, common carriage lost considerable ground to private carriage.

Finally, the quality and usefulness of the transportation facilities developed were not enhanced by the differing objectives and lack of coordination between the Bureau of Public Roads and the WPA. The basic approaches of the agencies differed sharply. It was inevitable that even if integration of transportation policies had been intended, it would have been extremely difficult to attain under these circumstances.

Policy Aspects of the Transportation Act of 1940

Following the outpouring of studies that extended over a decade, Congress, in passing the Transportation Act of 1940, again took action on the pressing transportation problems of the time. For in reality, the "old" problems remained unresolved while new problems, caused by a highly competitive situation within and among the various modes, arose.

One of the most significant aspects of this Act was a declaration of national transportation policy. It dealt with rail, water, and motor transportation. The policy stated that an adequate transportation system must embrace all three major forms and that each had its inherent advantages to be recognized and preserved. This concept, incidentally, was to appear in the 1960s under the rubric of "balanced transportation."

The declaration also placed in writing for the first time the goal of the country's transportation "plan" — the development, coordination, and preservation of a national system to meet the needs of commerce, the Postal Service, and national defense.

It is interesting that the Postal Service — reflecting the very early patterns of its linkages to transportation development and promotion — merited equal mention with commerce and national defense. And equally as noteworthy is the fact that air transportation, the mode for which the Post Office Department had played such an important part in bringing into being, was not covered by the Act.

Among other provisions of the Act was the elimination of the requirement of the Act of 1920 that consolidations or unifications conform to an ICC plan. The railroads could now develop and submit proposals on their own initiative. The criteria of what would be considered "in the public interest" in passing on such proposals, were also defined in more detail. Additionally, the ICC was prevented from prescribing railroad rates to protect the traffic of another type of carrier. And, finally, the "land grant" railroads were released from their obligation to carry mail and government property at reduced rates.

The Act of 1940 also mirrored the agitation of the railroad interests by including provisions for more effective control of domestic water carriers. In this connection, it was paradoxical that the mode of transportation which was the first to be developed in the nation's transportation network should be the last to come under the purview of the ICC.

In spite of fanfare to the contrary, the extent of regulation was not as effective as might be supposed. Exemptions from the Act constituted most of the traffic handled by the water carriers, particularly bulk traffic. Much of the transportation performed by contract carriers, and all of that carried by private carriers, were exempt. Thus, the consistency of a national regulatory policy, supposedly represented by the Act, was considerably more form than substance.

Also under the Act, Congress established a Board of Investigation and Research to conduct a far-reaching study of the transportation system — particularly inter-modal relationships, the subsidy question, and the tax policies applicable to the respective modes. In doing this, Congress itself recognized that the Act of 1940 represented a far-from-perfect answer to integrating national transportation policy.

No formal report was rendered by the Board during its four years of existence, although a number of pertinent recommendations were made. Among the most important were:

to create a federal transportation authority – this was thought of as a permanent body to create means for developing and effectuating national policy. It was also recommended that it have facilities for research;

to establish a national transportation advisory council – this would be an independent group of private citizens having knowledge of transportation, labor, finance, agriculture, and industry. It would report directly to the President and to Congress;

to establish an office of public transportation counsel – such would be an arm of the Department of Justice representing the interests of the "public," not otherwise represented in administrative and court proceedings involving transportation matters.[14]

With the work of yet another study group in hand, the question of national transportation policy thus began to qualify as one of the most thoroughly-analyzed problems with which the federal government had to deal. Nor were many of the recommendations regarding the need for a unified federal body to coordinate transportation policy development dissimilar. Indeed, the Board's findings added another name to the list of independent groups which perceived that the federal machinery for integrating transportation policy contributed as much, or more, to existent problems than it accomplished in solving them.

Effects of the National Resources Planning Board on
Federal Transportation Policy

The study of the National Resources Planning Board ranks as one of the most comprehensive of all examinations of national transportation policy in the United States.[15] Unfortunately, its impact was diminished by the fact that it became another phase of what could be termed transportation policy "studyitis." It was produced at a time during which far-reaching changes were taking place in transportation. Even more fundamental to the lack of attention that the report received was the fact that national concern had become completely absorbed in the conduct of World War II. There was little time or inclination to concentrate on long-range transportation planning.

Unlike most of the studies that preceded it, this analysis sketched the dimensions of the national transportation problem in both broad and fine strokes, fitting them into a cross-sectoral, nationwide pattern of planning. In fact, one of the primary aims was to develop an approach in which the transport system could be encompassed in the broader plans for the entire postwar economy. The only barriers which stood in the way of this objective were identified as " . . . our habits of thinking of our fiscal policy, and of our organization limitations."

At the same time, important specific problems were analyzed. For example, the study devoted considerable attention to the provision of terminal facilities, and concluded that this was the most neglected aspect of transport development. In another part of the study, the Board found that many airports were built in dangerous locations, that there was a good deal of ariport congestion, and that there was a need to segregate private from commercial flying. It is worthy of note that in spite of these "early warning signals" sounded from a highly competent source, all of these problems grew so in magnitude in the following three decades that they now present some of the most formidable challenges to present-day transportation planning.

The underlying premise of the study was that the development of an efficient system must recognize the controlling influences of consumer choice, the price system, and service, as well as other significant features. Thus, the Board identified a "bundle" of attributes which controlled allocation of traffic. It concluded that distribution of traffic could not be accomplished by government fiat or by arbitrary prescription.

Evaluation of Past Policies. In evaluating past promotional policies, the study found that an indiscriminate increase in all type of transportation facilities characterized the developmental role of government. It identified the "new" problem as one of shifting from expansion to coordination, greater efficiency and correction of inadequacies. In spite of this need at the national level, it concluded that the focus of policy remained concentrated upon more and more capacity. The report commented harshly:

Waste of public funds, vague and conflicting objectives, the absence of criteria to guide expenditure, questionable methods of financing, cost allocation, and administration have all furnished evidence of serious shortcomings.[16]

Nor was the study devoid of ideas to correct these deficiencies. For example, it generally favored the imposition of user charges. Secondly, it recommended that the costs and benefits for individual projects be calculated, and be fitted into a system of rational choice. Thirdly, it suggested that the public ownership or leasing of all basic transport facilities might be justified. But almost in the same breath, the study noted that financing schemes should not form the total bases for deciding the relative merits of transportation facilities. Again maintaining the broad perspective, the Board stated that such might be secondary, depending on what our national objectives were. Here, the Board clearly alluded to the need for fitting transportation policymaking into a broader national planning context.

The conclusions reached on regulatory policy set the pattern for most postwar findings on the same subject. In general, the study favored giving a larger role to competitive forces and greater latitude to the rail carriers in meeting the prices of their rivals. Here the Board was searching for a balance between competition and public control. And it was willing to see what experience would teach as a result.

But perhaps more significant in the long view was the observation made in the study that transportation facilities, rates, and services constitute important potential tools for broadly-based government planning. Specifically, it analyzed the direct relationship of transportation policy to diffusion and diversification of industries, suburbanization, rehabilitation of urban areas, housing and recreation, expansion of economic opportunities in undeveloped sections of the country, and wholesale rebuilding of central terminal areas.

In discussing transportation planning in these terms, the National Resources Planning Board proved to be well ahead of its time. The Board made it apparent that national leadership had failed to recognize important *system relationships* among the transportation programs in which it was engaged.

The absence of machinery for coordinating the projects of different transportation agencies was pinpointed as one of the central problems of national transportation policy formation. This point received further elaboration in a section of the report prepared by Wilfred Owen. He stated that although there had been comprehensive plans for various agencies of transport, there was a complete absence of broad plans to include all forms of transportation, all units of government, and non-transportation as well as transportation objectives. He noted, for example, that the airport plan had no connection with the highway plan, and that the latter was unrelated to railroad plans.[17]

Policy Recommendations. The Board presented a number of recommendations to rectify the undesirable elements of national transportation policy which it had identified. Highlights of these recommendations (many of which still sound very timely) include:

establish a unified transportation agency;

this "National Transportation Agency" would coordinate all federal development activites in relation to a carefully conceived plan. Its primary responsibilities would include determining whether individual projects were in accord with overall plans of the sponsoring agency, whether such projects formed desirable parts of the master transportation plan, whether, in view of business conditions, the timing and rate of transportation expenditures were properly adjusted, and whether a proper correlation existed among federal, state, and local transportation objectives;

rebuild and coordinate terminals;

increase public responsibility for basic transport facilities;[18]

particularly emphasized here was the need for more direct federal participation in assisting the railroads, including government credits for modernization and improvements;

encourage railroad consolidation;

the National Transportation Agency was to be empowered to develop and carry out plans for the economic consolidation of operating railroads. A limited number of systems cast along regional lines was envisaged;

undertake new and expanded highway building activities;

the need for development of a nationwide system on a larger scale than previously undertaken was recommended. However, the Board went further in outlining the needs for urban highway development, particularly express highways and off-street parking;

expand air transport;

the National Transportation Agency was to plan the conversion of the industry from war to peace, assist in the location and construction of airports on a vastly expanded basis, and accelerate the development of navigational aids. The Board also emphasized that, above all, a rational program for coordinating air transport with other forms of transportation was desperately needed.

Impact of World War II Transportation Planning

For the second time in little more than thirty years, the challenges of national involvement in a world war again forced upon the federal government the dire need for integrated policymaking for national transportation. But, as in World War I, the goals of these activities were relatively short-term, and directed primarily toward achievement of logistical support abroad and intensified production of war materials at home. Encompassing both of these classes of efforts was an atmosphere of emergency.

In response, the federal government again resorted to "crisis planning." One inevitable casualty was any hoped-for effectuation of the "Declaration of National Policy," contained in the Transportation Act of 1940. Indeed, by the war's end, many of the conditions for which it was designed would have undergone drastic change.

Scope of Federal Control

In general terms, the scope of federal guidance of transportation ranged from the function of broad policy formulation to selective operation and control of strategic facilities and services. Moreover, the nature of the policies adopted diverged sharply as they applied to the domestic modes (railroads, inland waterways, highways, and pipelines) and to the international modes (ocean shipping and aviation).

Federal planning for transportation drew upon some of the experience of World War I. But, in many cases the strategies reflected dissatisfaction with what had been done in 1917. Thus, although transportation planning again involved activities of prewar agencies, new wartime bureaucracies, the military, and diverse elements of the private sector, the nature of their relationships was vastly altered. In World War II, it was decided that private ownership and operation of the modes should continue, and be modified only as necessary by government control and direction.[19]

To assure maximum use of domestic transportation, the Office of Defense Transportation was established on December 18, 1941. The ODT formulated and coordinated transportation policies, estimated requirements growing out of the war effort, stimulated the provision of additional facilities as necessary, and served as the allocation agency for strategic transportation materials. It also cooperated with the ICC and other government agencies to eliminate duplication of effort.

On the other hand, the pattern adopted for dealing with the needs of ocean and coastal shipping was similar to that employed in World War I. It was almost completely taken over and operated by the newly-created War Shipping Administration (WSA), established on February 7, 1942. As a result, the WSA assumed much of the broad authority of the Maritime Commission.

Planning for the pipeline mode, including construction and operation, was made possible by the cooperation of the industry and a number of federal agencies, including the Petroleum Administration for War, the ODT, the War Production Board, and the Reconstruction Finance Corporation.[20]

And superimposed upon all of the agencies concerned with transportation, either as users or providers, was the Office of Emergency Management (OEM). This agency provided both a forum and a final decision point for resolving conflicting and competing demands made upon the wartime transportation resources of the nation.

The Role of the Military

At no point in the history of the United States did the military exert a stronger influence over transportation policymaking than during World War II. It provided many of the directions and the technological incentives to the OEM and other agencies. By and large, military needs took precedence in most decision-making.

This was most evident in aviation. Coordination of War Department relations with civil aviation was carried out through the Air Transport Command of the Army Air Forces. Airline priorities were established, and the military assumed ownership, or leased, over half of the available air cargo planes. In addition, virtually all of the new cargo craft produced during the war were assigned to the military.

Yet the importance of the private industry role, in comparison to the military and federal civilian roles, should not be minimized. For, a substantial number of civilian experts in the transportation field either advised or became part of these government agencies, thus precipitating a complex mix of perceptions, priorities, objectivies, and approaches directed toward wartime national transportation problems. This, inevitably, produced a pluralistic pattern of decision-making – one which was designed to deal with internal conflict through "structured competition."

Managing the Modes During Wartime

Railroads. The maintenance of a domestic economy, and the movement of personnel and goods to and from points of production and embarkation, relied principally upon the railroads. Their use was unparalleled, reaching a peak in 1944 of seventy percent of total ton-mile freight.[21]

In contrast to World War I, national planning activities during this relatively brief period were occupied with public-private relationships. The close cooperation of the Car Service Division of the American Association of Railroads and the ODT typified the method of operation used.[22]

Pipelines. Direct federal intervention in the pipeline industry made this mode a major beneficiary of federal wartime planning activities. In fact, its growth resulted, primarily, from a technological revolution sparked by government construction of large-diameter War Emergency Pipelines. Under the Cole Act of 1941, the federal government provided the risk capital for the "Big Inch Pipeline," which stretched from Texas to the East Coast.

Highways. The consequences of federal policy during World War II severely dampened the highway expansion that had been accelerated by Depression relief programs. Civilian motor vehicle production was virtually eliminated, and severe shortages resulted from rationing of gasoline and rubber for tires. These restrictions left little choice to travelers, and led to a revival of urban mass transportation for journeying to work, shopping, and general travel.[23]

Even though federal aid for highway construction was cut off in 1941, except for priority defense purposes, there was a growing appreciation of the importance of highways to national defense and interregional transportation. By the end of 1941, a total of 235,000 miles of federal aid highways had been designated – approximately the same mileage as belonged to Class I railways. In addition, there were approximately three million miles of rural highways in use.

Highway legislation continued to be considered during the war, although its evaluation was almost completely unintegrated with the consideration of other federal transportation policies. The results were summarized in a 1944 report of a Presidential commission, appointed in 1941 to study highway problems. This study proved highly influential in shaping the Federal Aid Highway Act of 1944.[24]

In effect, the Act of 1944 led to the designation of a National System of Interstate Highways to connect principal metropolitan areas. Although no special funds were authorized for such a system, it was made part of the primary aid program and, thus, became eligible for application of funding for that system.

The Act's greatest significance was its designation of a national system of highways. It set the stage for enormous postwar growth of federal influence on the nation's total roadway supply.

Aviation. Aviation came of age both domestically and militarily during the war. Despite the fact that many air facilities were appropriated for war purposes, the airlines doubled their volume of passenger miles and increased their freight business almost sixfold. This wartime reliance on aviation, in combination with technological advances and an enormously enlarged pool of trained pilots and ground personnel, set the stage for a spectacular postwar rise in aviation.

Here again, a marked parallel to the results of "crisis management" during World War I is to be found. That War provided the underpinning for the development of the aviation industry; World War II supplied the impetus for a new perception of the potentialities of aviation, as well as the wherewithal to attain them.

Shipping. Federal intervention in transportation, and its provision of integrated planning for an industry, was highly influential in intercoastal and ocean shipping. In 1942, much of the broad authority of the Maritime Commission was transferred to the War Shipping Administration.[25] The WSA requisitioned virtually all shipping under American registry. As a result, practically all of the vessels of the merchant marine engaged in overseas transportation were controlled by the federal government. But, the condition and supply of available shipping proved to be as deplorable as during the time of the country's entry into World War I, and, in response, another enormous shipbuilding program was initiated.

Delivery of oceangoing vessels in the United States, for the period 1939-45, numbered 5,777 and totaled 56.3 million deadweight tons. The program cost $14 billion and the WSA assumed responsibility for building, controlling and financing.

Federal control thus brought about yet another complete upheaval in both domestic and foreign shipping. The pattern established in World War I was adopted in part in World War II, except on a vastly expanded scale. And even though the country emerged from World War II with a strong shipping industry, it was one that had become almost completely dependent on aid and direction from Washington. Furthermore, the war resulted in heightened military influence on the industry and a new emphasis on the strategic national defense considerations that have since become so endemic to this mode.

Summary

The forces that have provided pressure for a unified approach to developing integrated national transportation policy have been relatively weak throughout most of the nation's history. In general, thrusts made in this direction sprang from early, fundamental needs to develop a nation; a slowly growing awareness that uncontrolled and uncoordinated federal transportation policies might lead to eventual chaos and disruption of a number of modes; and the needs imposed during periods of severe crisis in which the transportation facilities of the nation held the key to either regaining national economic health or winning victory in a world war.

The first attempts to develop integrated national transportation policy proved to be a failure. Any possibility of success for such an approach was destroyed by a host of side issues — political, economic, constitutional, and legal.

The studies of the 1930s and early 1940s provided an informational base for awakening interest in coordinated policy. Even the fact that they were conducted was important, for it indicated an appreciation of the existence of national transportation problems affecting most of the modes. In this regard, the work accomplished by the Federal Coordinator of Transportation and the National Resources Planning Board proved highly perceptive in examining national transportation needs in far greater depth than had been attempted before.

Nor were the studies without some effect. In the long run, they contributed to a broader understanding of the impact of transportation. A few aspects of this influence, in fact, were made explicit in the Transportation Act of 1940, and in subsequent legislation. Yet, in the long run, the influence of these studies proved peripheral. Federal transportation policy remained modally oriented, piecemeal, and characterized by expediency.

In retrospect, the most important steps along the road to achieving a small measure of integrated policy formation, on a national scale, have occurred during periods of crisis. The Depression Era engendered some cross-sectoral planning, particularly as it involved highways and the need for work-relief programs. But even this effort was characterized more by expediency than by a national commitment to reform policies. Here, transportation development provided a convenient ameliorant.

More significant as a force integrating to some degree the federal roles in transportation was the challenge imposed by the two world wars. World War I saw federal intervention in the transportation sector on a comparatively massive scale, particularly as it applied to the railroads and ocean shipping. World War II, although it employed somewhat less direct federal operation, totally immersed the nation's transportation activities in federal influence. Coordination of planning and control took on real meaning under the auspices of the ODT and OEM. Transportation bureaucracies, both traditional and wartime, exerted influences not experienced up to these points.

Closely associated with this integrative movement was the sharp rise in the weight of military influence and national defense considerations pertaining to transportation policy. Particularly affected were the shipping, aviation, pipeline, and highway modes. Areas of greatest impact were in the advancement of technology, and in the relative emphasis given to federal expenditures on the various modes. And not to be overlooked is the fact that from this point on, national defense would become one of the governing criteria — in some cases the most important consideration — in determining the nature and content of federal transportation policies.

In spite of these new influences on well-established practices, the basic lack of unity in developing, operating, and regulating transportation on a national scale still proved dominant. When integrated policymaking was attempted, it became almost synonymous with the existence of an emergency. And both the Depression and war emergencies were now over.

**Modern Currents of Federal
Transportation Policy**

3 Modern Currents of Federal Transportation Policy

The end of a major national crisis signaled the beginning of a new era of transportation development in the United States. Of primary importance in bringing about this change were the technological advances that had been scored in many segments of the transportation sector during the war. Another factor was the potential of an accelerating economy that possessed both the need and the wherewithal for proliferation of transportation resources, particularly for private transportation. A third important force was the sharp rise in the rate of population growth, and the subsequent suburbanization and decentralization of industrial locations. Also of great influence was the continuance of the important role of defense in transportation policy-making, resulting from the prolonged "Cold War" crisis.

In the face of these developments, how has national transportation policy adjusted? Has policy exhibited some new degree of flexibility or pursuit of new directions? Or have the practices of the past been largely continued?

This chapter analyzes modern-day developments in terms of five basic facets of policy formation. These include the "compartmentalized" modal practices which have continued or have been elaborated upon; the role of additional transportation studies in providing information and guidance in transportation policymaking; the appearance of new concern for the needs and possibilities of comprehensive planning, including a new emphasis on "maintaining the environment;" the recognition of federal responsibility for assisting in the search for solutions to urban transportation problems; and institutional changes in the federal transportation policy-making apparatus to achieve some degree of greater coordination.

These attributes of policy formation have been far from mutually exclusive. As a matter of fact, it is evident that, in some cases, new lines of approach have been undertaken to counter unforeseen consequences of other federal actions in the same arena. In retrospect, a number of policies adopted to solve short-term problems have proven self-defeating in the long term.

Illustrative of such practices is federal planning and development activity which vastly expanded the highway network on the one hand, and the late, but nonetheless important, initiation of other programs to provide "comprehensive urban planning," including that of highway facilities, on the other. In a similar vein, federally supported growth of interstate highways and commercial aviation accelerated the decline of interstate rail passenger service. Ultimately, these factors played important parts in necessitating creation in 1970 of the National Railroad Passenger Corporation (Amtrak), designed to rescue national rail passenger service from complete annihilation.

Another contradiction is illustrated by the passenger train discontinuances made possible by the Transportation Act of 1958 that helped to precipitate a series of "commuter crises," which subsequent federal grant programs were designed in part to overcome.

The analysis which follows elaborates on these major policy trends and seeks to establish a perspective of national transportation policy into which they can be placed.

Modal Orientation of Policy

The principal trend in transportation policy during the period since the end of World War II has been the continuation of relatively uncoordinated development and application of federal activities within each of the modes. This tendency mirrors the tremendous "sunk costs" of influence that are so important to the various transportation forms. These extend beyond the realm of private enterprise; they are to be found in the federal structure itself.

Aviation – the Burgeoning Benefactor

Perhaps no other mode of transportation has benefited more from wartime policies and postwar technological advances than aviation. Government policy, generated in a period of crisis in the form of defense contracts, provided the basis for transforming the aircraft manufacturing industry into a huge aerospace industrial complex. And thus a new dimension of federal transportation policy evolved – direct support for the accelerated growth of a complex, technically oriented transportation industry that gradually bound together the frequently divergent goals of private enterprise and the "public interest." As the imperatives of technological advance became more insistent, they served to blur lines separating private-enterprise planning and federal planning.

In the area of defense, for example, plans of the military increasingly called for the development of aircraft that were longer range, more maneuverable, and bigger. Within the Department of Defense, the military services competed vigorously with each other for funds to develop aircraft suited to their individual needs. It was inevitable that these needs would create a more competitive environment within which aircraft manufacturers would vie with each other for contracts to develop and build such aircraft. But it was also obvious that in some cases the direct civilian applications, or technological "spin-offs," might be substantial.

Policy innovations, however, were not confined to making possible the advanced development of equipment; airport facilities were also involved, as provided for in the Federal Airports Act of 1946. This Act ranks as the "giant step forward" made by the federal government to provide airport facilities on a nationwide basis. Up to this point, airports had traditionally been the responsibility of *local* government, with the exception of Depression construction programs and wartime activities.

But the horizons of aviation grew too quickly in the face of the limited resources of municipalities and the reluctance of the states to assist the cities. In this regard, state action on highway construction offers an interesting contrast to that in airport development. It is apparent that rural legislatures were more receptive to providing funds for highways that would help sustain a rural economy than to meeting the "peripheral" needs of intercity and international travel.[1] Once again it was a case of federal grants-in-aid filling a public expenditure "vacuum" to which no other level of government chose to respond.

The response was substantial. The first National Airport Plan included a forecast of requirements for 4,431 airports. In 1947, some 800 airports became eligible for either construction or improvement work.[2] By 1972, the Plan included 4,100 existing and proposed facilities, involving a development cost of over $2.1 billion. Through implementation of the Plan, federal planning for aviation advanced further than it has for any other mode of transportation, except highways.

This framework for developing national aviation facilities was designed by the CAA (now FAA), and revised annually. For a project to be eligible for aid, it had to be included in the Plan. Nor is there any question that the provision of matching funds provided a powerful incentive for broad participation in the program and the exertion of strong, direct federal power in national airport construction and improvement. Under the Act, Congress provided approximately $75 million annually in such grants. These funds have been applied to construction of runways, taxiways, parking aprons, lighting of runways, etc. Local airport projects were also given engineering advice and planning assistance.

Although the influence of federal planning for aviation proved substantial in the development of advanced aircraft and ground facilities, it achieved less initial success in dealing with the problems of air safety, traffic management and control. These matters came under intensive study in the immediate postwar years but little progress was made. Government policy simply failed to keep pace with the rapidly accelerating growth of the aviation industry. In addition, the problems of managing two separate control systems — one civilian and the other military — rapidly reached dangerous proportions.

Again the initial response was to do the expedient. Congress passed legislation establishing the Airways Modernization Board as an interim measure while it considered longer-term solutions to the problem. But the problem manifested itself tragically before detailed deliberation could take place. Early in 1958, two spectacular midair collisions took place. They were related to the fact that the civilian and military air-traffic control systems were allocating the same airspace.

These events heavily influenced the passage of the Federal Aviation Act of 1958. The Act created two independent aviation agencies. The Federal Aviation Agency replaced the CAA, and assumed its functions. In addition, the FAA took over the CAB function of establishing air safety regulations. The FAA also assumed the basic responsibility for allocating all airspace. This eliminated much of the duplication caused by the need for a nationwide network of military controllers.

In this case, the policy differences that had to be resolved were internal to the federal bureaucracy itself. Also under the Act, the ties of the CAB to the Commerce Department were finally broken and it became an independent economic regulatory agency. Since that time, the FAA has become one of the largest agencies in the federal government.

New Policy Emphases. The most far-reaching change in policy affecting aviation in the past decade is incorporated in the Airport and Airway Development Act of 1970. This legislation recognized that the national airport and air control systems were plainly inadequate to meet either current or projected needs. It called for the Secretary of Transportation to prepare and publish a new national airport plan that projects requirements for the next ten years. Furthermore, the Act made it mandatory that airports be related to the rest of the transportation system in the areas affected.

In broad terms, this new legislation provided obligational authority for the expenditure of $2.5 billion up to 1980 for airport development assistance. In addition, it commits the investment of not less than $250 million for air navigation during the same period.

The Act's companion legislation, the Airport and Airway Revenue Act of 1970, also reflects a basic change in the federal approach to giving financial support to further development and operation of the airport system. Basically, it incorporates one version of a user tax, under which the airlines contribute funds through taxes on fuel and certain equipment, and passengers provide funds by paying a ticket tax of 8 percent. These revenues flow into an Airport and Airway Trust Fund that, at least in theory, was designed to finance most of the future growth of navigational and airport facilities. Thus, "official" policy has moved further along the road toward attempting to achieve "modal self-support."[3]

Manipulation of Aviation Expenditures. Beyond these immediate goals, however, some pressing difficulties, enmeshed in the politics of transportation, have arisen. In Fiscal Year 1971, for example, the Nixon Administration limited grant authority to $170 million for all airport development and $10 million for airport planning. The unused trust funds were used by the FAA for its own operations, maintenance, and administration. In Fiscal Year 1972, the same pattern was followed, much to the dismay of aviation industry supporters, both within and outside of the Congress.

The net result has been funding of capital investments at levels that are distinctly below those envisioned by proponents of the 1970 Act and the diversion of substantial sums of user taxes from the trust fund to support the functioning of the FAA. Under this interpretation of the Act, the Nixon Administration varied the input of general fund contributions to the trust fund by scaling down development and navigational systems investments to fit the size of revenues available in the trust fund. This was done on the basis that the Act provides for a general fund contribution to the trust fund for the difference between user tax collections and *total program costs*. Thus, if the Administration wishes to reduce contributions from the general fund under this concept, the strategy would be to reduce capital and direct navigation system investments so that more expenditures, which had depended on support from the general fund in the past, would now be charged to the aviation trust fund.[4]

Late in 1971, the issue of diversion of aviation trust funds was explored fully by both houses of Congress. The result was the development of supplementary legislation which specified that no aviation trust fund monies could be diverted to administrative and operational expenses of the Department of Transportation (FAA), except those directly related to airport or airway improvements.

Aside from planning new facilities, federal aviation policy in the last ten years has also continued to focus its emphasis on technological advancement of aircraft and the promotion of domestic and international civil aviation.[5] Equally significant is the growing interdependence of civilian government, military, manufacturers and, in some cases, carriers, in executing highly complex projects. Work that had been undertaken to develop a supersonic transport (SST) is illustrative of the tremendous demands generated by the new transport technologies.[6]

These emphases of federal policy have not evolved without their costs. Not the least important among these has been the effect on policy priorities. Indeed, it has become apparent that the attention given to technological advances in the operation of increased numbers of aircraft, and to the development of airport facilities, has tended to lessen the attention given to policy matters of at least equal importance. This is most apparent in three categories of activities.

First, many of the "spillover effects" of airport activities on surrounding communities, particularly the problem of air pollution caused by aircraft, noise, and congestion on roadways providing airport access, have received late attention or no attention at all.

The problem of noise abatement is illustrative. Even though jet aircraft were introduced at about the same time that the FAA was created, it was not until 1966 that a federal program for noise abatement began. In fact, the initial FAA response was to maintain that the noise problem was not serious. From there it took the position that a problem existed, but it was one to be solved by the airport operator. Not until widespread pressure from communities in the vicinity of airports had built up was a program developed. This occurred, of course, considerably after the "jet age" had come into being.

Secondly, there has been little coordination of long-range planning for aviation with planning for other modes of transportation. The National Airport Plan was conceived largely in a vacuum. Subsequent activities, at least up to the early 1970s, have been based largely on aviation needs considered without regard to other modes. An associated aspect of this problem is the limited federal attention that has been given to the *total* needs of passenger and freight trips from points of origin to points of destination.

Thirdly, despite the growth of air traffic, both freight and passenger, many of the airlines continue to operate at a deficit – so much so that in 1970-1971 substantial cutbacks in services and employment were put into effect by most airlines. While the CAB has achieved commendable success in assisting the major trunk lines to attain a position of subsidy-free operation, it has been at the price of carefully controlling competition and blocking the entry of new lines. Nevertheless, a number of serious problems appear on the horizon. Although earnings have increased substantially since the introduction of jets, so has total indebtedness. It should also be noted that the reported rate of return on investment for the certificated route air carriers has plummeted in recent years, as shown in Table 3.1. Meanwhile, total indebtedness as a percent of total invested capital has risen steadily to well over 60 percent. And in 1971, the airlines suffered a loss of over $100 million, in spite of federal subsidies for local service carriers that have been recently maintained at a level of over $50 million annually.

This trend has now accelerated with the introduction of the "jumbo jets," "air buses," and the anticipated costs of acquiring other supersonic equipment. Indeed, the nation's airlines are now engaged in the biggest re-equipment program they have ever undertaken. They have received, or have on order, hundreds of new, wide-bodied aircraft costing from $16-23 million each. These adverse developments have sparked renewed pressure from the air carriers on the CAB to give carriers more leeway in setting fares and schedules.

Such crosscurrents of change again raise the question of what direction federal promotional policy will take in the future. The initial policy objective was to support aviation as an "infant" transportation industry. But the severe problems that have resulted from the tremendous costs of technological change, the continued pressure to maintain service to secondary nodes of air transportation demand, and the dependence of the industry on steady national economic growth, raise doubts about whether aviation can become self-supporting. The available evidence indicates it will not do so in the foreseeable future. And, certainly not to be overlooked, is the fact that if federal expenditures were made to broaden federal participation in meeting the costs of linking aviation with other modes of transportation, the overall insolvency of

Table 3.1

Rate of Return on Adjusted Investment, Domestic Operations of Domestic Trunk Carriers, 1961 – 1970

Calendar year	Rate of return on adjusted investment, investment tax credits *excluded* (percent)
1961	1.03%
1962	3.86
1963	4.01
1964	9.83
1965	12.21
1966	10.87
1967	7.74
1968	5.52
1969[a]	4.72
1969[b]	4.93
1970[b]	1.66

Notes: 1. Rates of return since 1965 are based on adjusted investment (i.e., total investment less equipment purchase deposits). Before 1965, they are based on total investment.

2. Investment tax credits, effective October 1, 1962, were excluded from the rates of return.

[a] All figures from 1961 through this entry include only operations in the 48 States and D.C., for domestic trunk carriers.

[b] These figures are on a 50-state basis (plus D.C.), including Alaskan and Hawaiian operations of domestic trunks, and Pan American.

Source: Department of Transportation and Related Agencies for 1972, Hearings Before a Subcommittee of the Committee on Appropriations, House of Representatives, 92d Cong., 1st Session (Part 2) (Washington, D.C.: U.S. Government Printing Office, 1971), p. 139.

aviation as a mode would further increase, making it even more dependent on substantial federal financial assistance.

Domestic Waterways Policy

The postwar period has witnessed little change in the well established character of federal domestic waterways policy. Here the incremental annual expenditure pattern established over a seventy-year period has continued. Individual port and river interests, as well as regional pressure groups, continue to compete for favorable consideration of their proposed projects by the Corps of Engineers. The political "in-fighting" has been typically confined to pursuit of large numbers of unrelated projects. In these activities, no concept of national transportation policy exists. Rather, the practices in effect continue to be characterized by numerous state and local interests "looking out for their own," in seeking economic advantage.

One of the significant deviations from this "standard" application of policy occurred with the enactment in 1959 of legislation authorizing United States participation with Canada in the development of the St. Lawrence Seaway. The Seaway Act created the St. Lawrence Seaway Development Corporation within the Department of Commerce. It was authorized to work in conjunction with the St. Lawrence Seaway Authority of Canada to create improved navigational facilities on the Seaway, and to develop power facilities. As a result of substantial pressures from competitive interests, however, the legislation required that the project be self-supporting and established a tolls structure to achieve this end. United States investment involved $140 million.

Space does not permit evaluation of the complete "story" of the St. Lawrence Seaway project, and of the bitter controversy that surrounded its creation and subsequent operations. This federal policy innovation was achieved through the concerted efforts of a united front of midwestern Congressmen opposing the forces of the railroad interests and representatives of the Atlantic Coast port interests. The stakes involved were hardly the "broad national interest" or the need to develop a "fourth coast." More fundamentally, the battle involved the loss of freight business by the railroads serving the North Atlantic ports, and the North Atlantic ports themselves. The principal objection raised dealt with the question of subsidizing the flow of commerce through the Seaway, in competition with individual port development efforts that relied primarily on local investment.

In 1970, Congress provided even more direct federal assistance to the Seaway Corporation by forgiving all of the interest due on the $140 million investment — about $22 million. The Seaway thus became a federally supported, "self-supporting project."

Ocean Shipping

In the modern period up to 1970, ocean shipping experienced a "planned decline." In some respects, the conditions that produced it appear similar to those which followed World War I. If any factor could be cited as most important, it would be the high domestic costs in virtually all categories, in comparison to foreign competition.

This decline took place in spite of the fact that *declared* national policy has:

... sought to maintain at all times a strong merchant fleet owned by American citizens, operated by American crews and fully capable of serving our international economic, military, and political commitments under all foreseeable circumstances, as well as the maximum possible freedom of competition among ocean carriers.[7]

In terms of fleet size alone, the merchant marine dropped from over 5,000 active ships at the end of World War II to a little over 1,000 ships in 1959. At the same time, the proportion of ships flying "flags of convenience" steadily increased. This type of shipping is not eligible for federal construction or operating subsidies, but owners incur other advantages, including the freedom to employ foreign crews at lower wage scales and to operate under less stringent safety regulations.

Thus, in spite of generous subsidies, federal policy designed to create a powerful, stable American flag fleet failed. As in the case of the actions taken to assist the railroads in the Depression, the federal government had not been able, at least up to 1970, to legislate a state of well-being for a segment of the transportation industry plagued by complex internal problems and economic circumstances heavily influenced by factors that transcend national boundaries. Among these problems are the difficulties of competing outside of shipping conferences which restrict competition, control rates, and pool cargoes; the higher costs of American shipbuilding and operation; and the disunity of the maritime pressure groups, particularly evident in the conflict of ship operators and the maritime unions, that has successfully undermined a viable maritime policy.

Is a continuation of the *status quo* likely? The answer must be negative, if actions taken during 1969-1970 are assessed carefully. For, in this period, the Nixon Administration proposed a new approach that received strong support from maritime-oriented members of Congress. Ultimately, this led to passage, late in 1970, of a major amendment to the Merchant Marine Act of 1936.[8] Its most important provision declared that "national policy" required the construction of 300 ships of various types and sizes during the period 1971-80. The expressed aim was to "restore the United States to the role of a first-rate maritime power."

If a resurgence of the maritime merchant fleet is the primary objective of this new "policy," the transfusion of economic blood into the domestic shipbuilding industry must rank a close second. In the last twenty years, United States shipbuilders, and the maritime unions, virtually priced themselves out of the world shipbuilding market. Even previous programs that offered a generous construction differential (55 percent of the cost of the same ship constructed in a foreign yard) had limited impact because only about ten ships a year were being built in the United States.

The new program will triple past output, although the federal subsidy for each new vessel is to be trimmed gradually to 35 percent by 1976. Nor are the costs of small consequence. Construction expense for the program is estimated at $2.7 billion. Furthermore, it is anticipated that the additional shipping capacity will swell the ranks of employed U.S. merchant mariners, increasing the costs to the government for payment of the wage differential between American and foreign seamen to as much as $6 billion over the next decade.

Pipelines

There has been little basic change in the policy stance of the federal government toward the pipeline mode since the late 1940s. As indicated earlier, World War II provided the impetus for rendering federal assistance to make possible technological advances. As much as any factor, this foundation of "know-how" enabled the large refining companies that dominate control of the pipelines (about 70 percent of pipeline mileage is owned by them) to capture 45 percent of the market for moving refined oils in domestic commerce.[9]

In general terms, the primary federal policy concern with the oil pipeline industry has concentrated on regulation of common carriers. Just which oil pipelines are to be considered in this category has still not been resolved. But with the increase of products which may be made suitable for transport through pipelines, this question will become increasingly important.

Railroads

Federal transportation policy affecting the railroads in the modern period, at least up to 1958, followed the traditional, and passive, patterns established prior to World War II.

The relative position of the railroads, both in transporting passenger and freight traffic, has been declining steadily since the end of World War II. Much of this decline can be traced to the effects of new transportation technology, and heightened competition provided by other modes of transportation. Related to the latter factor, of course, are the generally more favorable regulatory and promotional policies that apply to the modes with which the railroads compete.

Also important in explaining this decline are problems of increasing passenger deficits, high costs and shortage of capital, labor "featherbedding," high state and local taxes, and the disruption caused by the Korean War.[10] This complex mix of dampening influences stemmed from policies generated within the railroad industry itself, as well as by virtually all levels of government.

New "Emergency" Legislation. Although Congress acted to deal with certain of the financial problems of the railroads in the late 1940s,[11] its most important action was passage of the Transportation Act of 1958. This legislation stemmed from the generally poor financial condition of the railroads, which, by 1956, had reached disturbing proportions. These industry-wide conditions made the raising of new investment capital difficult, a problem that was aggravated by steadily rising losses in passenger operations and the business recession of 1957.

For one of the few times in its history, the railroad industry of the nation presented a "united front" in appealing to Congress for corrective action. Lengthy hearings followed, in which broad publicity was given to the problem.[12] Over the hearings loomed the spectre of ultimate failure of a number of the "weak" roads, if corrective action were not taken. The outcome of these considerations was the Transportation Act of 1958.

The Transportation Act of 1958 was designed to provide emergency relief, to ease yet another transportation policy crisis. And although the provisions of the legislation involved a number of inter-modal considerations, action was taken with a "tunnel view" of the railroads alone.

Under the Act, the ICC assumed jurisdiction over the discontinuance and level of service of passenger trains and railroad ferries. The law also made it possible to abandon rail service in a number of cases, unless the ICC ruled otherwise, after the filing of a thirty days' notice of discontinuance.

This provision threw a number of metropolitan areas, served by suburban commuter railroads, into a panic. Obviously, no provisions for alternate services had been planned and the prospect of thousands of railroad commuters diverting to the roads held the promise of utter chaos. Yet this factor received scant attention while the legislation was under consideration. Indeed, at this point in time the representation of these metropolitan interests appeared almost non-existent. On the federal level, it was an area in which a genuine "policy vacuum" existed. In this respect, a significant federal transportation policy was enacted in a way undistinguished by foresight or planning.

Under the Act, the rule of rate-making was amended to instruct the ICC not to determine the level of rates applicable to one mode of transportation on the basis of their effects on another mode. Similarly, the ICC was not to use its rate-making power to serve as a traffic allocation mechanism among the modes of transportation. This provision created somewhat of a dilemma for the ICC since the Commission was charged with the responsibility of simultaneously enforcing it and the declaration of national transportation policy, which calls for giving consideration to the transportation system *as a whole*. Execution of the provision has also been complicated by the lack of agreement on what cost basis should be used to determine minimum rate structures. This is not a new policy problem, but its lack of resolution continues to muddle the application of regulatory policy.

It should also be noted that under the Act, ICC authority to exercise power over intrastate rates was affirmed and the ICC was authorized to guarantee loans for railroad capital improvements and maintenance work. But few loans had been applied for. One observer ascribed this lack of enthusiasm to the rigid conditions of securing loans and the improved financial condition of a number of railroads.[13]

In the field of freight transportation, the nation's railroads have gradually recovered from their desperate position of the 1950s. Rail transportation now handles almost 800 billion ton-miles annually. Even so, this volume is only slightly above the previous peak performance that was achieved in 1944. Furthermore, the tonnage is dominated by bulk-type commodities such as coal, grain, and lumber. The trend toward losing more highly valued commodities to trucking, although somewhat slackened, has continued.

In general terms, it may be said that the principal effect of federal policy affecting railroad freight has been negative, if anything. The principal reason is that governmental influence is not directed toward development or promotion; it is concentrated primarily on detailed regulation, as it has been during the past seventy years.

If railroad freight transportation is surviving in spite of limited growth, and with a dwindling share of the total "transportation market," what of passenger transportation? In comparison, railroad passenger service, whether viewed nationally or in countless local situations, represents a "disaster area." In only four of the last forty-two years have passenger operations turned a profit. None of those years occurred after World War II. In the period from 1958 to 1968 alone, intercity passenger miles declined from 18.4 billion to 8.7 billion; passenger train miles declined from 246 million to 124 million; route miles, over which passenger service was operated, dropped from 106,000 to less than 60,000; and, the national passenger deficit climbed from $82 million to $198 million.[14]

The Creation of Amtrak. Although a number of factors, in addition to those cited above, played important roles in precipitating federal action to deal with the matter of intercity rail passenger transportation, it was the Department of Transportation that exerted the strongest pressure for creation of a national corporation to tackle this problem. This action took positive form with the passage of the Rail Passenger Service Act of 1970, signed into law late in the year.[15]

This Act set as its goal the organization and maintenance of a modern, efficient intercity railroad passenger service as a fundamental part of a "balanced transportation system." It further called for the designation of a basic national network, and created the National Railroad Passenger Corporation (Amtrak), a quasi-public organization directed by a fifteen-member board. Eight are appointed by the President and the remainder are elected by the stockholders.

The Corporation has been designed to function on a profitable basis, although it initially received federal assistance as follows: $40 million in grant funds to establish the Corporation, $100 million of guaranteed loans, and $200 million in funds for loans to be made to participating railroads or to guarantee loans of railroads turning over their passenger operations to the Corporation.

And, as almost a critical commentary on the regulatory quagmire of the Interstate Commerce Commission, the Corporation was exempted from ICC provisions governing rates, fares and charges, abandonments and extensions, discontinuances, and regulation of routes and services. Paradoxically, virtually all of the railroads that will participate in the development of the system have been seeking exactly this kind of freedom for many decades, as basic requirements for profitability and efficient operation.

Lest ardent "railroad buffs" conclude that this move signaled a new era of positive federal policy to redevelop national passenger service, it should be noted that when the Nixon Administration revealed the plan for the network, it represented a sharp contraction of existing service. Specifically, the plan to implement the legislation called for a further reduction of the national total of passenger trains in daily operation to 184 — a cut of about fifty percent of the number in operation in 1970.

Emphasis was placed on high-speed corridor service linking most of the major metropolitan centers of the country. But there were significant omissions, particularly on the West Coast, that the Administration was hard put to justify — except on the basis of assuring profitability. Congress, after all, had decreed that the Corporation must return a profit.

The original plan has been expanded somewhat in response to pressures emanating from many directions, all seeking preservation of what they consider "essential services." This "final" designation took effect May 1, 1971, and must remain in effect until mid-1973, at which time the question of "essentiality" will be opened once again.

In its short history, Amtrak has been less than a financial success. For the time being, the goal of making nationwide passenger service a "profitable" venture, while at the same time improving service, has drifted far out of reach. In fact, late in 1971, the Nixon Administration was forced to request additional appropriations. In mid-1972, an additional $227 million was provided by Congress to carry the Corporation through to January 1, 1973. The Corporation estimated that its operations would incur a deficit of over $150 million before the magnitude and facilities of the "system" could be revamped once again.

Obviously, Amtrak has fallen heir to many of the difficulties that have plagued the passenger railroad industry for decades — low ridership, immense needs for equipment and facilities, and spiraling labor costs. Amtrak has limited control over such expenses since it contracts with the railroads to provide service. It does not own trains or employ operating personnel.

For the present, Congress has acceded to this request for further financial assistance. But the long-range prospects for revitalizing intercity railroad passenger transportation appear dim.

In retrospect, the policy shift that led to the creation of Amtrak is a "holding action." Without it, such rail operations were doomed. But what appears disturbing is the continuation of the federal policy view that railroad passenger service, unlike other modes of transportation, should be profitable; that it must not become the beneficiary of direct or indirect federal subsidies — this in the face of federal subsidization that abounds, directly and indirectly, in the other transportation modes. In this sense, the Act reinforced past practices of evolving transportation policy mode by mode, but with particular emphasis on maintaining rail passenger service on a "profit basis."

The Highway Mode

The tremendous impact of compartmentalized federal policies within individual modes of transportation has become most apparent in the highway field during the modern period. It was particularly manifested in the most costly and far-reaching piece of legislation ever enacted for transportation purposes – the Federal Aid Highway Act of 1956.

The Federal Aid Highway Act of 1956. The Federal Aid Highway Act of 1956 was a product of forces that exerted influence from a number of diverse sources. Following World War II, it became apparent that much of the highway system of the United States had become functionally obsolete. As automobile and truck production increased, existing facilities became congested in short order. Although a federal highway system had been authorized for construction, there was considerable reluctance to commit substantial funds for its implementation.

Yet pressures for more highway capacity continued to mount. These were soon met by a flurry of state activities in constructing toll roads to serve those routes where demand appeared heaviest. During the period from 1946 to 1957, for example, a total of 3,262 miles of toll roads were constructed. In many respects, this action bore a striking similarity to very early state attempts to construct toll roads in the absence of a federal effort toward this end.

It soon became apparent that toll roads would not be enough and that the scale of potential development exceeded the financial capabilities of most states. As one consequence of increasing pressures, a committee headed by General Lucius D. Clay was established in 1954 to study the highway problem. Its report laid the basis for the Federal Aid Highway Act of 1956.[16]

The forces that led to the passage of the Act represented a powerful combination of interests. They have been described as the " . . . most unique and massive coalition of single-minded pressures ever to hit the American scene."[17] But these sources of influence did not stand alone. In part, they were augmented by the questionable linkage of development of the Interstate Highway System to national defense needs. However, even more fundamental was the rising concern about economic recession, and the obvious effect a public-works program of such great magnitude would have in stimulating the economy. Indeed, the policy motivation involved here bore a strong resemblance to Depression road building practices. As had happened often in previous applications of federal transportation policy, the ostensible means employed to achieve transportation goals were, in part, designed to serve other purposes.

Under this Act, grants administered by the Bureau of Public Roads are made to the states for construction and improvement of Federal-aid highways. These cover ninety percent of the costs of completing the 41,000-mile National System of Interstate and Defense Highways (since expanded to 42,500 miles), and match state funds on a 50-50 basis for primary, secondary, and urban programs. The federal share is further increased in those states with large areas of public domain.

The law initially authorized expenditures by the federal government of $46.2 billion over a period of thirteen years. Additional funds have been provided in subsequent legislation, raising the estimated amount of money to complete the system to about $70 billion. In addition, consideration continues to be given to even further expansion of the system.

Of major significance as a *policy departure* from previous highway legislation was the creation under the accompanying Revenue Act of the Highway Trust Fund, from which highway expenditures were to be made. In effect, it earmarked certain taxes assessed on fuel, motor vehicles and motor vehicle materials for use in highway development. It is assumed that, in the long run, the Trust Fund will provide the money to finance federal commitments under the program.

Experience with this method has proved successful enough to encourage institution of similar arrangements for application to federally-financed aviaiton facilities (discussed previously), and urban transportation improvements. Both of these policy innovations will be analyzed further in Chapter 7.

The consequences of implementing the 1956 Act have been both direct and indirect. The program provided the primary premises from which changes took place, not only in transportation patterns, but in the vast network of national community structures as well.

It is doubtful that the framers of the Highway Act of 1956 realized how far-reaching the implications of the interstate highway program would be. Whether made consciously or not, a basic policy decision favoring development of highways and private auto transportation as the nation's primary transportation mode seems, in retrospect, to have been part and parcel of the Act. Among the consequences of the Act, tending to support this conclusion, are the following:

(1) The 90-10 aid formula for interstate highways has proved virtually irresistible in attracting public transportation expenditures by the states. The aid formula affected the overall ordering of state expenditures, including those for mass transportation. Furthermore, the formula induced pressure within the states to participate in the Interstate system, as opposed to the more traditional system of primary, secondary, and urban roads for which 50-50 funding was available. In some cases, the latter might have received much higher state and local priority but the cost *to the states* was considerably higher. Thus, the provisions of the Highway Act of 1956 induced the placement of some of the highest priorities for public spending on the Interstate System.

(2) The Act helped to assure that intercity transportation of both passengers and goods would be dominated by the auto and truck, respectively. Moreover, the construction of superior interstate highways, both bypass and direct service routes, helped to assure that metropolitan transportation would also become auto-dominated.

(3) Construction of the new Interstate System has speeded the post-World War II trend of suburbanization of population, and decentralization of industry mentioned above. Without the new capacities provided by the system, and the numerous direct linkages and high speed arteries that have been developed, it is likely that this trend would have been slower, and would have involved higher population and industrial densities. Thus, the new arteries, more than any other

single factor, have affected the character of metropolitan peripheral growth, with corresponding effects on the central city.

(4) Most of the design and construction of the new system have taken place largely without the benefit of comprehensive transportation plans for the affected areas. While the highway plan itself was integrated with other elements of roadway planning, it was, at best, an attempt at optimization of only one subsystem of the transport network of the country. Further, beyond the concerns of transportation planning, the development of the Interstate System was not related, until the late 1960s, to the problems and processes of cost-sectoral urban planning.

Motor Freight Carriers

Federal policy applicable to motor freight carriers has reflected little basic change in the modern era. In general, trucking has experienced a continuation of the steady growth that had preceded World War II. In addition, the industry itself capitalized on expansive highway development policies to capture a greater share of the intercity market. However, it should be noted that while absolute tonnage has increased, the share of freight carried by intercity trucks has tended to stabilize at around twenty-two percent – reflecting, in part, the policies of the Transportation Act of 1958, the more aggressive practices employed by the railroads, and the technological advances made by the pipeline industry.

In effect, federal highway policy provided many new "rights of way" for truckers, and thereby opened new markets. And, since the industry is characterized by relatively low capital equipment costs and comparatively small economies of scale, the general effect has been to sharply increase competition within the industry as well as the competition that the entire industry offers to the rail mode.

National regulatory policy governing the motor freight industry continues to be elaborated upon through the ICC. Here the basic prewar model remains largely intact. As indicated earlier, common carrier trucking is characterized by much of same type of regulation applied to the railroads – a labyrinth of restriction and control.

This attribute, as much as any, may explain why private- and contract-motor freight carriers, as opposed to common carriers tightly controlled by the ICC, now account for an increasing proportion (almost one-third) of total national expenditures for transportation goods and services. The present lack of flexibility and adaptability of common carriers make it impossible for them to meet demands for service. Particularly at issue is the ICC practice of using "average cost" to establish rates for common carriers; in practice these often prove non-competitive.

But in spite of many cogent criticisms, no immediate change in federal policy is in the offing. Common carriage is experiencing a "creeping crisis," which is approaching disastrous proportions. Until that stage is reached, it is likely that the regulatory, "case-by-case" approach will continue to be the primary instrument of federal policy in the trucking industry.

National Transportation Policy Studies in the Modern Era

A second major characteristic of the modern period has been the revival studies of national transportation policy. As was the case in the latter half of the 1930s, motivations for undertaking these evaluations had sprung from a number of diverse sources.

Reorganization Studies of the Hoover Commission

One of the most comprehensive evaluations of national transportation policy that took place after World War II resulted from a reorganization study of the first Hoover Commission.[18] The study provided broad coverage of the entire range of transportation policy questions, and proposed both substantive changes in policy content and in federal institutional arrangements.

The primary finding of the Commission was that federal policy has failed to pursue the objective of considering "total transportation requirements." It noted that the fragmentation of responsibilities, among a host of promotional and regulatory agencies, had negated any possibility of effective development or coordination.

The Hoover Commission, however, found itself in sharp disagreement with its staff task force in seeking a solution to these problems. The Commission favored combining transportation related functions under the Department of Commerce, while the task force favored creation of executive transportation functions in a new Department of Transportation.

The recommendation for a new department was finally rejected by the Commission. It thought it inadvisable to set up a department devoted entirely to the problems of one industry and noted that Congress had given the Department of Commerce broad responsibilities in the field of transportation which should not be reallocated.[19]

This reasoning appears curious. Certainly it would have been a simple matter for the Commission to recommend a reorganization of the sort recommended by the task force. The primary purpose of the Commission was to study the need for reorganization; the many recommendations it submitted to Congress demonstrated that historical precedent was hardly sufficient grounds for maintaining organizational arrangements that literally cried for change. So, too, rejection of the proposal on the premise that only one industry was involved appears weak. For, even at that time, transportation represented not one industry, but a complex mixture of industries accounting for about twenty percent of gross national product. In retrospect, it appears likely that such a policy change was rejected because of the desire of the Department of Commerce to retain its transportation functions.

As it turned out, the subsequent establishment of the position of Undersecretary of Transportation in the Department of Commerce probably impeded the progress which might have been made in creating a Department of Transportation before 1966. This may be attributed not to the calibre of the men who held the position, but rather to the fact that its existence lessened the pressure to achieve policy coordination on a broader scale than could be done in the Department of Commerce.

The Brookings Institution Study

The Brookings Institution study of national transportation policy clearly identified the polarity of regulation as opposed to development and promotion. The authors, Charles Dearing and Wilfred Owen, outlined their reorganization proposals accordingly. On the regulation side, they proposed creation of a National Transport Regulatory Commission that would carry out the functions of the separate regulatory agencies. To handle the executive problems of promotion and subsidy, the authors recommended creation of a Department of Transportation. The scope of the new organization's responsibilities were envisioned as encompassing planning and research, program analysis of promotion and subsidies, transportation requirements, and investigation of the possibilities of government ownership of selected facilities.

But the contribution of this study went considerably further. Major questions were raised about offering federal subsidies to develop secondary roads (which the authors considered a primary function of local and state government), to airports, particularly where traffic was dominated by privately operated aircraft, and to river and harbor projects. These challenges were pointed directly at the justification for such federal assistance, not the level of expenditures involved.

The Brookings study also examined the complexities involved in the simple proposition that users should pay for transportation projects from which they benefited. In particular, the study noted that user charges might be justified in terms of the economic allocation of resources, if problems of multiple uses of transportation facilities and difficulties of assigning costs in a practical manner could be overcome. However, it was also observed that planning transportation facilities solely on the basis of total cost would not necessarily achieve the *kind* of transport system desired. In fact, it was pointed out that exclusive reliance on the economic aspects of decision-making in transportation could mean national catastrophy.

The authors concluded that expressions of concern over national security are seldom found in the actual conduct of federal transportation activity. In other words, policy rhetoric dwells on it but little operational effect results. The state of preparedness of transportation facilities and equipment before 1941, for example, was found to be as much a matter of good fortune as anything. In addition, the study criticized the lack of information available on railroad equipment and motor vehicles available for use in time of emergency.

And what of the many problems stemming from formulation of transportation policies on a modal basis? The most serious shortcoming highlighted was the lack of a planning strategy which would trace the divergent lines of federal action through to their logical consequences. Here, Dearing and Owen analyzed the impact of this lack, particularly the resistance to physical- and service-coordination among modes, the indifference shown toward the conflicts and inconsistencies in regulatory policies, and the regulation of aviation, apart from other modes, on the grounds of technological uniqueness.

The Sawyer Report[20]

At about the same time that the Brookings Institution was engaged in its study, the Department of Commerce was conducting its own reevaluation of national transportation policy. The report which resulted was in the nature of a brief review; certainly it failed to reflect any analysis in depth.

The report began on the note that " . . . development of an adequate and low-cost transportation system is the keystone of federal transportation policy." After reviewing the evolution of national policy, it analyzed the numerous factors outside of those justified on economic grounds, that had important bearing on the content of policy. In general terms, the report was preoccupied with matters of *national defense*. It pointed to both the legitimate transportation considerations that defense generated and the excesses of federal financial participation in projects that it engendered.

Its primary recommendation was to place the responsibility for federal transportation policy in one location. The report concluded that:

An organization which had the general responsibility for evolving the Nation's basic transportation (except for the administration of regulatory functions), would appear to furnish a good nucleus for any necessary wartime control agency or agencies.[21]

The Weeks Report[22]

A change to a Republican administration, and renewed business pressure to reexamine the competitive facets of transportation policy, led to yet another study that culminated in the Weeks Report.

Its major conclusion stated that the transportation sector was operating in a general atmosphere of "pervasive competition," and that regulatory programs and policies ought to be adjusted accordingly. A secondary but nonetheless important conclusion asserted that a strong system of common carrier transportation was paramount to the public interest. The report recommended that this be accomplished by, first, placing more carriers under common carrier regulation, and, then, easing these controls and relying more heavily on competitive forces to achieve low cost transportation.

Some serious questions can be raised about the findings of the Advisory Committee. Perhaps its greatest weakness was to underestimate the complexities of the transportation market in concluding that transportation had become more competitive. For example, the unit of output in transportation is considerably more complex than the homogeneity of the "ton-mile" would suggest. Yet the "ton-mile" was the common denominator relied upon by the Advisory Committee in assessing the efficacy of the transportation system. It simply fails to account for such factors as speed, flexibility, safety and dependability, and the differing elasticities of demand for service that are involved. Nor did the report take into account the fact that transportation runs the gamut from nearly perfect competition to near complete monopoly.[23]

The report also argued for excess common carrier capacity in the interests of national defense. However, it failed to answer the question of how such excess capacity *and* a profitable system of common carriage could be maintained simultaneously in an atmosphere of vigorous rate competition. The principle involved is that price competition eliminates excess supply. Since such excess capacity has almost never been held out of commercial competition, it is difficult to see how the objectives of maintaining sharp competition and extra transportation capacity for national defense could be achieved at the same time.

The Mueller Report[24]

Continued concern over the lack of comprehensive consideration of transportation policy prompted the study that resulted in the Mueller Report. For the most part, it concerned itself with the needs for more research in transportation, particularly costs, user charges, and user benefits. Also advocated was a census of transportation to fill the many informational gaps in transportation data. Finally, the report placed emphasis on a strategy of gradualism in bringing about policy changes.

The value of this study was primarily one of pointing up the informational needs that had been obscured or taken for granted in earlier evaluations. But, it had little impact in bringing about any significant changes in substantive policies.

The Doyle Report[25]

The lack of resolution of pressing concerns involving transportation stimulated the Senate Committee on Interstate and Foreign Commerce to undertake its own intensive investigation of national transportation policy. Unfortunately, the study took longer than anticipated and the study group was forced to submit, as its final report, the preliminary findings of the evaluation. Nevertheless, of all the postwar studies of transportation policy, the Doyle Report ranks, by far, as the most detailed and thoroughly documented analysis of the status of United States transportation policy. Numerous well-supported conclusions were reached that were to prove substantially correct in years to follow.

It noted, for example, that if the trends of the 1960s continued, private and exempt carriages would account for half of all intercity freight movement by 1975. The report thus reflected a dim view of the future of common carriage, indicating that if traffic levels continued to fall many common carriers simply could not survive.

The study also found that government organization for formulating and implementing national transportation policies contributed to the lack of rational administration of the sector. In particular, it noted a need to coordinate regulatory and promotional activities.

The report also observed that Congress itself had fragmented its inquiries into the transportation problems of the nation, and had examined only small parts of the total spectrum. At one point, the report concluded that the federal government contributed to the economic plight of regulated carriers through its use of the provisions of Section 22 of the ICC Act, which allow for negotiation of low rates for government transportation. The magnitude of this problem is indicated by the estimate made by Earl B. Smith, former Director of the Transportation and Communications Office of the Defense Department, that repeal of this provision would cost the defense establishment $200 million a year for freight and $15 million for passengers. The point he did not include, however, is that this comprised income which common carriers failed to receive as revenue.[26]

Turning to another arena of policy formation, the report found that the federal government had an important role to play in solving the problems of urban transportation by revising regulatory policy, conducting planning and research activities, and using the availability of federal programs in metropolitan areas as a lever to institute comprehensive planning.

Numerous ideas for organizational change were also presented in the study. (In fact, the number of changes recommended may account for the lack of attention that some of the study's recommendations received.) Most of the changes suggested for the federal structure had been made before, but there were several innovations. These included:

Creation of a Department of Transportation. However, organization at the Assistant Secretary level was encouraged along functional lines rather than by clientele or mode of transport;

Consolidation of the CAB, ICC and FMB into a single Federal Transportation Commission;

To speed the adjudicatory process in transportation, creation of a *Transportation Circuit Court of Appeals;*

Chartering of a National Rail Freight Car Corporation and consideration of a National Railroad Passenger Service Corporation. (As discussed, this approach was adopted in late 1970 with the establishment of AMTRAK);

Institution of a House and Senate Joint Committee on Transportation to serve as a focal point for coordinating legislation related to national transportation policy and for long-range planning purposes.

It is difficult to assess the true impact and ultimate significance of the Doyle Report. Nor is it easy to determine the weight its findings were given when changes in federal comprehensive transportation planning requirements were legislated at a later point, or when legislation creating the Department of Transportation was finally enacted. But it proved very rich in specific data on national transportation trends and supported many of its recommendations with both information and informed opinion, not opinion alone.

As noted, the major problem of the report was its lack of focus. This might well be explained by the short supply of both funds and time, which ultimately forced this "preliminary" examination to serve as the final product. It was the last of the major studies of national transportation policy to be conducted in the 1960s.

Comprehensive Planning and Environmental Planning Requirements

A third influential factor affecting the formation of national transportation policy in the modern period has been the deliberate effort to make provision of increasing amounts of federal assistance contingent upon the institution of comprehensive and environmental planning processes by recipient units of government.

The "pacesetter" for this policy was the Housing Act of 1961.[27] This Act signaled the rejuvenation of American urban transportation and helped to pave the way for favorable consideration of the Urban Mass Transportation Act of 1964. In particular, the law contained a provision under which federal urban planning assistance was made available for " . . . comprehensive urban transportation surveys, studies, and plans to aid in solving problems of traffic congestion, facilitating the circulation of people and goods in metropolitan and other urban areas, and reducing transportation need." Further, the Act called for federal assistance to state and local government " . . . to facilitate comprehensive planning for urban development, including coordinated transportation systems, on a continuing basis." At least in urban areas, then, the interdependence of transportation planning and general community planning was formally recognized.

Since that time, the requirement for comprehensive planning, including that for transportation, has been incorporated in other legislation, such as that creating the "Model Cities" Program. In addition, similar provisions have been included in every piece of legislation dealing with transportation development. In this regard, programs designed to cope with problems of urban transportation, and the institution of very new programs, such as those discussed earlier – intercity rail passenger transportation and aviation facilities development – call for achievement of the goal of "balanced transportation" and "comprehensive planning."

A provision incorporating this approach was also included in the Federal Aid Highway Act of 1962. It stated that, beginning in 1965, federal grants-in-aid for highway projects within urban areas would be allocated only where there was a continuing, comprehensive transportation planning process carried on cooperatively by the states and local communities. Thus, only in the last several years has the powerful lever of highway fund allocation been used to force at least some measure of integrated planning.

As indicated earlier, however, the effectiveness of this measure presents another matter for consideration. The primary problem is that the highway network authorized by the Federal Aid Highway Act of 1956 had been planned for a long period and few basic changes in it have been made up to now. In fact, all but small parts of the system have been constructed, or are committed to construction. In the long run, it would appear that if any flexibility is to be exercised in integrating the elements involved in comprehensive planning, most of the highways now under construction, or planned, will have to be accepted as "givens."

Very closely associated with the growth "comprehensive" planning requirements, and yet in another respect a concern with a rather different source and orientation, was the increasing recognition in the late 1960s of the importance of ecological and environmental planning. As far as transportation planning is concerned, this emphasis first took meaningful form in the Transportation Act of 1966 that created the Department of Transportation (discussed in the next chapter). Among other responsibilities assigned to the Secretary was that of withholding approval of projects that required use of park, recreational, or other public lands, unless there was no reasonable alternative. Even if such lands were authorized for use, the law required that all possible steps be taken to minimize adverse effects.

Stronger teeth were put into the federal apparatus for environmental planning with the passage of the National Environmental Policy Act of 1969.[28] It required that all agencies contemplating any action take into account environmental impact, adverse effects, alternatives to the proposed action, relationships between short term uses and long term productivity, and irreversible and irretrievable commitments of resources. Since that time, the thrust of federal policy concerning the environment has become the responsibility of the Environmental Protection Agency located in the Executive Office of the

President. As a consequence, the entire range of national transportation policy has taken on a new complexion at the operational level.

Currently, each piece of new legislation covering the various modal programs has dictated that planning will take into account environmental effects. Thus, highway development now falls under this policy; creation of new airports, and the operations of existing ones, are to incorporate adequate provisions for protection of the environment. The Urban Mass Transportation Assistance Act of 1970 declares as a national policy that special efforts be made to preserve the environment in planning, designing, and constructing such facilities.

In retrospect, it appears that if the previous decade asked, "What price progress?" the next ten years will ask, "What price environmental protection?" Because of its unique relationships within the system of federal transportation policymaking as a whole, this subject will be explored further in Chapter 8.

Recognition of a Federal Role in Solving
Urban Transportation Problems

The fourth basic characteristic of the modern period affecting national transportation policy has been a recognition of, at least, limited federal responsibility in the search for solutions to urban transportation problems. In many respects, this trend has been closely associated with the employment of the comprehensive planning requirements just noted. Again the Housing Act of 1961 was instrumental in providing initial federal funding for urban transportation projects. The Act initially authorized $50 million for federal loans to be used for the acquisition and improvement of mass transportation facilities in urban areas, and $25 million for transit demonstration grants which did not involve "major long-term capital improvements."

But perhaps the greatest single impetus given to this change in federal policy direction was the Transportation Message of President John F. Kennedy, delivered in 1962.[29] The President devoted one section of the Message to consideration of the urban transportation problem and the need for both long-term federal assistance and emergency aid. Much of the current federal transportation policy stance in urban areas reflects basic approaches suggested by President Kennedy.

Several specific recommendations included in the Message were eventually adopted. These dealt with continuing demonstration grants for mass transit, requiring comprehensive planning in urban areas as a prerequisite for qualification for highway grants-in-aid, and initiating further urban mass transportation legislation. However, the amount of funds authorized was somewhat less than President Kennedy had suggested.

Up to the 1970s, the Urban Mass Transportation Act of 1964 served as the chief instrument through which the federal government has rendered assistance to urban areas in seeking solutions to their transportation problems.[30] The Act was designed to encourage improved mass transportation systems, particularly their area-wide use for urban development, and to provide assistance to state and local governments in financing such systems.

The Act authorized a $375 million grant program: $75 million for 1965, $150 million for 1966, and $150 million for 1967. And again the requirement of coordinated urban transportation planning, as part of a comprehensively planned development of urban areas, was included in the Act. A federal grant for a project was not to exceed two-thirds of the "net project cost" — the part that could not be financed from revenue. Grants could be applied only to project capital costs. These limits, obviously, stood in sharp contrast to the program for funding construction of interstate highways, which provides ninety percent of funding for planning and construction from the federal government's Highway Trust Fund.

New Developments in Funding Urban Mass Transportation

The year 1970 witnessed the emergence of a more sweeping approach to urban transportation problems in the form of the Urban Mass Transportation Assistance Act.[31] Developed within the Nixon Administration by the Department of Transportation, the Act provides for a federal program of assistance that would amount to $10 billion over a twelve-year period. It authorized the incurrence of obligations amounting to $3.1 billion, distributed in the initial period of implementation as follows:

not to exceed $ 80 million prior to July 1, 1971
not to exceed $ 310 million prior to July 1, 1972
not to exceed $ 710 million prior to July 1, 1973
not to exceed $1260 million prior to July 1, 1974
not to exceed $1860 million prior to July 1, 1975
$3100 thereafter

This funding provision was designed to allow for planning and commitment of funds and projects over a five-year period, as an alternative to the establishment of a mass transit trust fund that would provide revenues for expenditure on a revolving basis. While the legislation allows for obligation of funds, its principal difficulty is that it cannot guarantee the actual appropriation of the funds planned. That remains the prerogative of each succeeding Congress.

Questions remain about the liability to which city and metropolitan governments would be exposed if Congress failed to appropriate in accordance with the above schedule. Indeed, just such problems have arisen in the early 1970s. Performance has not gone according to plan, due to both Congressional actions *and* Nixon Administration policies regarding the spending of appropriated funds. These developments will be explored further in Chapter 7.

Had an "urban mass transportation trust fund" been established, many of these difficulties would not have arisen. But it would have presented other and, perhaps, equally serious problems. Foremost is the question of from what source revenues to support a trust fund would be derived. Highway users and airport users provide the revenue for maintenance of the Highway Trust Fund and the Airport and Airway Trust Fund, respectively. What would be the source of revenue for an urban mass transportation trust fund? Clearly, the "market" involved could not supply the level of funding required.

Perhaps the greatest deficiency of the Act of 1970 is the magnitude of the federal commitment. Testimony before Congress, prior to its passage, indicated strong sentiment for a funding level at least double that finally approved. In fact, much testimony contended that the major metropolitan areas of the country had already developed plans for mass transportation systems that would require $20 billion in federal aid in the next decade.

Added to this important factor is the historically well-established reluctance of Congress to step off into a bottomless abyss of funding mass transportation improvements for metropolitan areas. This reluctance is evidenced by the low level of funding provided for this purpose in the mid- and late-1960s. In 1970, federal outlays for such purposes totaled $161 million, in 1971 they amounted to $215 million, by the end of fiscal year 1972 it is anticipated that they will amount to about $327 million. In light of experience, therefore, "massive" jumps in assistance can hardly be expected in the near future – in spite of much rhetoric to the contrary.

The other important legislation of the modern era bearing on urban transportation problems and the changing content of some aspects of national transportation policy was the High Speed Ground Transportation Act of 1965. Its passage was indicative of concern at the federal level for the long-term consequences of growing urban transportation needs.[32]

Unfortunately, when modern federal transportation policy is assessed in terms of its responsiveness to national urban needs, it appears more significant in intent than in commitment. The aggregate funds appropriated to date for urban transportation purposes are quite small indeed, especially when compared to other federal transportation programs with a distinctly modal orientation, such as highways, aviation, and waterways. Again, it is becoming increasingly apparent that the dimensions of the urban transportation problem are so huge, and the demand for the input of federal funds so large, that an extremely cautious federal government attitude has been fostered.

Institutional Changes to Achieve Coordination

The fifth major aspect of national transportation policy in the modern period has been the revamping of federal institutional arrangements to bring about greater policy coordination and integration. The outstanding development in this direction was the formation of the Department of Transportation which occurred in 1966, and the beginning of its functioning in 1967. Because of its potential significance and impact, the next chapter is devoted to this subject.

Summary

The period since the end of World War II has witnessed the continuation of a tortuous and complicated course of federal transportation policy formation.

In many respects, the patterns that have been carved out bear a remarkable similarity to, and elaborations upon, those of the past. One example is the revival of transportation policy studies closely resembling one tactic employed in the latter half of the 1930s. As in that period, the results proved indirect at best and provided little positive guidance that the Executive Branch or Congress could follow in drawing up specific policies or legislation. In a sense, several studies constituted more preachment than program.

Also illustrative is the continuation of the modal orientation in promotion and regulation. Certainly the magnitude of public investment in highways, aviation, and inland waterways has risen so sharply that it dwarfs federal efforts in other transportation endeavors. And, it is equally evident that only within the past few years have commitments of federal funding been made with some consideration of their impact on the character and development of transportation in the nation as a whole.

In the formulation of transportation policy, it is, also, only recently that *social imperatives* have received a weighting that even begins to approach that of political, economic, and technological considerations. This shift in policy content has manifested itself in the small but increasing emphases now being placed on the needs for "comprehensive" planning, and the recognition that the federal government must play a stronger role in helping to solve urban transportation problems. Even more recent – so new, in fact, that it has yet to compile a record of performance – is the application of federal transportation policy to environmental planning.

At the same time, it should be realized that an increasing number of transportation programs, although largely retaining their modal character, are being transformed into longer-term plans. In particular, the year 1970 witnessed this shift in direction being applied to aviation, urban mass transportation, maritime development, and intercity rail passenger transportation. Serious shortcomings remain in each of these programs, reflecting the continued absence of a comprehensive national strategy for determining priorities and assuring adequate federal financial support. But a start has been made on introducing a more realistic time perspective.

These new trends, reinforced by the reorganization of many federal transportation activities under the Department of Transportation, may set the stage for an overall reorientation of national policy. But whether new directions will be followed, in the face of the overwhelming momentum of past practices, remains in serious doubt.

The Department of
Transportation

4 The Department of Transportation

This chapter is concerned with analyzing the formation of the Department of Transportation and evaluating some of the most important directions it is pursuing in evolving "national transportation policy."

Certainly creation of the Department is significant enough to the content and evolution of national transportation policy to justify its recording solely as a historical landmark. Indeed, some fourteen legislative attempts had been made over the past hundred years to bring about such action. And over and above these attempts were the many studies and recommendations, both public and private, that sought the same end. While these proposals often differed substantially in content, they shared one common thread — creation of a federal organization that could unify transportation policy.

The successful effort in 1966 was characterized by a significant amount of the "in-fighting" that has become such a common part of transportation decision-making in the United States. In retrospect, this struggle represented a microcosm of all of the conflicts that had proceeded it. The concerns and tactics that surfaced during the re-structuring of federal Executive transportation responsibilities shed a bright light on the problems of adapting the goals of vested interests and the public interest. The process of creating the Department also demonstrated how often these goals are incompatible. Consideration of this proposal, for a change of far-reaching proportions, brought into clear focus the stakes involved in existing policies, the fears and hopes engendered by suggested changes in the existing power structure, and the compromises and adjustments that had to be made if a Department of Transportation were to be created.

In the analysis that follows, primary attention will be directed toward reviewing and evaluating the process that made the DOT a reality, outlining the primary functions of the Department, analyzing a number of the more important roles that have been assumed by the Department, and summarizing some of the major proposals which have been made by DOT affecting both urban and other types of transportation. The chapter concludes with a general assessment of the realities and potentialities of the Department's role in influencing the substance of federal transportation policy.

Prelude to Action

A number of important steps served as a prelude to action on creating a new

Department of Transportation. One aspect of this process that occurred in 1962 was the series of national transportation goals proposed by President John F. Kennedy. As demonstrated by subsequent events, these were to have long-lasting influences, both in emphasizing the need for a Department of Transportation and in redefining the objectives of federal transportation policy.

Most important were his recommendations that greater reliance be placed on the free market as a means for allocating traffic among the modes of transportation and that governmental regulatory procedures be selectively relaxed. Secondly, imposition of user charges was advocated as a means of recovering, to the greatest degree possible, the cost of federal investments in the various modes of transportation. Thirdly, he stressed the need for closer coordination of urban transportation planning, and urban land use planning. Fourthly, his plan called for improvement of the competitive position of public transportation *vis-á-vis* private transportation. Finally, President Kennedy sought to make transportation activities of United States carriers engaged in international trade more self-sufficient, thereby reducing the federal subsidies required.

As one of the first steps in his strategy to reorient transportation policies, President Kennedy requested that legislation be passed to exempt railroads and water carriers from having their rates for hauling certain commodities regulated by the ICC. He was particularly concerned by the unequal regulation applied to minimum rates for transport of agricultural and fishery products, and for bulk, and the fact that some carriers were exempt while others were not.[1] But the proposed legislation never survived controversy within the halls of Congress.

In the next two years, a number of other efforts were made to provide "equal competitive opportunities" in the common carrier transportation industry. However, all were to no avail. Attempts were also made to repeal the "Commodities Clause" and to institute changes in selected, federal rate-making policies. All failed.

These experiences (and indeed the long history of failures before them) made it abundantly clear that if changes were to be made in transportation policies, a direct assault on rate structures was not the road to success. For, in fact, such tactics served only to intensify inter-modal conflicts and to solidify the fragmented nature of federal policies.

When the Johnson Administration assumed office, the President formed a coordinating group to take up the "old saw" of streamlining national transportation policies. The group was organized within the Department of Commerce and charged with the responsibility of finding ways to reduce the economic waste of existing policies, reduce regulation, increase competition and coordinate the plethora of agencies spending government funds in transportation.

At this point, indications were that primary attention would be given to changes which could be made without new legislation and without creating a new department. However, it soon became apparent that neither of these constraints could be effectively realized. Ultimately, President Johnson became convinced that a new Department of Transportation would provide the only logical foundation stone for a broad reorientation of federal transportation policy.

The President's intention to recommend the new Department was first indicated in his State of the Union Message in 1966. At that time, a special task force composed of representatives of most of the agencies expected to be directly affected by the Department, under the chairmanship of Assistant Director of the Bureau of the Budget Charles Zwick, began the job of drafting the bill and developing plans for setting up the Department.[2]

On March 4, 1966, President Johnson sent a special message to the Congress setting forth his reasons for recommending that a Department of Transportation be created.[3] On the same day, Senator Warren G. Magnuson and Representative Chet Holifield introduced companion bills, S. 3010 and H.R. 13200, which had been drafted in the Executive Branch.

The special message stressed that the United States was the only major nation in the world which relied so heavily on privately-owned and privately-operated transportation. At the same time, however, the President noted that this reliance was made possible only by the extensive latitude that had been given to private enterprise by various levels of government, and by tremendous investment of public resources.

The following offices and agencies, with all of their respective functions, were recommended for transfer to the new department:

a. The Office of the Undersecretary of Commerce for Transportation, including its Policy, Program, Emergency Transportation and Research staffs;
b. The Bureau of Public Roads;
c. The Federal Aviation Agency;
d. The United States Coast Guard;
e. The St. Lawrence Seaway Development Corporation and the Great Lakes Pilotage Administration;
f. The Alaska Railroad;
g. The Maritime Administration, including its construction and operating subsidy programs;
h. The aviation safety functions of the Civil Aeronautics Board and the railroad and motor carrier safety functions of the ICC;
i. Certain functions of the Army Corps of Engineers relating to bridge commissions, bridge tolls, and obstruction of navigable waterways;
j. Bureaus, to be established, to administer the motor vehicle and highway safety legislation then progressing through the Congress.

The roles that the new Department was to play were envisaged by President Johnson as follows: coordinating transportation programs; encouraging the introduction of new technology; improving safety throughout all methods of transportation; supporting high quality, low-cost service; using planning and systems analysis to strengthen the national transportation system; and developing investment criteria, standards, and analytical techniques for use in evaluating transportation investments.

Transportation safety received particular attention. In fact, the President recommended that a National Transportation Safety Board (NTSB) be created under the Secretary, independent of the operating components of the Department. The Board's five members were to be appointed by the President. It was proposed that the Board absorb the safety functions of the ICC and the CAB, undertake studies to determine causes of accidents, evaluate the adequacy of existing safety standards and set new ones, and enforce compliance with such safety standards as might be established.

As far as economic regulation of the various modes of transportation was concerned, it was recommended that this be continued in existing agencies. This reflected the widely held view that while planning, and providing financial assistance, were appropriate functions of the Executive Branch, economic regulation ought to remain an independent function. Thus, the airline subsidy program was to remain with the CAB, while the subsidy programs of the Federal Maritime Administration were to move with it to the new Department.

The message recommended several steps which were to cause more than a mild stir. One was that the Secretary of Transportation should become involved in the planning of water transportation projects, with the understanding that the navigation portion of such projects would remain under the jurisdiction of the Corps of Engineers. The implication of this recommendation was that nontechnical, economic criteria for such investments could be better analyzed by the Secretary of Transportation. Where multipurpose water projects were involved, the Secretary was to work with the Water Resources Council. The Council was established by the Water Resources Act of 1964 to formulate the principles, standards, and procedures for Federal participation in the preparation of comprehensive regional and river basin plans. Its membership then included the Secretaries of Agriculture; Interior; Army; Health, Education and Welfare; and the Chairman of the Federal Power Commission.

A second controversial change was to charge the Secretary of Transportation, upon the approval of the President, with *developing and issuing standards and criteria* for the economic evaluation of *all* federal transportation investments. This became commonly referred to as "Section 7," during the period when the proposed legislation was being reviewed by Congress.

A third recommendation that stirred conflict was that the ultimate "home" for locating federal responsibility for urban transportation not be decided immediately but be studied by the Secretaries of Transportation and Housing and Urban Development for a year. This was to result in a recommendation to the President of how the programs could best be administered.

Reaction to the Proposal

The last words of the Transportation Message had scarcely been recorded when "first returns" reflecting various fears, doubts, suspicions, and questions began to be voiced. One important issue raised at the outset, but never explored in detail, was the future of governmental use of Section 22 of the ICC Act, under which it obtains favorable, negotiated rates from common carriers. Critics pointed out that the federal government was the biggest single user of transportation and that if the new Department of Transportation could control such shipping it would have a tremendous impact.[4]

But more basic and important to the transportation industry across the country was a deep concern about the prospect of change itself. Misgivings were expressed that the new Department would meddle in regulation and become involved in "politics." This revealed an interesting attitude. It presumed that, up to this time, the formation and implementation of transportation policies had been a "non-political" process.

Nor were other fears lacking. Some critics charged that the new Department would engage in a "wholesale take-over" of the nation's transportation.[5] Certainly many elements in the freight shipping industry, within almost all modes, were most concerned with the potential impact on regulatory policy which a new "umbrella agency" would have. J. W. Bush, new chairman of the ICC at the time, outlined a similar concern several weeks after the President's State of the Union Message, and announced his opposition to the transfer of any regulatory functions to the new Department.

So it was that even before Congress formally began hearings on the bill to create the new Department, an editorial in *Life* concluded:

Thus, we may have to settle for a Department of Transportation whose spirit is willing even though its jurisdiction is weak.[6]

In spite of the rumblings that immediately preceded hearings on the bill and the fact that history was overwhelmingly against achieving success in creating a new Executive Branch Department, the Administration remained optimistic. In fact, just before the hearings began an Administration official indicated that Congressional approval appeared assured because the proposal was " . . . just a managerial shift, a grandstand play that looks like it is doing something. But nothing is going to happen in the bread-and-butter areas. The proposal contains no new programs. It contains nothing for industry to get upset about."[7]

Congress Defines the Issues

Contrary to the above prediction, both the affected industry and the Congress became upset rather quickly over a number of provisions of the proposed legislation. If any single aspect of the legislation could be identified as most crucial to Congress and industry, it was the matter of the intent of the bill. Specifically, was the Administration simply creating a "holding company" organization to coordinate national transportation planning? Or was the proposed legislation not only an attempt to create such a mechanism, but also to define new transportation policies and directions designed to change power relationships? Would this reorientation drastically increase the thrust of federal influence in the transportation sphere?

Clearly, the early understanding was that the new Department would simply serve as a device to bring together agencies engaged in transportation activities which had been scattered about the federal bureaucracy. Indeed, this concept had been the principal theme of recommendations for establishment of a new Department which have been made since the 1930s. It had virtually always been viewed as the first step on the road to unifying federal transportation.[8]

Most of the testimony of government witnesses tended to substantiate this general theme. For the most part, the testimony was restricted to discussion of the difficulties imposed by a faulty, fragmented administrative structure. This emphasis upon *form rather than substance* appeared deliberate, indicating that the statements had been cleared for policy consistency through the Bureau of the Budget and the White House.

The statement of Charles Schultze, Director of the Bureau of the Budget, was representative of this general approach. He emphasized the lack of a central point for coordinating federal transportation activities, and outlined some of the inordinate program emphases which resulted. In addition, he appealed to economy-minded Congressmen by indicating some of the financial savings which would result from a centralized transportation management system. The tone of his argument emphasized more the administrative "tidiness" that the new Department would make possible than changes that would be made in specific transportation policies.[9]

Whether the proposal to establish a Department of Transportation was designed as the first step in a long-range program to bring about substantive coordination of transportation policy, and the elimination of conflicting policy objectives, is open to question. However, in some quarters it has been suggested that if the legislation had spelled out policy changes in lengthy detail, it would have been doomed to failure at the very beginning. It appears that the more plausible tactic of, first, getting the Department established and, subsequently, proposing new policy was the one chosen by the Administration. In this sense, the strategy was designed to be more pragmatic than heroic.[10]

Transportation Investment Standards and Criteria – A Primary Issue

As indicated earlier, the proposed legislation carefully avoided spelling out substantive transportation policy – with one notable exception. The exception was Section 7, which provided that, subject to Presidential approval, the Secretary of Transportation "shall develop . . . standards and criteria . . . for the formulation and economic evaluation of all proposals for the investment of Federal funds in transportation facilities or equipment." However, this responsibility was not to extend to the following:

1. acquisition of transportation facilities for the Federal Government's own use;
2. interocean canals outside of the contiguous United States;
3. defense features which originated in the Department of Defense;
4. programs of foreign assistance.

It is particularly noteworthy that the Administration sought to exempt its own internal transportation programs from the measurement of costs and benefits which it desired to apply to external programs. While this was, and remains, an important policy matter, some Congressmen were concerned about even more fundamental issues. Such concern was reflected in the statement of Senator Warren G. Magnuson, Chairman of the Senate Commerce Committee, in which he questioned how these provisions would affect the *prerogatives of Congress* in determining the manner in which federal funds would be allocated. Further, he questioned the source of information from which standards and criteria would be developed. Senator Magnuson advocated the development of a series of regional economic analyses for "... the purpose of flexibly planning and guiding investment in both the public and private sectors."[11]

Senator John L. McClellan proved equally blunt in expressing his concern about Section 7. In his specific questioning of General MacDonnel of the Corps of Engineers, he asked:

Is not the real purpose of this to give a veto power to the Department of Transportation over proposed projects that you might recommend? Is that not what it adds up to in its final analysis?[12]

Although such an intention was repeatedly denied throughout the hearings, most of the members of the Senate Operations Committee appeared less than convinced. As a result, considerable emphasis was placed on establishing a clear and complete record of the meaning which the proposed legislation was intended to convey.

Yet the undercurrent of concern over Section 7 ran deeper than the matter of defending the general "prerogatives of Congress." More basic was the threat that it posed to the long-established system of Congressional control and trade-offs of specific public works projects. Again, Senator McClellan was most candid in discussing the specific points that concerned him. For example, at one point he noted:

My state has abundant water resources, and we intend to develop them. We are in the process of developing them. Call it pork barrel if you want to, but it is pork for the Nation, because it strengthens the economy of the Nation, and the whole Nation benefits from it. I am not willing to let a Secretary of Commerce or a secretary of anything else make the final decision as to the benefits that may flow therefrom, and set up some standard or criteria that I have got to observe in passing judgment on it.[13]

When the bill came up for consideration before the House of Representatives, the implications of Section 7 again became a focal point. In an effort to meet the criticism which had been generated (and possibly to protect the future prerogatives of the Corps of Engineers itself), Lieutenant General William F. Cassidy, Chief of Engineers, testified that the proposed legislation would have no effect on the evaluation of projects by the Corps.[14] He characterized the role of the new Department as one of providing certain basic data on transportation for use by the Corps and of submitting comments on reports prepared by the Corps in the same way as other departments. But he was unable to spell out the exact relationship that would exist between the new Department and the Corps on water resource development projects.

The provisions of Section 7 also raised other serious questions. Congressman George H. Fallon, Chairman of the House Committee on Public Works, voiced disapproval of the potential for major shifts in the power to make transportation investment decisions which was implied in the bill. He recommended that the provisions be changed to limit them to an *advisory* role for the President and Congress.[15]

Congressman Fallon's particular concern was that the Secretary of Transportation could disapprove highway construction, and rivers and harbors projects without regard to the Federal Aid Highway Act or public works legislation. In other words, he feared that the legislation might be interpreted as giving the Secretary of Transportation veto power over Congressional authorization and appropriations for the highway program, and the rivers and harbors program. He also raised the point that if Section 7 were enacted, the Secretary might take it upon himself to transfer Highway Trust Funds for other purposes.

The tremendous influence of Congressman Fallon's testimony became even more apparent in the House Report on the bill.[16] The Report excepted from Section 7 programs such as the Interstate Highway System and the Highway Trust Fund, Federal grants to localities for airport purposes, and river and harbor projects. Some members of the Committee expressed concern that Section 7 might be used to establish national transportation policy without seeking approval of Congress, and that so many categories of activities had been exempted from its application that undue emphasis might be placed on the remainder.

Nor was this the total extent of opposition which Section 7 engendered. Various representatives of the merchant marine interests interpreted this provision as frustrating all maritime policies.[17] Similarly, representatives of the airlines saw their interests endangered by the provision. And in the eyes of many trucking firms and barge operators, Section 7 smacked of a railroad industry plot to better its position at the expense of everyone else.[18]

Interestingly enough, inland waterway interests made a positive gain as a result of the controversy surrounding Section 7 when the Bureau of the Budget changed the method for computing waterway benefits in an effort to assist in passage of the bill. The previous system was based on making an allowance for rail and highway rate reductions that would follow completion of a waterway. It only counted as a waterway benefit the freight movement and freight benefits it would provide after rival carriers had lowered their charges. The new system allowed the anticipation of rate reductions to be counted as a benefit.

In the final analysis, representatives of the various modes disliked the prospect of entering into direct competition for funds, with priorities set on the basis of public investment criteria and standards established by a Secretary of Transportation. Each of the modes of transportation had always regarded itself as unique, and its requirements for federal funds as separate and distinct. Each had established its individual ties throughout the federal bureaucracy and in the Congress. Thus, it was hardly surprising that in their pursuit of self-interest they viewed with considerable trepidation the prospect of centrally-determined priorities and estimated benefits.

Other Important Issues

While the initial reaction of many segments of the transportation industry regarding the Department of Transportation was to prefer to be "included out," such a course of action was most strongly urged in the case of the Federal Maritime Administration. This reflected a highly complex situation, involving Congressional, maritime industry, and union dissatisfaction with maritime policies. In general, dissatisfaction ran deep regarding the manner in which the Maritime Administration had fared in "the basement" of the Commerce Department, and the prospect that its situation would not be improved by a shift to another department.

Congressional pressure took the form of a recommendation by the House Committee on Merchant Marine and Fisheries to the Committee on Government Operations that a separate Federal Maritime Administration be established.[19] Support for this recommendation was mounted by a maritime pressure group involving both unions and owners. Under the banner of "Save Our Shipping" (S.O.S.), the campaign resulted in a deluge of 18,000 letters and telegrams to Congress advocating an independent Maritime Administration.

Adding fuel to the fire was the fact that the House Republican Policy Committee criticized the bill as inadequate and no answer to the "maritime crisis." In the background lurked the fear that a new Department might undertake a major revision in existing subsidy policies, and subject the questions of ship standardization, ship manning scales, maritime labor wages, and subsistence allowances to much more critical review. It was also feared that the proposal to permit American flag operators to have ships constructed in foreign shipyards would receive favorable consideration. Some of these fears, in fact, were borne out by subsequent events.

The fear of loss of independent identities among virtually all modes of transportation became apparent throughout the hearings. The intensity of their respective arguments was uneven, however, and failed to rival the level of acrimony reached in the drive for an independent maritime agency.

As far as the FAA and the aviation industry were concerned, there was considerable reason to expect that continued high priority would be given by the new Department to the various programs either planned or under way. For the highway mode, the relative security of the Highway Trust Fund, and the presence of many advocates in Congress, seemed to assure neither loss in prestige nor influence in the new Department. Nor were the railroads displeased with the prospect of the new arrangement, for they could only gain from securing some representation in the bureaucracy where none had existed previously. Thus, while the desire for an "independent" status existed in some quarters of the various modes, it was not strong enough to overcome those forces which saw potential gain resulting from Cabinet-level representation on matters affecting transportation policy.

Closely associated with the controversy over Section 7 – but not completely coincident with it – was the concern of a number of Congressmen that the long-range plan called for a "strong" Secretary – one who would "make policy." For some members of Congress, the testimony of Secretary of Commerce Connor was not at all consistent with the "umbrella agency" concept that they had been considering. In his appearance before the Senate Committee on Government Operations, he indicated that the new organization would make possible substantive changes in transportation policy, not simply pull together a group of existing agencies.[20]

The reaction of the Congress was to try to "build a wall" around the Secretary of Transportation so that he could not change programs already authorized by Congress. This tactic served to assure the fulfillment of all existing arrangements, and established a precedent for carefully circumscribing the powers of the Secretary in the future.

Although the Administration proposal provided for the continued orientation of federal transportation policy on a *modal basis,* the bill avoided making the designation of the modal administrators as Presidential appointees. Both the Senate and House members reviewing the legislation insisted that the Administrators be subject to the political process of appointment, and not be solely determined by the Secretary, subject to Presidential approval. They felt that if the primary building blocks of the new department were to be, as "advertised," the modal administrations, such recognition should be an intrinsic part of the appointment process. In effect, this device also served to reduce the prerogatives of the Secretary.

Both the House and Senate took particular interest in maintaining an independent and impartial status for the regulation of safety in transportation. Of all the concerns expressed, the one which occurred most often was that the accident-investigation function of the CAB, even though it was transferred to the new Department, maintain its unbiased orientation. The original plan would have tied this function much more closely to the FAA and to the Secretary. Likewise, Congress generally advocated a more independent role for the National Transportation Safety Board than had been proposed by the Administration. This point of view generally reflected the attitude that if such were not done, the Department of Transportation would frequently be placed in a position of investigating itself – a situation which might lead to more self-protection than honest fact-finding and criticism. The Senate Committee went even further in recommending that all safety decisions of the modal administrators be final and not subject to Secretarial review.[21]

The Administration proposal held in abeyance the questions of relating urban planning and transportation planning, and of which Department should assume responsibility for urban transportation planning. As indicated earlier, it recommended that the Secretaries of Transportation and HUD study the problem for a year and make an appropriate recommendation. But this approach was not received with much enthusiasm in Congress. The close questioning of the HUD representatives, in particular, revealed an overriding Congressional attitude that the urban transportation problem was so basic to what they visualized as the responsibility of DOT that it could scarcely be omitted.[22]

A related point was raised by Senator Ribicoff. He criticized the great potential for duplication of effort which would exist between DOT and HUD. He questioned why this matter could not be resolved immediately; otherwise, he maintained, the goal of centralizing federal transportation policy-making would still remain unattained.

In addition to the gap in coordination of urban transportation planning, a number of important additional aspects of federal transportation policy remained uncoordinated. The House Report pointed out, for example, that spending for air traffic centers and aviation systems would be under the control of the Secretary, but airport construction would not; that alteration of bridges in the interest of navigation would continue to be considered, but not highway bridges and feeder roads; that the Secretary would control funds for marine navigation and shipping aids, but not for other phases of ship safety and water navigation.[23]

To this list might have been added the point that even if the Maritime Administration had become part of the new Department, there would exist a major inconsistency between the economic regulation applied to the aviation mode and the maritime mode. The subsidy program applicable to air carriers, of course, was to remain with the independent CAB, while the subsidy function of the latter was to fall under the direct jurisdiction of the Department of Transportation.

Under the bill, the regulation of the nation's oil pipelines was to shift from the ICC to DOT; yet no provision for a modal administration to handle it was provided. This situation provided the basis for a caustic observation in the House Report on the bill. It stated the only conclusion which could be reached was that if a transportation mode has been so successful that it has never had cause to come under Federal regulation, then it does not desire to be represented in a Department of Transportation, whose objective is to meet the future needs of the United States.[24] This point became all the more important, when, at a later point, the new Department of Transportation was charged with the responsibility for safety regulation of gas pipelines.

This position of the House Report represented almost precisely that taken by the oil pipeline industry in opposing a shift in jurisdiction over it from the ICC to the Department of Transportation. In general, it felt that there was lack of necessity for the shift, and that it had compiled an outstanding safety record. But, perhaps the most important objection to the change went unexpressed. Put simply, such a change of jurisdiction held a number of risks that did not exist in the long established ICC-oil pipeline relationship.[25]

Other Lesser Issues. A number of lesser issues concerning the proposed legislation occupied the attention of Congress, and merit only brief review here. The Administration proposal called for transfer of the car-service function of the ICC to the new Department; the House Report, however, favored no change in its location. For its part, the Senate Committee made a special point of the need for preserving the natural beauty of the countryside, public parks, recreational land, refuges, and historic sites affected by the development of transportation facilities. It also insisted that research and development on aircraft noise abatement be made a specific responsibility of the new Department.

After the House and Senate Committees had completed their work on the proposal, the bill still faced the hurdle of passing both the full House and Senate, and surviving the "give-and-take" of a conference committee. Although the bill passed the Senate, in what fairly could be called a "modified version," it was almost decimated in the House. In the latter case, the powers of the Secretary were severely restricted; Section 7 was dropped completely, and the Maritime Administration was excluded from the Department. In this form, it was considered a "skeletal version" of the original Administration proposal. As a result of the work of the conference committee, however, the final bill restored some of these potential "losses."

DOT Becomes a Reality

The legislation creating the Department was approved on October 15, 1966.[26] It provided for the inclusion of the agencies recommended in the original proposal, with the exception of the Federal Maritime Administration which remained in the Department of Commerce.

One of the primary objectives included in the legislation was the development and recommendation to the President and to the Congress for approval of national transportation policies and programs. The intent, as discussed earlier, was to restrict the latitude of departmental policy-making power. In Section 4 of the Act, it was specifically provided that:

Nothing in this Act shall be construed to authorize, without appropriate action by Congress, the adoption, revision, or implementation of (A) any transportation policy, or, (B) any investment standards or criteria.

Section 4(f) of the Act also empowered the Secretary to preserve cultural, aesthetic, scenic, and historic landmarks affected by highway development, and to search for viable alternatives in such cases.

In Section 7, the standards and criteria to be developed and revised by the Secretary for federal transportation investments were to be promulgated only upon the approval of Congress. And, to the categories of activity that were excepted in the Administration proposal, Congress added water resource projects and grant-in-aid programs. Thus, the legislation made the framework for investment standards and criteria virtually meaningless by eliminating the great bulk of the "money programs" for which it was intended.

The Act noted that among the factors to be considered in establishing standards and criteria are the projected growth of transportation needs and traffic in affected areas, the relative efficiency of various modes of transport, the available transportation services, and the general effect of proposed investment on existing modes, as well as on the regional and national economy. It is interesting to speculate on the effects which consideration of such factors in developing standards and criteria would have on programs involving billions of dollars, such as highway aid, urban transportation aid, and rivers and harbors investments. But all of these fall into the "excepted" category.

As far as the safety provisions of the legislation were concerned, these reflected the attitude of Congress during the period that the bill was being considered. Section 5 established a National Transportation Safety Board. In addition to accident investigation and review functions, the Board received the power to review certificating and licensing actions taken by the Secretary or an administrator. Nor did Congress fail to underscore the "independence" of the NTSB. The legislation required that the following actions be made public: Board recommendations to the Secretary or to administrators, all special studies, and every action requesting the Secretary or an administrator to take action. The Board was specifically made independent of the Secretary, with its members appointed by the President and consented to by the Senate.

The legislation also made the Secretary of Transportation a member of the Water Resources Council on matters involving navigational features of water resource projects.

And finally, the Act charged the Secretaries of DOT and HUD with cooperating on their respective transportation policies and reporting within one year on the organization and location of the urban mass transportation function to the Executive Branch. This took about one and one-half years. The agreement was announced in mid-March, 1968, indicating a general division of policy responsibility as follows:

Department of Transportation – To become responsible for promoting and helping to finance research and development on operating systems involving conventional modes such as trains and buses.
Department of Housing and Urban Development – To promote planning of urban facilities (such as transit) along with schools, hospitals, and other community institutions as part of overall urban planning. Thus, its role in transportation emphasized the relationships that it bore to other urban concerns and the need for their coordination through HUD.

Under the arrangement, DOT assumed responsibility for urban research and development, most transportation grants-in-aid, and demonstration projects. It was also agreed that both departments would act jointly in testing systems incorporating advanced technology and in proposing the use of unconventional vehicles and propulsion systems.[27]

What did these general guidelines result in as far as actual program shifts were concerned? The record indicates that the bulk of research and development projects shifted to DOT. Of the forty-six positions in HUD which had been devoted to urban transportation, thirty-eight were transferred to DOT. In all, only fifty projects, involving $3 million, were retained in HUD. For the most part these were concerned with particular aspects of comprehensive planning in urban areas, or were so close to completion that to shift them to DOT would have been impractical.[28]

To provide the administrative apparatus for handling these additional responsibilities, the Urban Mass Transportation Administration was created in the Department of Transportation. It was to be considered parallel to the modal administrations concerned with rail, highway, and air transportation. The nature of its functions, however, is inter-modal.

Department Structure – A "Holding Company"
in Transition

When DOT became operational in 1967, it took the form of the "holding company" that had been anticipated. But a primary component – the maritime mode – had been excluded. This led to a series of attempts to entice the Maritime Administration into departmental membership. This was done, initially, by developing programs that would have sufficient appeal for maritime interests to relent in their resistance to such a move.

In early 1967, for example, then Secretary Boyd proposed a plan to provide about $200 million annually for five years in construction subsidies to build fifteen United States flagships a year, as compared to the program that had been providing $120 million annually for thirteen ships. But there was a price. The arrangement also would have permitted foreign built ships (bulk carriers), to qualify for operating subsidies. And, foreign-built ships would have been allowed to operate in coastal trade.

United States shipbuilders flatly opposed the idea of national flagships being built in foreign yards. In fact, George Meany, President of the AFL-CIO, commented acidly: "Maybe we should get our Secretary of Transportation from some foreign yard."[29]

In May of 1968, Boyd returned with another maritime proposal, this time linking the expansion and improvement of the subsidy program to the size of the fleet needed for national security purposes. Again Congress and the maritime industry were highly critical and found the DOT approach almost totally unacceptable. So vigorous was the response that they were able to push a bill through Congress to establish a separate Maritime Administration, which President Johnson subsequently killed with a "pocket veto." Since that time, as reviewed in Chapter 3, legislation has been passed to undertake a long-term program of maritime expansion and rebuilding. MARAD remains in the Commerce Department; for the time being at least, this "prodigal" mode will not become an integral part of DOT.

Even without the Maritime Administration, the addition of the Urban Mass Transportation Administration to the other modal administrations – Coast Guard, Federal Aviation Agency, Federal Highway Administration, Federal Railroad Administration, and St. Lawrence Seaway Development Corporation – gave the Department substantial operating responsibilities. The respective powers of the administrations under the law were to be far-reaching, inasmuch as they reported to the Secretary. In fact, it became abundantly clear during hearings on the DOT bill that Congress would insist on this direct kind of access, if such had not been included as part of the Administration's legislative proposal. Moreover, if the primary purpose of establishing the organization was to bring together sundry transportation agencies scattered about the federal establishment, would not this be a rather natural organizational arrangement?

Significant Organization Changes – The Assistant Secretaries

Significant changes have been occurring in DOT since 1967 that affect these original power alignments and policy content. Not overly emphasized during consideration of the creation of DOT, but moving into positions of ever greater prominence during the past few years, are the Assistant Secretary positions. These were functionally organized to provide policy assistance to the Secretary, and to coordinate functions common to the overall mission of the department as a whole. Several changes have already been made in this structure and, in some cases, reorganization has taken place immediately after organization. In fact, there was an initial proliferation of offices within the structure that prompted

Congress to caution against making the Secretarial superstructure too cumbersome and fragmented. As Chart 4-1 indicates, Assistant Secretaries now operate in each of the following areas: Policy and International Affairs, Environment and Urban Systems, Safety and Consumer Affairs, Systems Development and Technology, and Administration.

Policy and International Affairs. Perhaps the key position at this level exists in the area of Policy and International Affairs. This Assistant Secretary formulates, reviews and analyzes domestic and international transportation policies and programs affecting the movement of people and goods. Such responsibility places him in a pivotal role to influence all but the strictly modal programs involving operations. And with the growing awareness of the interdependence of all of the facets of transportation upon one another, the likelihood is that the position will continue to weigh heavily in all basic policy considerations involving the Department.

Most vitally affecting future policy was the charge to this Assistant Secretary to undertake a National Transportation Needs Study. This is to provide a basis for a DOT definition of the goals and objectives of national transportation policy in terms of requirements, costs, systems, and economic impact. The study was scheduled to be forwarded to Congress in 1972; it is to contain DOT legislative and expenditure recommendations covering fiscal years 1974 through 1978, and outline relationships between proposed federal programs and the longer-term needs of states and localities.

Systems Development and Technology. The Assistant Secretary for Systems Development and Technology oversees the Department's efforts in this area to assure that they are well-planned, coordinated, and implemented. He also provides assistance to the Secretary on technical and scientific matters. More specific functions falling within the province of this component include coordination of programs involving departmental telecommunications, and research and development activities relating to abatement of noise. Responsibility for coordination and integration of Departmental research efforts is particularly crucial since all of the modal administrations carry out numerous research activities within their individual areas of responsibility.

Administration. The Assistant Secretary for Administration deals with the huge problems of administering the department and providing a source of expertise on organization and management. It represents the only top position that falls under civil service, and is expected to provide continuity. Specific tasks include personnel and training, organization and management, administrative operations, investigations, security, logistics, procurement, and auditing. In addition, special administrative services are provided to various modal administrations on a reimbursable basis.

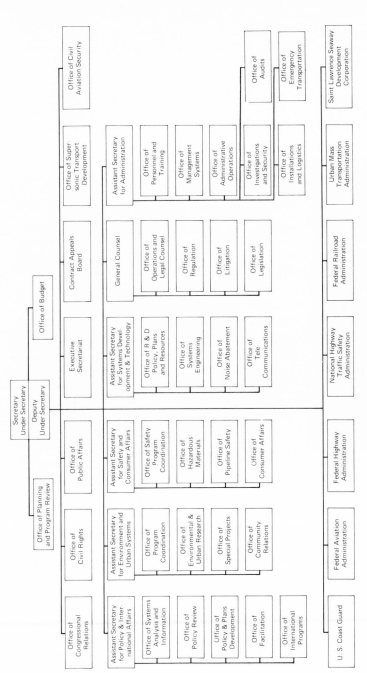

Chart 4.1. Department of Transportation. Source: *Department of Transportation and Related Agencies Appropriations for 1971*, Hearings Before a Subcommittee of the Committee on Appropriations, House of Representatives, 91st Cong., 2d Sess., (Part 3) (Washington, D.C.: U.S. Government Printing Office, 1970), p. 583; *Department of Transportation and Related Agencies Appropriations for 1972*, Hearings Before a Subcommittee of the Committee on Appropriations, House of Representatives, 92d Cong., 2d Sess., (Part 3) (Washington, D.C.: U.S. Government Printing Office, 1971), p. 791.

Safety and Consumer Affairs. The latest major reorganization within the Department of Transportation, occurring in fiscal year 1971, created a new Assistant Secretary for Safety and Consumer Affairs. This position was formerly assigned to Public Affairs. Obviously, this reorientation of departmental efforts provides a significant response to the growing needs of coordinating and bringing a focus to the safety programs of the modal administrations. Moreover, the consumer component of the new organization reflects the growing impact of "consumerism" on government in general. In this case, the Assistant Secretary is charged with the responsibility of viewing the provision of transportation services from the point of view of the recipient.

In addition to these broad responsibilities, the new Assistant Secretary also administers the Department's program related to the movement of hazardous materials and the natural gas pipeline safety program.[a]

Environment and Urban Systems. The other recent organization to come into being at the Assistant Secretary level is that of Environment and Urban Systems. It was established in fiscal year 1969 to deal with the problem of achieving balance between human values and engineering values in the development of transportation systems. In substantial part, its creation was a direct outgrowth of the National Environmental Policy Act of 1969 described previously. The Assistant Secretary is responsible for departmental compliance with this Act. Basically, this responsibility introduces new environmental considerations in the transportation planning process. Most fundamental is concern for approaching problems of land use that will bring about both "balanced transportation development" and ecological compatibility.

Responsibility for making recommendations on Section 4(f) of the Transportation Act of 1966 has also been placed in this Office. It will be recalled that this part of the legislation requires that the use of park, recreation, and similar public lands not be approved for any project unless there is no alternative. When such lands are used, all possible measures must be used to reduce the adverse effects. With the continued emphasis being placed on such factors in the transportation planning process, it is likely that rapid expansion of staff and resources in this area will continue for some time in the future.

A number of transportation projects throughout the country have been substantially modified, or indefinitely postponed, by the Secretary of Transportation on the bais of their environmental incompatibility. Illustrative are the proposed Miami Airport in South Florida, the Riverfront Expressway in

---

[a]It is worth noting that pipeline operations have traditionally been classified as a mode of transportation, comparable to rail, aviation, waterways, and highways. Yet the DOT organization planners chose to place responsibility for it directly under an Assistant Secretary, rather than to establish another modal administration. Moreover, the most recent organization to be created at the modal administration level is the National Highway Traffic Safety Administration. This is in addition to the Federal Highway Administration, which has been part of DOT since its creation.

New Orleans, Louisiana, and the North Expressway in San Antonio, Texas. The Everglades Jetport threatened the quantity of the water supply reaching Everglades Park and South Florida. At stake were the animal and plant systems native to this part of the country. Development of the airport was limited by DOT to that of a training facility, and further consideration as a commercial center was indefinitely deferred. The Riverfront Expressway threatened to drastically alter historic parts of the city and destroy one of the most picturesque views of the city. Likewise, in San Antonio, expressway development posed a threat to maintaining the character of the city. Other alternatives were to be explored in these two highway cases. In the past several years, the number of additional transportation projects coming under similar scrutiny has mushroomed to include many more highway and airport projects, as well as bridge projects.[30]

Increasing expressions of national concern for ecology and the environment have also reacted upon the character and content of research and development activities of the Department of Transportation. Thus, the Department's recommended budget for fiscal year 1972 contained provisions for a number of studies that would enable future integration of transportation and environmental planning.

One projected study would be concerned with developing specific techniques to ensure that presently unquantifiable amenities and values be given appropriate consideration in decision-making processes. Another would determine procedures for estimating the degradation potential of transportation alternatives. One aim would be to identify ways in which transportation projects could be utilized to improve the environment and the quality of life.

Yet other studies plan to focus on the assessment of the *total costs* of projects which deplete the urban landscape and their open-space areas. The overriding goal is to improve the "state of the art" of transportation planning in metropolitan areas. Also planned are continuing studies of the potential impacts that new or expanded transportation facilities would have on the resource base, including water quality, fish and wildlife, soil and mineral deposits, woodlands and wetlands, and scenic and recreational sites.

In total, well over $1 million would be spent on these explorations. They are indicative of the far-reaching impact that the provisions of Section 4(f) of the Department of Transportation Act and the National Environmental Act of 1969 are having on federal transportation policy.[31]

Shifts in Policy Emphasis

In summary, DOT is reviewing transportation projects in terms of values that have not been given high priority by engineers, planners, and elected officials. By and large, these values are those held by people and communities relating to nontechnical factors such as open space, parks, historic sites, recreational areas, revitalization of downtown areas, improvement of accessibility to jobs, preservation of neighborhoods, and reduction of all types of pollution.

The evolution of these emphases suggest several important directions of future DOT development.

First, the Office of the Secretary itself is moving quickly to consolidate both expertise and power with which to administer the Department. Centralization of policy-making is occurring at the same time that decentralization of operating responsibilities to the modal administrations is taking place.

Secondly, a substantial effort is being made to develop policies and programs in inter-modal terms. Increasingly, more program justification is presented in terms of the interrelatedness of development rather than as the separate modal programs of the past. Again, this is only the smallest of beginnings, but it is discernible.

Thirdly, the power that was characteristic of the individual modal administrations, when they became a part of DOT in 1967, is slowly but systematically being reduced and channeled toward the functionally-organized Assistant Secretaries. In spite of some "raised eyebrows" in Congress and among vested interests, modal administrations are being gradually stripped of their former full-fledged capabilities to perform their own public affairs work, research, liaison, administration, etc. Much of this change began with the "counterpart" studies that DOT undertook upon its creation. These focused on those staff functions that were executed by individual modal administrations, such as the Federal Aviation Agency and the Federal Highway Administration, on a department-wide basis.

An example of this trend is contained in the budgetary submission made by DOT for fiscal year 1971. In that year, it proposed that the Office of the Secretary be increased by 397 positions – the most substantial increase requested by the Secretary since the Department was created. But even more significant was the fact that 187 of these positions were to be transferred from the administrations " . . . to consolidate certain staff functions which the Secretary has decided can better and more efficiently be carried out on a centralized basis." Needless to say, the modal administrations were less than happy with these harbingers of things to come.

Finally, the relative size and capabilities of the Secretary's staff are growing at a rapid pace, enabling him to rely increasingly on his immediate staff for policy guidance and to lessen substantially dependence on modal administrations for such assistance, as was the case when DOT was created.

These significant shifts in power and influence still represent but a start toward introducing new perspectives and relationships within the organization. Nor are they backed by a clientele or group of vested interests, as are the modal administrations. This factor will undoubtedly limit the degree to which the roles of the modal administrations can be diminished. Nevertheless, I would conclude that these changes portend policy inputs that will differ substantially from the past, and have important consequences for the future.

Changes in Program Content and Direction

In addition to these changes that have occurred, linking policy content with organizational arrangements, many other significant shifts in program and direction have taken place. Several of these will be reviewed in substantive fields of policy formulation such as mass transportation, cross-modal financing, regulation, and safety. Again, the coverage is intended to suggest the range and nature of policy evolution rather than to comprehend the full scope of all that has happened.

Mass Transportation. The Department of Transportation has been established for only a few years and is still developing mechanisms for dealing with urban mass-transportation responsibilities. Yet, if precedent can serve as a yardstick, the fundamental question that it will face is the one that HUD faced before it — what level of funding for transportation programs will be sought and provided?

As an illustration, total federal funds obligated for mass transit through 1967 were $373.7 million. Of this amount, $320 million went to seventy-five projects in fifty-seven urban areas. Demonstrations totaled $45.6 million through 1967 for sixty projects — most of which were of the improvement type.[32] Altogether, the Housing Act of 1961 and the Urban Mass Transportation Act of 1964, as extended, authorized $675 million for the period years 1965-1969.

More recent data indicate that mass transit outlays totaled only $161 million in 1970 and $215 million in 1971. The 1972 projection is $327 million.

Since its establishment within DOT, the Urban Mass Transportation Administration has continued the past record of "footdragging" on development of a program commensurable with national needs. Funding levels have really changed little from previous years. The pattern has been for the Administration to request funding quite inadequate for meeting urban requirements. Compounding the problem, Congress has then usually moved to cut even these amounts.

As noted earlier, the Urban Mass Transportation Assistance Act of 1970, with its contemplated obligation of $3.1 billion in the first five years and $10 billion over a twelve-year period, could alter this record for the better. But whether even these amounts will be enough to meet minimum national requirements remains very much in doubt.

That the funding problem continues to be serious has been made evident on numerous occasions. But one of the most conclusive examples came to light during fiscal year 1971. As a result of its budgetary review for that year,

Congress limited the amount of money that UMTA could obligate to $600 million. Subsequently, this amount was further limited by the Office of Management and Budget of the Nixon Administration to a level of $400 million. Of this amount, only $269 million was designated for capital improvement grants.

Some proponents of the Urban Mass Transportation Assistance Act interpreted the provisions of the law to mean the DOT would simply have to request Congress for the authority to obligate the $3.1 billion immediately. It has not done so; neither has Congress departed from the customary process of providing *annual* appropriations and obligational authority. So far, the net result has been the provision of funding levels for mass transportation that are only slightly higher than those provided in the years prior to passage of the Act.

The budget request for fiscal year 1972 included a request for $497 million in capital grants. And UMTA has maintained that by the *end* of the five-year period, the $3.1 billion will be obligated. However, the problem with this reasoning, as well as with the annual budgetary process, is that most mass transit systems cannot start projects of substantial magnitude because continued federal funding is not guaranteed.

But the frustration does not end there. At that point UMTA had received requests for grant assistance amounting to *$2.6 billion.* And even this amount represented a small percentage of those that would be made if adequate funding were available. The federal policy response continues to be one of doling out relatively small sums, entirely out of proportion to the size of mass transportation problems being faced all across the nation.[33]

Nor do planned expenditures compare favorably with the level of *actual* transportation investment being made in highways. Spending through the Highway Trust Fund has been proceeding at a rate of $4 billion, or more, *annually.* During the last twelve years, the Interstate Highway Program has spent roughly five times the amount projected for urban mass transportation assistance in the next twelve years.

Apart from the mass transportation programs that were shifted from HUD, are the High Speed Ground Transportation Program and the Northeast Corridor Transportation Project transferred to DOT as part of the shift of the Office of the Undersecretary of Transportation from the Department of Commerce. Both programs were initially carried out under the supervision of the Federal Railroad Administration, although they obviously involve more than this mode. Since that time responsibility for them has been moved to the Assistant Secretary for Policy and International Affairs.

The potential implications of these programs for future urban transportation policy could become highly significant. Because of the many technological, and other facets of the projects involved, analysis of their specific content will be explored in Chapter 6.

Attempts to Achieve Self-Support. Another major policy thrust of the new Department has been to propose legislative changes that would move toward putting federal investments in the various modes on a self-supporting basis. This was reflected in the Airport and Airway Development Act of 1970, discussed in the previous chapter. Likewise, departmental support for legislation that would impose user taxes on waterways offers another example of the movement toward linking transportation beneficiaries and the costs of transportation-facility improvements. These moves draw heavily on the model of the Highway Trust Fund in particular, and federal highway financing in general.

Transportation Safety. Another important function of DOT already involved in a major transition is the range of safety programs conducted by both the National Transportation Safety Board and the modal administrations. The Board was established within the Department as an independent organization to investigate all civil aviation accidents, conduct special transportation safety studies, and make recommendations for the purpose of preventing accidents and promoting safety in transportation. The Board was expected to investigate only "major" surface transportation accidents and to rely on the modal administrations within the Department to develop safety programs.

National transportation safety priorities have made little sense from the very beginning. The major consequence of policies adopted is that the NTSB has devoted the vast bulk of its resources to aviation safety, and worked on safety problems of surface transportation only sporadically and, then, on an "exception basis." As a result, a marked, inverse relationship has developed between federal expenditures for aviation safety and aviation accident rates.[34] Meanwhile, enormous problems of transportation safety have engulfed the modes of surface transportation. Grossly inadequate attention has been given to them.

Several recent changes may affect relative emphases of the future. One is reflected in the Federal Railroad Safety Act of 1970.[35] It makes the Secretary of Transportation responsible for rules, regulations, orders, and standards for all areas of railroad safety. In effect, railroad safety will become, for the first time, a *nationwide* program rather than a fragmented collection of controls spread over various federal and state jurisdictions. Part of the Act is devoted to instituting control mechanisms for the transportation of hazardous materials.

But the major shift in safety emphasis occurred with the elevation of the National Highway Safety Bureau to a position coequal with the modal administrations. The Highway Traffic Safety Administration is now independent of the Federal Highway Administration and reports directly to the Secretary. This change was designed to increase the visibility and stature of the Bureau, and project a concern for safety in closer accord with the magnitude of the problem.

Money spent on highway safety programs has risen sharply in the last two years. In 1971, $46.2 million was committed; requests for 1972 spending rose to

$89 million, in large part to fund the Alcohol Countermeasures Program. Another hopeful sign was that the year 1970 witnessed the first reduction in national traffic deaths – 55,300 – which was 1,100 less than 1969.[36]

These changes took a long time to come to fruition. They are revealing, however, in demonstrating the difficulties of making programs responsive to needs, even when the activities involved are housed within a new agency. In these cases, past practices and concerns were initially carried along with the agencies that were relocated within DOT. Nonetheless, a case could be made to show that such disparities in safety priorities might not have come to light so readily had not DOT been created.

DOT has also attempted to affect the policies of the regulatory agencies, particularly the Civil Aeronautics Board, Interstate Commerce Commission, and the Federal Maritime Commission. Specifically, in mid-1967, then Secretary Boyd asked the ICC to keep in mind the potential inflationary influence of national trucking and railroad general freight rate increases which were under consideration. In response, Chairman William H. Tucker indicated that he did not think the appeal would "cut much ice," because the ICC weighed all important factors in its deliberations and the request really concerned nothing new. When the ICC subsequently granted increases, DOT filed a protest with the Commission asking for consideration of the "broader range of economic considerations." In addition, DOT attacked the decision on the grounds that the Commission had not given sufficient consideration to productivity and rate of return factors.

Since these first experiences, the lot of DOT in these activities has improved somewhat. The scope of Departmental intervention has expanded to matters of airport congestion, new air services, intermodal coordination, and carrier conference agreements. These are in addition to intervention actions on rate proposals. In the latter connection, the Department feels it has been quite successful in convincing the ICC that new criteria for justifying rate increases ought to be established.

If the past approaches of the regulatory agencies are a reliable guide, one may conclude that DOT still faces a long and difficult struggle in influencing policy at this level. Before these agencies, it is considered as one of a number of interested parties. It is not looked upon as the "defender of the public interest," for that is a role the regulatory agencies reserve for themselves.

A Perspective on DOT

Over and above the observations which have already been made in this analysis of the Department of Transportation, there are a number of additional considerations which deserve mention.

Foremost is the obvious fact that DOT has been in operation for a comparatively short time. And even during this period it has been receiving new organizational elements and new responsibilities. Its organization and program structures remain incomplete and in states of transition.

Nor can the factor of size be ignored. With its employee population totaling almost 115,000 and its annual budget approaching $10 billion, it is one of the largest elements in all of the federal bureaucracy. The sheer magnitude of the task of "organizing for action" will command the time and attention of its top administrators for an indefinite time to come.

The circumstances surrounding creation of DOT invited criticism that, in retrospect, appears both premature and an underestimation of the impact of subsequent developments. Hugh S. Norton, for example, concluded two months after the Department was created that " ... the mountain has ceased its labor and produced a mouse."[37] Norton viewed the process of creating DOT as a "farcical performance," and criticized the new organization for not being a true consolidation. Other observers interpreted the legislative process of creating DOT as continuing the "non-policy" of the past – distributing its largesse according to the political imperatives of the moment.[38]

While the process of bringing the Department into being might well be criticized, such conclusions regarding its potential for the future appear somewhat extreme. A more realistic assessment of the Department's potentiality was made by Richard Barsness when he noted that while DOT suffers from important statutory restrictions, it should be able to influence national transportation performance gradually. Such an incremental growth of power would be rooted primarily in future developments, and the role DOT could play in assisting new facilities, technology, techniques, and methods of funding.[39] This strategy contains a good deal of merit, since it would de-emphasize problems of reforming the past and concentrate instead on stimulating innovative perspectives for the future.

Perhaps the greatest significance of the formation of the new Department lies not so much in the specific detail of its organization and the changes made, or in the basic purposes spelled out in the legislation which created it, or in the programs that it has either proposed or in which it has had a part thus far. Most important is the fact that DOT, for the first time, provides a focal point within the Executive Branch for consolidating and coordinating many basic elements of national transportation policy. As has been discussed in earlier chapters, this point has long been recognized as a necessary and vital "first step." Without such a mechanism, there would be no grounds for even entertaining the possibility that policy contradictions and fragmentation could be lessened.

Of course it should be noted at this point that the never-ending process of reorganizing the structure of the federal government, in time, may once again drastically alter the DOT mechanisms that have been evolving over the past seven years. President Nixon has proposed a sweeping set of recommendations for revamping the domestic departments of the federal government. If enacted, the Department of Transportation would be divided mainly between the newly-proposed Department of Economic Affairs and the proposed Department of Community Development. Under this arrangement, most of the operating programs would fall under the Department of Economic Affairs. Highway programs and urban mass transportation programs would become the responsibility of the Department of Community Development.[40]

Just what new courses of action DOT will adopt over the next several years have yet to be determined. In its present form, DOT has one of the most complex and difficult missions in the federal government. As noted earlier, the Presidential message calling for its creation carefully avoided policy declarations on key issues. On the surface, the concern was with structural form – not substantive policy. In reality, the real significance of the process which led to formation of the Department may lie in what was left unsaid, and in the questions that were not asked.

DOT has an opportunity to carve out a role for itself in coordinating transportation policy without a great many specific commitments on how it will proceed. On the other hand, it must continue to face the enormously difficult task of bringing together the efforts of as diverse a collection of agencies as has ever been placed under one "departmental roof" in a reorganization. And this task may act as a brake on the imagination and innovation that the Department brings to its tasks.

By the time Congress finished emasculating the bill creating the new Department, the powers of the Secretary were carefully circumscribed and limited. He was to "recommend" policy to the President and to Congress. But, in practice, literal interpretation of this provision has proven difficult, if not impossible. The numerous programs of DOT require frequent interpretation of policy; one may question at what point such interpretations, in effect, become new policy. In those areas where discretionary powers exist, and these are many, the Secretary has already played policy-making roles that have been both weighty and controversial. Beyond this point, of course, is the plain fact that Congress has neither the time nor expertise to make decisions on the vast range of policy matters that now face and will continue to face DOT. It must rely heavily on the Department.

Establishment of the Department may lead in time to a reevaluation of the basic approach which the federal government will take toward national transportation matters. In particular, it may develop that, unlike the past, *initiation* of programs may increasingly become the dominant characteristic of federal transportation policy. In 1966, then Secretary Boyd revealed the implications of such an approach when he stated:

In the past, we have left our transportation system pretty much alone, depending on competition to work things out. Planning, particularly by government officials, was considered akin to socialism and thus taboo. Times have changed, however, and planning now is respectable and necessary. So we can get on with the job.[41]

In its optimism, however, this point of view reflects two serious flaws: The first is that the Department must operate within a number of restrictive statutory provisions. In the long run, much more may be accomplished by persuasion than by reliance on the limited, formal powers at hand. The second flaw is that DOT has only a *share* of the role of the federal government in national transportation policy-making and implementation. So pervasive are the decisions made in transportation that their effects can be fundamentally altered by the regulatory agencies, the courts, Congress, and the President himself. To ignore the fact that the Department is a part, albeit a large one, of a highly complex, interactive federal system — many parts of which are concerned with transportation policy matters — could easily lead to a serious misinterpretation of the relative success or failure that the Department experiences in the future.

Cost-Benefit Analysis—The Highway Models

5

Cost-Benefit Analysis — The Highway Models

As indicated in the previous chapter, pressure for the "scientific" evaluation of public transportation investments has been mounting steadily. The primary motivation appears to be the desire for greater rationality in decision-making affecting transportation. Closely allied with this factor is the dissatisfaction felt in various quarters with effects of political "bargains" and "pork barrel" measures on past transportation development decisions. Such rarely utilized a broadly-based review of the comparative merits of transportation subsystem alternatives for meeting national needs.

The relative importance attached to approaches that would inject "precise measurement" into the transportation investment process was demonstrated by the stress placed on the proposal to make the Department of Transportation responsible for setting *standards and criteria* for transportation investments. If it had been adopted in its original form, this legislation would have made the Department responsible for "across the board" cross-benefit analysis of *all* proposed transportation projects.

This chapter deals with the possible application of cost-benefit analysis to national transportation investment decisions. Considerable interest has been expressed in this question; indeed, some are willing to have it play a crucial and, perhaps, deciding role in future federal modal policies. Yet in many respects, cost-benefit analysis, as it might be applied to the entire national transportation system, remains an "unknown quantity."

Its most far-reaching applications thus far have occurred in the field of highway planning. Surprisingly little work in such analysis has been done, at least comparatively, in the other modes of transportation. And even more rare is cost-benefit analysis of alternative *inter-modal* projects. But experience indicates that the use of cost-benefit analysis in highway planning offers substantial grounds for evaluating its potential for broader application to other modes of transportation, as well as inter-modally.

In a sense, this examination is designed to serve a dual purpose. First, in terms of long-range government investment in transportation, the highway mode dominates all others. Therefore, evaluation of the bases of the decisions that contribute to such magnitude of expenditure would be useful. Secondly, the primary factors that have justified specific outlays for highways share many traits and considerations applicable to weighing possible investment in projects within other modes of transportation.

Yet another point is pertinent to the analysis undertaken in this chapter. In spite of the fact that Congress ultimately decided to hold the reins of transportation project decision-making in its own hands when it created the Department of Transportation, pressure to bring about a greater stress on the role of economic rationality continues.

It is also quite apparent that, in spite of the lack of a formal provision of power to the Secretary of Transportation to establish the "ground rules" of future decision-making, the new forms of project justification in transportation will be well-armed with the results of Executive Branch cost-benefit analysis. The question then would involve determination of the relative weight that economic rationality should have, in reaching political decisions on transportation policy.

The future role of cost-benefit analysis in transportation decision-making is not at all clear. Some see it as offering the possibility of substituting factual criteria for "uninformed" intuition and judgment. This possibility has been accepted, at least outwardly, by many professional administrators and political officials. In its ideal form, cost-benefit analysis would thus make it possible to simplify and clarify the decision-making process, thereby rendering the most desirable alternatives obvious.

Others are much less sanguine about its potentialities. It may be that these critics will "bide their time" until they can gain deeper insight into the positive contributions of the quantitative approaches that have emerged, as well as the "window dressing" that has been used on occasion to befuddle, rather than to inform.

The analysis of cost-benefit approaches does not lend itself to discussion in general terms. To be meaningful, some of the specific content of the methods employed must be examined. In this way it may be possible to determine the practicality of employing such approaches on a broad scale throughout the field of transportation.

This chapter focuses on a number of crucial questions. What are the dimensions of the "models" that govern highway planning decisions? What procedures are followed in determining how the links of the highway system are forged? At what level are highway planning decisions made, i.e., is the orientation dominated by a macro-approach or micro-attention — or some combination of the two? What are the strengths and weaknesses of the cost-benefit analysis models in highway planning? Can existing models be transferred to the analysis of federal transportation investments in other modes of transportation?

In order to establish a perspective for dealing with these questions, the analysis will cover various models used, or recommended for use, in making decisions on highway projects. These include the approaches taken in engineering economy, marginalism, and collateral effects. The analysis will then examine systems approaches which advocate a more broadly-based assessment of transportation projects and their impact on the *total* community or region.

Finally, the chapter will evaluate the potential of cost-benefit analysis, using the experience gained with it in the highway planning sphere, as a tool for decision-making across the whole spectrum of federal transportation investments.

Background

The basic impetus for applying cost-benefit analysis to the development of the national highway system was provided by the Highway Revenue Act of 1956. This legislation created the financial mechanism for making the Interstate Highway System a reality.[1] In addition to establishing the Highway Trust Fund — thus providing an explicit relationship between federal highway expenditures and highway-related taxation — this legislation required a study by the Bureau of Public Roads to determine how the costs of federally aided highway improvements could be more equitably allocated. In 1961, the Bureau submitted a report to Congress summarizing its research, and that of state highway departments and other agencies. Congress subsequently developed a report of its own, summarizing its conclusions on the question of highway costs and benefits.[2]

The studies of the nature and measurement of highway benefits and costs attempted to answer five broad questions:

1. How do the benefits of highway investment arise?
2. How can these benefits be measured?
3. By what mechanism are these benefits distributed to individual members of the population?
4. What effects does the financing system for highway improvement have on the size and distribution of benefits?
5. How can net highway benefits be quantitatively estimated?

It should be emphasized at this point that these studies were undertaken to explore possibilities of going beyond the traditional methods of measuring highway costs and benefits, i.e., the long-accepted approaches of "engineering economy." After detailed examination of the above questions, it was generally concluded that alternatives to the use of "engineering economy" were fraught with numerous difficulties and pitfalls. Thus, the validity of "engineering economy" was again substantiated and, at least up to about 1970, remained the basic and accepted method of determining highway cost-benefit relationships.

The Engineering Economy Model

"Engineering economy" usually represents the application of highway economic studies at what could be termed the "second level" of analysis. Under this concept, the "first level" of planning analysis would be the factors involved in a decision to develop a highway route or system. Most often, however, this crucial aspect of the decision-making process is taken as a "given," involving as it does numerous considerations which transcend economics. Thus, when engineering economy is applied to specific projects, general routes and corridors for new highways have already been selected.

Robley Winfrey summarized the "state of the art" in the late 1950s in the following terms:

In contrast with industry, the current, most frequent highway economic analyses have to do with the selection of alternates for a project already accepted for construction. Thus, the solution for choice of "with or without" — economic justification of constructing or not constructing the project — is the infrequent solution.[3]

The Basic Premises

The underlying premise of engineering economy is that the location and design of a highway should be thought of as a problem of economy — one capable of quantitative analysis.[4] The basic objective is to determine, by one method or another, the "best uses" and priorities for investing limited funds. To achieve these ends, the following general principles are employed:

1. Complete objectivity — not subjectivity — is required in estimating, forecasting, and selecting the factors to be measured and in pricing them;
2. Decisions are to be made on the basis of alternatives;
3. The expected consequences of the various alternatives are to be commensurable with investments insofar as practical. In this regard, the analysis of economy is wholly *money based*;
4. Only *differences* among alternatives are considered relevant for comparison. "Sunk costs" are considered irrelevant, unless they affect the future alternatives. Analysis of investment increments are favored over average unit costs;
5. Criteria for decision-making should recognize the *time value of money* and related problems of capital rationing;
6. Relative weights should be assigned to account for the degrees of *uncertainty* associated with the various forecasts concerning consequences. Moreover, judgments should be made regarding the *sensitivity* of the decision to changes in the different forecasts;
7. Market and extra-market consequences should be separated, and explicit weights should be assigned to each.[5]

It is often assumed that the techniques of "engineering economy" in highway planning are relatively consistent in application. Yet analyses performed take a number of different forms, and vary extensively in their scope and assumptions. The trait that they share in common, however, is their confinement to examination of *road user consequences*, which compares input costs to output benefits.[6] Subject categories cover:

> Route location
> Geometrics of design
> Materials
> Traffic controls
> Improvements
> Stage construction
> Highway costs (construction, maintenance, administration)
> Road user consequences (operating costs, accident costs, time value, intangibles)

The methods of computing costs in engineering economy vary considerably — again demonstrating the point that "technical-solution" techniques are not always clear-cut, easily understood, or uniform in their applications. Nor is this a small point in terms of its impact on policy judgments in the highway planning field. Indeed, the alternative approaches available to planners in choosing among different projects may result in divergent solutions. The following analysis of the most favored methods gives some indication of how this may occur.

Annual Economic Cost Method

Under the annual economic cost method, the total annual cost of a highway improvement is taken as the *sum* of all annual costs of capital recovery, plus the annual costs of maintenance and operations, plus the annual costs of the road users, plus the annual costs of accidents and time delays. Annual costs are computed for the existing facility and for each of the alternative proposals for improvement. The alternative resulting in the lowest annual cost represents the best solution.

The procedure for developing the annual cost of a capital investment to be recovered in *n* years, with interest, is to multiply its first cost by the appropriate capital-recovery factor. This uniform amount, if charged at the end of each year for the assumed useful life of the project, will exactly repay the initial investment with interest.

But this approach is not without its problems. Nor does it lack in opportunities for manipulation. Most critical is the point that the sensitivity of the interest rate chosen, as well as the estimated service life, may markedly distort the outcome. A number of highway projects have incorporated such distortions in past years. Projects submitted to the Bureau of Public Roads, for example, have on occasion indicated service lives of fifty, seventy-five, or even one hundred years — ignoring problems of obsolescence, inadequacy, physical wear and tear, etc. In several cases, such unrealistic assumptions have been accompanied by interest rates of only two or three percent.

Rate of Return Method

The rate of return method of comparing alternative costs and benefits for highway transportation projects has been borrowed from private industry. In this case, the interest rate is the unknown quantity in the problem. Most commonly, when two alternatives are compared (for example, one may have a lower capital investment and higher maintenance, operation, and road user costs, while the other has a higher capital investment and lower maintenance, operation, and road user costs), this unknown interest rate is thought of as the prospective rate of return on the excess of investment in the alternative with the higher overall investment. Therefore, the method involves determining the rate of interest at which the two alternatives have equal annual costs. Desirable alternatives are those that show a rate of return in excess of what is considered to be the minimum attractive return on investment.

Here again, some important questions of public policy arise. What considerations, for example, ought to enter into the evaluation of any proposed investment in highways?[7] Should rates of return on public expenditures be comparable to the rates of return in private enterprise? If they can be compared, should the controlling element in selecting a minimum attractive rate be the *opportunity cost*? Would this approach lead to the selection of more transportation projects other than highways, or to the greater retention of funds in private hands?

The use of the rate of return method has served to focus much greater attention on the impropriety of using extremely low interest rates (three percent or lower, for example) and the suggestion that the minimum rate of seven percent — applicable to many regulated public utilities throughout the United States — be employed uniformly.[8]

Benefit—Cost Ratio Method

There are several approaches to the use of benefit-cost analyses in highway planning. However, the most common and accepted has followed the concepts developed by the American Association of State Highway Officials.[9]

In its most basic form, the ratio represents the amount of *savings to highway users* for each dollar invested in a highway facility.[10] To achieve this end, the benefits and costs are discounted for the appropriate time period, using a formulation such as the following:

$$\text{Net Benefit Ratio} = \dfrac{\dfrac{B}{(1+i)^n}}{\dfrac{C}{(1+i)^n}}$$

The method calls for computation of highway costs and road user costs from which road user benefits can be determined. Highway costs include both construction and maintenance. Road user costs include the actual costs of vehicle operation, the value of time spent in travel, the costs of accidents, and the costs of impedance.[11]

This method employs part of the annual economic cost method described earlier. The amortization of the investment in the result of applying the capital recovery factor for a pre-chosen rate of interest, at an estimated service life, for the calculation of the capital recovery costs during a given period. Under this method, the rate of depreciation and consequent salvage are undetermined.

Although it is often contended that when this ratio is greater than unity, the project is justified; this does not mean that such projects will then be undertaken. As has been demonstrated in practice, high priority highway projects frequently have ratios of from 3 or 4 to 1, as well as 10 or more to 1. As a result, "small ratio" projects often fail to be implemented because of the always present scarcity of public investment funds.

The benefit-cost ratio has been characterized as a technique to collect and organize relevant data by some conceptually meaningful criteria to determine the relative preferredness of alternatives.[12] But even under this conceptualization there can be problems, particularly if totaling and averaging are practiced indiscriminately. Quade, for example, criticizes cost-benefit studies for using some ratio of *total* costs to benefits as a measure, when in fact they should measure benefits *at the margin*.[13] In addition, of course, benefit-cost analysis is subject to some weaknesses characteristic of the methods analyzed previously. Particularly sensitive are the effects of the selected interest rate and the assumed service life.

Highway User Benefits and Costs

This section analyzes the adequacy of present techniques for measuring costs and benefits that are largely confined to highway users. For, no matter which cost-benefit method is employed, this category of data must be an integral part of the analysis. For the moment, this sets aside the basic questions that have been raised by critics of engineering economy on the questions of collateral effects, secondary benefits and "disbenefits," spillovers, etc. These are discussed later in the chapter.

As already noted, it is frequently assumed that the various approaches of the engineering economy method are based on precise "scientific" premises that accurately portray the factual bases for decision-making on highway projects. But as the following analysis indicates, this assumption is subject to serious question.

The Value of Motorist Time

One of the primary justifications for expanding the nation's highway system is the value of the time savings that will accrue to user motorists. But how is this value measured in dollar terms? In practice, several methods are employed.

A frequently used approach goes as follows: If a certain cost is incurred in replacing a two lane road with a four-lane road to save motorists travel time, the total time saved may be divided into the total cost to obtain a unit value of the cost of time. This approach, of course, requires data on average daily volumes and projections of these volumes, as well as of estimated costs and benefits.

A second method involves use of a "trade-off." In this case, the value of time of a person wishing to travel at an average of sixty-five mph rather than fifty-five mph is computed by measuring the increase in fuel, tire, and other costs resulting from such an increase.

Yet a third method assigns a value to the time of the motorist. While this may sound simple enough, the determination of what the value should be, i.e., a single value such as an average, differentiated single values for occupational groups, probability distributions of potential values, etc., comprises a complex problem.[14]

The guide for evaluating motorists' time that had been most widely employed and accepted is the standard of the American Association of Highway Officials — $1.55 per hour. So far as can be determined, the value chosen was arbitrary. Nor have other estimates of the value of time been lacking.[a] Mohring, for example, concluded that on the basis of his studies around 1960, travel time was worth from $0.50 to $1.00 per hour.[15] On the other hand, Hummel took the approach that average hourly income in the state should be used. Thus, at the time of his study he assigned a value of $2.74 per hour because that was the average hourly income in the State of Virginia.[16]

Vehicle Operating Costs

Another major component of *road user utility* relates the costs of proposed

---

[a]It should be noted that the value of time has been the subject of voluminous literature which cannot be included here. However, in spite of this attention, there is no agreement on a methodology for defining such values. Yet it is evident that the results of such calculations may "make or break" the desirability of most projects.

highway improvements to savings in vehicular operating costs. This approach again usually relies on estimated average daily volumes and estimates of time and mileage saved. Operating costs have been developed (using AASHO guidelines) for varying classes of vehicles on per mile, time delay basis. This relates fuel and oil consumption, tire wear, costs of wear and tear in congested traffic, etc., for the existing facility as opposed to the proposed facility. Net savings of the improvement then are employed as part of the calculation of the cost-benefit ratio.

The Costs of Accidents

Engineering economy requires that if accident reduction is to be a part of the calculation of benefits and costs, it must be translated into *dollar terms*. As in the case of other factors to which dollar values are assigned, the calculation makes no allowance for secondary effects.

Factual bases for determining the costs of accidents are indeed flimsy. One approach employed in the past was to rely on a Massachusetts study which drew upon statewide insurance and claims data which were aggregated and then averaged over the parties involved.[17] Average costs computed were as follows:

$5,800 for a fatality
$ 960 for an injury
$ 225 for property damage

Such measures have been applied nationally to help justify highway improvements. In 1958, for example, the Chicago Area Transportation Study compared the accident cost rate per million vehicle miles for arterial streets ($6,202) and for the new Congress Expressway ($1,282). The capitalized difference at an interest rate of five percent and an assumed life of 25 years yielded savings per mile in the order of $2 million.[18]

Perhaps in no other aspect of its application does the engineering economy method demonstrate a weakness than in applying dollar values to accident prevention. Nor is the problem one of overstating values. Indeed, the error undoubtedly lies in the other direction. There is little basis, as an example, for concluding that court settlements reflect accurate or realistic costs. The cost of an accident can be imputed far into the future to cover total income which would have been earned in a lifetime in the case of a fatality, the partial losses of income which would result from injuries in the case of a less severe accident, and the numerous collateral losses which are incurred by families, employers, and associates as a result of accidents.

Of course, the most important aspect of all is the question of whether dollars can ever serve as a legitimate measure of the value of a person's life or an injury to his person. And, then, there is also the question of whether the provision of additional highway capacity *induces* an increased volume of traffic, thus contributing in the long run to an increase in the *absolute number* of accidents that occur.

The Cost of Strain and Discomfort

The cost of strain and discomfort represents another major group of costs normally used in engineering economy. Again, the values involved are "squeezed" into monetary terms by defining a common denominator — really a surrogate — for these elements. This is a summation of speed changes on a trip which is taken to represent the whole catalog of impedances to uniform driving.[19]

In effect, this approach is similar to that used in determining the value of time. When speed drops below that desired or feasible, the "strain-discomfort" factor comes into play, ringing up dollar values on the cost side of the ledger. By the same token, avoidance of such impedances can be credited as a benefit for a new, alternate project under consideration.

Up to this point, primary attention has been given to the standard approach to highway cost and benefit analysis — the engineering economy model. Its application has dominated the field of highway planning. And it is highly likely that as cost-benefit analysis plays an increasingly large part in federal allocation decisions affecting *all modes* of transportation, long-standing highway experience with engineering economy will be drawn upon. But this is not to say that the shortcomings and omissions of the standard method have not been noted.

The Marginalism Model

In some quarters, it has been suggested that engineering economy be put aside in favor of the marginalism model. Under this concept, the cost of producing an additional unit of highway improvements would just equal the amount that the highway user would be willing to pay for that unit.[20] In this approach, efficiency of resource allocation for highways would be maximized at this point, since the added value to the highway user would equal the marginal cost of the highway investment required. This method also implies that if the values of collateral effects cannot be obtained *at the margin* in the market through the price system, it is inappropriate to use them in developing cost-benefit analysis.

While various models for applying these concepts have been developed in theory, their application is severely limited by the nature of highway benefits and costs. One problem, for example, is that the value of highways at the margin has no relation to the cost of production. This occurs because the price of the service is indirect. Indeed, it leads one to the conclusion that direct pricing of highway services would be required before marginal value and cost comparisons would be feasible.

A second major problem of this method, even if some kind of direct costing and pricing existed, would be the development of data in a usable form. As is apparent in the analysis of the engineering model, severe difficulties are now encountered even in obtaining over-simplified data on *average* costs and values in a number of categories of information. Of course, the approach of marginalism would also encounter the basic problems of realistic rates of interest, service lives, etc., that are faced in the engineering economy method.

Collateral Effects Model

Perhaps no approach in highway planning has received more attention in recent years than the collateral effects model. It extends analysis to include the *indirect effects* of highways.

This method of measuring costs and benefits is basically a "welfare economics" approach, which takes into account externalities or spillovers that result from highway projects and accrue to the *non-users*.[21] Unlike the factors considered in the engineering economy and marginalism approaches, certain of the relevant considerations cannot be translated into dollar terms. But wherever it seems at all feasible, such a translation is attempted.

Up to about 1970, most highway planners concentrated their efforts on defining the non-user benefits (as opposed to "disbenefits") that result from highway improvements. This point of view was reflected by Robert G. Hennes:

Policy decisions, which include considerations of social benefits and social costs, will not necessarily agree with policy decisions that consider only vehicular benefits and highway costs. It is important that highway users should not pay the entire cost of improvements which are built differently than traffic considerations alone would require.[22]

Some of the *non-user* benefits he noted include:

— increased employment;
— income generated by building materials and equipment used;
— development of new industrial areas;
— provision of functional boundaries for inconsistent land uses;
— provision of scenic views and access to open spaces;
— alterations in patterns of retail distribution;
— elimination of blighted areas;
— provision of rights-of-way for utilities;
— illumination of surrounding areas;
— provision of sidewalks;
— creation of structures to prevent erosion, flood damage, and drainage problems.

This listing is included to convey some idea of how far-reaching considerations of spillovers are. Numerous possibilities exist for further expansion. Of course it should be noted that a parallel list of "disbenefits" resulting from highway projects could also be developed, although the author fails to deal with this aspect of the problem. Also unanswered, and perhaps impossible to calculate, is the *percentage* of gains realized which should be credited to the highway improvement variable. Again, the interrelationships involved are extremely complex and very difficult to trace precisely.

Analyzing Highway Collateral Effects –
The "State of the Art"

The "state of the art", in analyzing highway collateral effects remained relatively unsophisticated up to about 1970. Indeed, there were few studies undertaken to determine the impact of improved highways and their secondary effects. As Stroup and Vargha noted ten years ago:

Although much has been done, much remains to be discovered about the identification and measurement of changes which follow highway additions, much remains to be done in explaining how and why these changes occur, and who or what groups are affected, and how.[23]

Much of what has been done more recently has concentrated on the *economic* impact of "improvements." Perhaps the principal one is the identification of "redistributive effects" as "net benefits."[24]

Closely associated with this problem are the increasing number of questions being raised about the *distribution* of benefits. This concerns the significance of the form benefits assume, i.e., concentrated, large returns for a few, broadly dispersed distribution to many, benefits for selective economic income groups, etc. Obviously, the claim for an aggregate benefit sheds very little light on this important aspect of analysis.[25]

Another problem, common to some applications of welfare economics, is that of multiple causation. Sorting out the specific impact of highway improvements from the impact of other developments and activities can be extraordinarily difficult. Yet another problem involves the interaction which takes place among variables through time. And perhaps as important as any of the problems of measuring collateral effects in highway planning is the paucity of useful quantitative information.

Effects Receiving Some Attention

It is, of course, simpler to conclude that highway transportation has far-reaching social effects, than to identify and measure them with any precision. But the questions now being addressed as principal concerns of the collateral effects method are of vital concern to the future of *national transportation policy* and its repercussions in other sectors. These include:

1. Aesthetics — the view of the road, the view from the road, and highway induced effects;
2. Agriculture — access, effects on productivity and relocation;
3. Commercial effects — changes due to relocation, dislocation, population change, bypass effects, community price changes, rentals, land use, and land value impacts, etc;
4. Community Government — effects on services, facilities, parks, recreation, public policies and laws, and goals;
5. Construction — its impact socially, economically, etc., both immediately and in the long run;
6. Employment — changes in patterns and amount;
7. Environment — effects of noise, air pollution, vibration, and drainage patterns;
8. Industrial — changes in development, locations, land use, and land value;
9. Institutions — changes in accessibility and patronage;
10. Population — impact on growth, density, geographic shifts, and distribution;
11. Public Utilities — dislocations, distribution patterns, and costs;
12. Residential Neighborhoods — effects on rents, costs, quality of neighborhood life, community stability, linkage patterns, land development, property values, social life, etc.;
13. Road User — impact on safety, costs, benefits;
14. Spatial and Geographic Changes — impact on relationships of local, metropolitan, and regional life;
15. Urban Form and Development — effects on land use and values, patterns of development, and the Central Business District.[26]

Yet even these subjects of collateral effects studies fail to identify some of the major components of the national economy that relate directly to the costs and benefits of highway improvements — the huge automobile manufacturing, parts, equipment, and service industries, as well as the oil industry. Without the "benefit" of an ever-expanding highway network, what would be the impact on their outputs?

Another significant impact in terms of collateral effects are the other modes of transportation. To what degree are net benefits produced as opposed to redistributive benefits? In what forms do "disbenefits" appear?

Empirical Study Results

In spite of the fact that the areas above constitute most important subjects for research, empirical studies conducted thus far have been of a more limited scope. Many of these studies of costs and benefits deal with the impact of highways on land values. Furthermore, since studies in the highway field have been conducted largely from a *position of advocacy*, most of the emphasis has been placed on benefits to the exclusion of diseconomies.

In measuring the impact of highway bypasses, for example, Horwood found that they have differential effects on communities, with the least benefit derived by towns of less than 5,000 and by highway-oriented businesses. By the same token, greater benefit accrued to larger centers and to non-highway businesses.[27] He also found a propensity on the part of industry and commerce to locate along beltway routes, and that land values rose in proportion to proximity to them.

Flaherty found the impact of bypasses to be differentiated for quite another reason — the effect of local community policies on how adjacent land is used. Unrestricted zoning produced the results noted by Horwood. But where complete land use plans were developed, the impact of bypass development was controlled accordingly. [28]

The question of community response and economic stimulation has been dealt with by McKain in his study of the impact of the Connecticut Turnpike on towns in Eastern Connecticut. As he noted, the highway, measured in terms of costs and benefits, was used as an instrument of *social change*:

Until recently, highway planning has been concerned with existing or anticipated needs. Highways were considered the effect of social change, not its cause. If a new road happened to bring benefits to an area, this was considered an unexpected bonus. And if a highway improvement brought economic hardship, this was dismissed in the name of overall progress.[29]

McKain observed that this expressway was extended into this area for the avowed purpose of stimulating the economy of that area. Following its completion, most towns experienced growth in manufacturing employment, tourist business, immigration of population, and real estate value.

The impact of highway improvements has also been measured by other "before and after" studies. Goldstein, for example, found that transportation cost reductions induce other changes that increase output above the magnitude of the savings. Applying input-output analysis in tracing the effects of a highway improvement program, he concluded that such savings have a multiplier effect of between 1.9 and 3.8.[30]

Such conclusions are, of course, open to question in terms of whether the criteria used were appropriate and whether the full range of applicable factors were included. Frequently in such approaches, the bases for such judgments prove to be short term and uncomprehensive. Furthermore, unrealistic boundaries are often placed around the impact area under study.

The development of land in the vicinity of new highway interchanges has also received increasing attention as part of the examination of the collateral effects of highway improvements. Again the focus has been economic, with infrequent attention given to the *costs* of increased congestion, reduction of travel amenities, increased air pollution and the like. Not unexpectedly, the general findings have tended to be highly positive. Some researchers, in fact, have concluded that such lands experience no losses at all and that the only serious question to be answered is *how great the net benefits will be.*[31]

The positive side of highway impact studies has also gotten a boost from those who have examined its effect on the development of utilities. The most common conclusion is that the location of gas, telephone, electric, sewer, and water lines would involve additional costs if special rights-of-way had to be provided. Of course it should be noted that this still leaves open the question of *who* receives the benefit from these savings — the rate-paying public or the utility management and stockholders.

Collateral effects analysis is essential to obtaining a more complete picture of the costs and benefits of highway planning. But it is also readily apparent that such analysis presents enormous problems of developing data, tracing causation, defining "net" benefits and diseconomies, and dealing with non-quantifiable factors. Yet to ignore collateral effects or externalities because the data required to place dollar values on them is lacking may well "assume away" the most far-reaching implications of a project.

The Systems Approach to Highway Planning. As the preceding sections of this chapter indicate, great weight has been given in the past to micro-analysis in developing the numerous links which comprise the national highway system. For the most part, engineering economy has dominated the methodology of highway planners. Up until recently, collateral effects analysis had received only limited acceptance.

By and large, most of the applications of cost-benefit analysis to highway planning reflect the kind of emphasis it has received in other areas of public investment in the United States. As Maass indicates, this means that projects and programs are ranked in terms of one criterion — economic efficiency.[32] Such occurs in spite of the fact that the objective functions of most government programs are highly complex, and in some cases may make the goal of economic efficiency relatively low ranking.

A number of strategies have been suggested to broaden the scope of highway cost-benefit analysis. Outside of the models of marginalism and collateral effects, it has been suggested by some that a limited *systems approach* be applied to analyzing inter-modal interaction. In essence, this would involve measuring the impacts of specific transportation projects and programs on *all modes*, i.e., the entire transportation system of the area affected.

Critics point out how enormously complex such an undertaking would be. Their major concerns include:

1. Integrated systems planning would be so complicated that it would fall of its own weight;
2. It would not provide for an acceptable degree of timeliness for decision-making — even with computers;

3. A perfect model could not be constructed.[33]

On the other hand, proponents of the "transportation systems approach" interpret the more accepted practices as having even more drawbacks. They contend that planning for pieces of individual modes, with little or no regard for impacts on other modes, at best results in "sub-optimization." Since such an approach is largely micro-level, its possibilities for achieving an optimum system are automatically nil.

Describing this as a practice of highway planners, Mishan notes:

The piecemeal methods of engineers in the face of traffic problems differ only from those of the economist in being cruder. They turn on the location of "growing points" in the traffic, and on a variety of formulae, based on traffic growth relative to road capacity, that yield critical ratios purporting to justify increased investment. These formulae are supplemented by *ad hoc* decisions on building bridges, circuses, bypasses, diversions, fly-overs and fly-unders, whenever something "has to be done."[34]

Mishan develops an economic argument in which he concludes that the practices of the engineering economy method are invalid. In fact, he theorizes that the benefit measures used may be *inversely* related to the actual benefit. To illustrate his point, he traces the impact of indiscriminate increases in roadway capacity and auto use, particularly on other modes of urban passenger transportation. Mishan finds that the inevitable result would be complete elimination of transportation alternatives.

Mishan's approach to the costs and benefits of highway development would provide a basis for the broad scale evaluation of inter-modal costs and benefits of specific projects. It would do this by defining the boundaries of the system to include all of the transportation modes. But this leaves open the question of the externalities that are not directly associated with effects on the various modes of transportation. One answer to this criticism would be to extend what the collateral-effects approach has been in practice to a more encompassing "total systems" approach.

The Total Systems Approach

Preceding chapters have emphasized how basic the development of transportation is to the quality of national life. Attesting to this fact are the enormous changes in national *spatial* patterns brought about by the expansion of all forms of land, water, and air transportation.

In the period since World War II, particularly, highway expansion has been a predominant force of transportation in forging the molds of fundamental change. Mass suburbanization of population and decentralization of industry comprises but two of the products of this expansion.

Within specific areas, basic relationships have been transformed. The lifelines of the nation, almost daily, take some new shape. Each state finds its network for transporting people and goods modified; cities experience altered patterns of commerce and journey-to-work, particularly in the central business district; suburban areas suddenly find themselves on the "main line" of highway transportation — or excluded from it. Neighborhoods of small homeowners find "instant mobility" at their back door, usually accompanied by smoke and noise. Changing patterns of highway capacity mount pressure to modify land uses in all areas, bringing increased values for some and decreased utility for others. Indeed, the skeletal framework of road transportation often signals the creation of new businesses and industries, and the demise of others less well located. Such are some of the fundamental attributes of transportation development.

It is increasingly being maintained that to ignore these close relationships between highway improvements and area development in cost-benefit analysis is to be totally unrealistic. Or as Robert Dorfman has noted, such practices are akin to carefully measuring the effect of the rabbit in a horse-and-rabbit stew, and completely ignoring the taste of the horse.[35]

The recent literature of highway planning displays a fundamental reorientation toward planning in total systems terms. Much more frequently now, such transportation planning recognizes its effects on a wide range of policy variables. Indeed, new models of transportation systems being developed perform in part as goal-seeking apparatus. Thus, plans are not only modified to conform to existing goals but also to identify and reach new goals. In this sense, they are considered "self-adaptive."[36]

Under this approach, the first step in analyzing alternative transportation plans is to determine the tasks that the transportation system performs. A broad, continual evaluation of these system outputs frequently leads to identification of values and goals that are not being fulfilled but to which transportation could make a contribution. Without such an examination of the interactive quality of the system, the outcomes of the planning process would not only prove narrow, but highly misleading as well. In this way, the total systems approach seeks a higher level of rationality.

However, one should not interpret the methodology of total systems planning as dismissing the importance of engineering economy. It recognizes that economic efficiency is important, i.e., plans should seek to derive the most return for a given investment. But the approach points out that no universal metric prevails for defining the "return." Thus, it would give equal or greater weight to considerations of plan "effectiveness," i.e., the degree to which overall *goals* are attained.[37]

In broad terms, the total systems approach is conceived of as taking into account economic, social, political, aesthetic, and other factors produced or affected by proposed changes in the transportation network — a *macro-system* orientation. This broad-scale approach thus must account for and anticipate "feedback" between transportation and the important variables that influence the vitality of an area. It would do so by studying the statistical, as well as qualitative, relationships among travel, population settlement, industrial development, and land use, and relating them to appropriate economic and social indices. From these it would be possible to develop "models of systems performance."

Meyer alludes to the possibility of a more comprehensive approach in suggesting that it may be necessary to couple a model of the transport sector to a general macro-aggregative model of the economy, as well as to more specialized models. Such would clarify the relationships of transport projects with other important variables outside of economic efficiency.[38]

Garrison notes that large-scale urban transportation models have gone through two phases of development:

1. Models that distributed expected land uses and then allocated complementary transportation facilities;
2. Models in which transportation and land uses have been allocated simultaneously in the light of their effects on each other. These have also recognized the need to have explicit development goals and alternative schemes for achieving them.[39]

Yet even these models have their shortcomings, and Garrison anticipates that the "third generation" will deal with data on a more timely, sophisticated level. In particular, he foresees the need for models incorporating enough richness of detail to account for hour-to-hour fluctuations in transportation demand, and instant information on the short-run "random shocks" which change flows of travel. In short, models of the future would use "less history and more current information."

Difficulties of Applying Comprehensive
Systems Approach to Cost-Benefit Analysis

In many respects, the broad-scale application of a comprehensive systems approach to highway cost-benefit analysis is still more of a goal to be achieved than a present-day reality. A number of factors mitigate against its immediate utilization:

1. The practices and procedures of engineering economy are firmly embedded in administrative structures at all levels of government which carry out highway planning. They emphasize precise measurement of a limited number of variables, thus making planning problems more manageable — at least for the planners. Yet much of this "precision" is open to serious question. In addition, it should be noted that estimates of costs and benefits, even in these terms, are subject to manipulation;

2. There remains a lack of understanding of the specific casual relationships

between highway projects and the complex set of variables operative in the areas affected;[40]

3. Available data are inadequate in comparison to the information demands imposed by a comprehensive systems model. By and large, they fail to describe and evaluate the relationships of transport to most of the factors in which there is a planning interest. This necessitates considerable reliance on speculation.

4. The full extent of non-quantifiable factors on both the benefit and "disbenefit" sides of analysis are inadequately identified and treated. This gives rise to enormous problems of assigning weights and relative significances, in combination with factors for which dollar values are available. One approach to dealing with this problem is suggested by Hill, who stresses the importance of making all factors considered in a cost-benefit analysis as explicit as possible and evaluating them in terms of bundles of benefits and "disbenefits."[41]

5. The "state of the art" in building comprehensive transportation models is not sufficiently advanced to handle the huge array of interactive processes involved. There is an absence of knowledge for determining desirable levels of aggregation, the manner in which time is to be accommodated, and how changes in variables should be reflected.[42]

Imposing as they are, these difficulties do not appear insurmountable. To be sure, future solutions will undoubtedly incorporate procedures which at times are unacceptable to the "purist" — be he economist, highway engineer, social scientist, or politician. But the overriding thrust is in the direction of more comprehensive, rational approaches to complex decision-making. And this emphasis is certain to be increasingly aided by advances in computer technology and the mounting experience of researchers studying the anatomy of national transportation, urban areas, suburban development, and rural change.

Summary

Cost-benefit analysis in highway transportation is in a state of transition. Even though engineering economy, with its narrow conception of measuring the impact of projects in terms of economic efficiency, remains dominant, its validity is subject to increasing challenges.

In a sense, limited, partial efforts to achieve a confined rationality are themselves recognized as irrational in the larger view. Given that government transport investment decisions have often included such objective functions as regional development, relief to distressed areas, income redistribution, controlling monopoly, dampening inflation, providing for the national defense, and fostering national unity, it appears illogical that measurement of the benefits and costs of such projects should be confined to the narrow criterion of economic efficiency. Transportation projects produce differential effects; the means chosen for their measurement must reflect this characteristic. In the long run, efforts to expand on the collateral effects method, particularly the total systems approach which is still being developed, seem to offer a viable method for dealing with this phenomenon.

At this point in time, it is clear that the "state of the art" of cost-benefit analysis in highway development is not sufficiently advanced in application to be accorded overriding influence in the making of transport decisions. But this is not to say that future refinements and progress will not provide it with such a capacity. If such occurs, prospects would appear promising for transferring many of the lessons of highway cost-benefit analysis to other modes of transportation.

The potential strength of cost-benefit analysis lies in the framework for evaluation that it can provide. For all of its weaknesses, it still has the strength of forcing a rigorous examination of all pertinent evidence. In a broadly conceived context, it would incorporate both quantitative and qualitative data and seek to clarify their complex relationships. If basic distortions can be avoided, it would lead to more informed judgment than would otherwise be possible.

In many respects, the various explorations of how it could be utilized most effectively represent "pioneering" in every sense of the word. In fact, its current status might be described as a set of worthwhile goals in search of a more suitable methodology. If this is gradually achieved, its ultimate influence on national transportation policy can be projected to grow commensurately.

The Policy Implications of
Technological Change

6

The Policy Implications of Technological Change

Perhaps no other single factor renders the facilities of the national transportation network more volatile and unpredictable than advancing technology. Changing technology not only has served to increase capacity and efficiency within the modes of transportation as they emerged; more fundamentally, it has effected the partial or, in some cases, the complete displacement of the role of one mode by another. In this respect, science inexorably moves toward the ultimate goal of "frictionless" transportation in which passengers and goods move between origin and destination in the most efficient manner.

Previous chapters have illustrated just how critical the effects of technological advance have been to the fates of individual modes in the past. No single carrier has remained dominant long in providing the means for moving the people or materials of the nation. Concomitantly, the consequences of changing technology have also helped to assure a continuing trend away from monopoly control of national transportation.

Even within the individual modes, technology has fomented unique differentiation, providing the basis for increasingly specialized services and facilities. One consequence of this characteristic has been the drastic and continuing shift in the relationship between public and private transportation. This is well illustrated by the changes that have occurred in intercity passenger transportation and in motor carrier transportation. Another has been the revamping of long-established transportation methods to such a marked degree that in some cases they now bear little resemblance to those they replaced. Recent developments in the field of cargo containerization demonstrate this point.

Another major dimension of the impact of technological change upon transportation concerns innovations in other fields. Here science has done more than alter the character of transportation; it has also modified the product being shipped by moving it in a different way.[1] Some examples include the bulk movement of certain alcoholic beverages, such as wine shipped in tankers from California to the East Coast, bulk movement of sugar, cement, chemicals, and coal. In certain cases, the need for shipment has been eliminated altogether, as illustrated by the growing utilization of "mine-mouth" generation of electricity by using coal.

Nor is this type of far-reaching change limited to the transportation of goods and materials. For technological change may drastically affect passenger travel as well. This fact is perhaps best illustrated by the close relationship between many of the functions provided by *both* transportation and communication. In the future, for example, it may be expected that widespread employment of technological advances such as closed circuit television, video-phones, facsimile reproduction, advanced data processing, and others will even more drastically alter both the volume and composition of intercity and intracity travel.

Technological change in transportation must be viewed as one part of a total panorama of change. Changes constantly take place within the transportation sector and affect virtually all of its elements and their interrelationships. Simultaneously, other components of the economy also undergo continuous modification and metamorphosis, resulting in the creation of new transportation needs, the elimination of outmoded routes and facilities, and the forging of new links in an increasingly complex network.

Thus, the process of developing "tomorrow's transportation" is highly interactive, extremely sensitive, and dominated by uncertainty in all of its dimensions. In examining this aspect of transportation planning, Wilfred Owen has observed the frequency with which transportation expenditures have proved to be unwise, unneccessary, or untimely. He noted that " . . . transport by its nature provides unparalleled opportunities for making mistakes."[2]

This chapter and the one that follows analyze the role of the federal government both in encouraging and adapting to technological changes in transportation. They are not intended to encompass the entire range of transportation research and technology. Rather the purpose is to analyze the nature of the problem *as a whole*, and to review several of the most crucial aspects of transportation policy that are evolving.

Primary attention will be given to defining the nature of the federal role in transportation technological change; reviewing a number of innovative approaches to future transportation problems; analyzing the thrust of several "high priority" programs of the Department of Transportation, including the work of the Office of High Speed Ground Transportation, the Northeast Corridor Study, and the Supersonic Transport Project; evaluating federal responses to the problems of achieving "coordinated" transportation and improved interface transfers; delineating the barriers to optimizing the gains made possible by technological advance; and analyzing approaches to introducing changes in the presence of traditional constraints.

Nature of the Federal Role in Technological Change

The nature of the federal role in influencing technological change is becoming ever more complex. In this connection, Wilfred Owen provided what is still an apt description of the "transportation problem." He said:

It has long been hypothesized by scientists on the Moon that Earth might support some type of superior intelligence. I can report, after a preliminary study of Earth transportation, that this assumption is groundless.

Indeed, it is surprising that Earth people have decided to expand their transport system into space when they have so much trouble moving in the space they already have.[3]

A related point might be made regarding the federal role in providing for national transportation. Indeed, the task of simply dealing with the problems of existing modes under present conditions would be enormous in itself. But the nature of the challenge is infinitely magnified by the very nature of technological change, so much of which occurs beyond the purview of federal control or influence.

The relationship of the federal role to technological changes in transportation shares many of the attributes and difficulties associated with formulating and implementing national transportation policies. For here, too, a most difficult policy question must be faced: What national purposes should the transportation system serve? How much should be allocated to fulfill these purposes and sub-purposes? What phases of technological research should be a federal responsibility? What should be the relative weights of the economic and noneconomic objectives?

The nature of the federal role in providing for technological change is influenced importantly by the private-public interdependence in transportation development. Characteristics of this complicated intertwining have been analyzed in previous chapters, particularly as they concerned the inevitable time lag between the appearance of problems and actions taken to ameliorate them.

In the modern era of rapid technological advance, this challenge has intensified. Not only has the national capacity for divergent new forms of transportation grown, but also the industrial base to produce the hardware of transportation in staggering numbers. Examples of the former will be discussed in this chapter. As far as the latter factor is concerned, one need but note the capacity of the auto industry to produce 10 million or more cars a year to appreciate by how much the challenge of transportation technology has grown in the short span of three decades.[4] Significant, if less dramatic, advances have also been scored within the other modes of transportation. These accentuate the complexity of evolving a relevant and, at the same time, flexible role for federal fostering of technological advances and the management of their consequences.

The Role of Technology

Another major aspect of federal policy in supporting technological advance in transportation concerns the relative weights to be given to *improving on existing technology versus development of new technology.*[5] Indeed, the long history of national transportation development reveals a strong preference for directing technological efforts at achieving marginal improvements of existing systems. Thus, the maritime industry has improved capacity, power, and propulsion of shipping; limited attention has been given to development of shipping with markedly different operational characteristics. Similarly, the auto and truck of modern times are the refined successors of the originals; the modern bus has undergone few functional changes; the present-day railroad, with very few exceptions, operates on roadbeds laid at least 40 years ago; few changes have been made in trackage or in the basic functional concept.

Technological progress has been substantial in some selected areas; however, it again largely represents improvement at the margin. And even the most recent and advanced mode — aviation — has achieved its present state through a series of technological changes made at the margin. Of course, it might well be contended that at least in the case of aviation, the contrast between pre-World War II aviation and the present-day development of supersonic jet aircraft, jumbo jets, STOL, V/STOL and the like, is so great that it constitutes "new technology." This argument, however, ignores the outstanding marginal improvements that were made in the 1950s and 1960s, which provided the technological basis for present-day planning.

In general terms, the past lack of enthusiasm for the risks and costs of researching and developing dramatically different forms of transportation appears consistent with the general tenor of federal policy involvement. As has been demonstrated, existing facilities represent powerfully situated "sunk costs" for both the public and private spheres. Thus, the strategy of marginal improvement presents a more conservative, pragmatic approach to technology; it offers the possibility of making resultant innovations more manageable.

Such provides an interesting contrast with the colorful "technical" solutions to transportation problems that contribute so frequently to the "Sunday-supplement syndrome." Experience shows, all too sadly, that these treatments appeal to the popular imagination largely through futuristic and slick presentation. But few find their way to practical implementation.

Regulation and Technological Change

While government influence on technical change is normally most closely associated with effects on research and development activities, and their resultant products and systems, another important facet of federal influence on transport technology concerns the effects of regulatory policy. In some cases, such policies retard or instigate technological advance, while in others they affect its composition and relative emphasis.

Many of the positive effects of regulation on technological advance have related to transportation safety. Control of the ICC over common carriers, engaged in interstate land movement of passengers and freight, stimulated substantial technical advances. Examples include railroad braking systems, and motor carrier operating specifications and safety requirements.[6] Regulation of the aviation mode has stimulated the development of highly sophisticated systems of on-board navigation, all-weather instrument landing systems, automatic altitude reporting systems, computerized control systems, and the like.

But there is also a negative side to the effects of regulatory policy. This principally concerns the activities of the ICC in maintaining inter-modal cost relationships. And it has been the railroads, more than any other mode, that have suffered from this weighty deterrent to technological advance. The nub of the problem is the continued heavy reliance on "value of service" pricing in determining rate structures. This approach rests on the principle of "what the traffic will bear." A second aspect of the problem is the continued practice of "umbrella rate setting," which, in effect, works like a "giant handicapper" in dividing traffic among different modes of transportation.[7]

How does this rate setting practice relate to technological change? The primary tie involves incentives for change. Specifically, if shippers are forced to pay rates which exceed actual rail costs by a significant margin, they will turn to alternative forms of transportation. Likewise, if railroads develop technically advanced equipment or operational systems and then are precluded by the ICC from reflecting the resultant savings in their rate structure, the potential advantages to the carrier, as well as to the economy, are lost.

The development of 100-ton "Big John" hopper cars by the Southern Railway illustrates the problem. These were designed for the handling of bulk grain movements. When the railroad established a rate level reflecting the savings made possible by these cars, it was immediately opposed by the competitive water carriers. For two years, the attempts of the Southern to benefit from this new technology were thwarted by the ICC. And the final rate structure established by the Commission incorporated only part of savings made possible by this technological advance.

This constraint on the railroads, in fact, may explain their strong disposition to concentrate their innovative efforts on the area of expense curtailment, rather than upon sweeping system changes. As long as a deliberate, gradual approach to technological advance is taken by regulatory agencies, the modes affected will be forced to adhere to the strategy of limited change. To do otherwise would not only lead to losses, but also to possible financial ruin. In this way, the present regulatory framework can make revolutionary technological advance self-defeating.

Impact of Federal Policy on Metropolitan
Transportation Problem

As has been discussed in earlier chapters, the impact of the federal role in meeting the problems of metropolitan transportation — both intercity and intracity — were relatively minor up to the period of the 1950s.[8] Even at that stage, when the Interstate Highway System was begun, the needs of urban areas for carefully designed facilities to fit their individual circumstances clearly took second place to considerations of the efficiency of roads as parts of a *national* highway system. Under this concept, the major metropolitan areas were gradually linked in a highly "efficient" highway network. Unfortunately, consideration of its effects on other modes of transportation occurred after the fact.

In this sense, federally sponsored advances in highway construction technology literally overwhelmed the usage and capabilities of the modes with which it competed. Having provided the means for metropolitan transportation to become so "unbalanced," the question now arises: Should this role of advancing the technological applications of highway research be continued with the same intensity, be modified, or be changed abruptly?

A related, and perhaps more important, policy question concerns the stress which the federal government wishes to put upon the use of transportation development projects to shape the future dimensions of urban growth. As has been discussed, the basic motive for furthering transportation technology may not be the provision of transportation capacity at all. If the past can be used as a reasonable guide, national defense, accelerated redevelopment of depressed areas, economic "pump-priming," and, most recently, minority group access to jobs, homes and education, and control of inflation, may become the *real* objectives of what is termed "transportation policy."[9]

The dimensions of the metropolitan planning problem have thus far exceeded the abilities of policymakers at all levels of government to deal with them. This being the case, it is hardly surprising that the role the federal government should assume in advancing transportation technology in urban areas is, at best, unclear. Again the question arises: Should transportation serve existing or anticipated needs; should it venture into the arena of creating its own demand? The former alternative adjusts to conditions and projected trends; the latter alternative attempts to design the desired community in advance, and then employs transportation development to transform the plan into reality.

The second alternative suffers from lack of agreement on what constitutes "ideal metropolitanization."[a] Which criteria are to be employed in determining "optimum" population densities; "ideal" mixes of facilities for shopping, health services, education, recreation, and community services; suitable access to employment opportunities; efficient and aesthetically pleasing combinations of

---

[a]The then President of the Ford Motor Company gave vent to his frustration concerning this problem when he noted that if population is concentrated in too small an area, we have "urban congestion." If population is spread out, we have "urban sprawl." Both conditions, he observed, were most frequently attributed to the automobile.[10]

land uses?[11] If some agreement on these questions cannot be reached, this approach to determining the nature of the future federal role in advancing transport technology would have to rely on speculation, arbitrary judgment, or political bargaining.

To these difficulties must be added the point that federal participation in the search for technological solutions to metropolitan transportation problems began very "late in the game." Consequently, limited opportunities exist for planning systems *de novo*. And even where new systems can be considered, their relationships with existing competitive or companion modes must necessarily become part of the evolution of the federal role.

Associated with these points is the view that no significant reduction in land use requirements would result from large-scale development of mass transit systems to downtowns. In fact, Meyer, Kain and Wohl concluded that *with or without* mass transit, American cities would decentralize, and that the patterns of land uses, population growth, and employment location are essentially the same for both transit-oriented and highway-oriented cities.[12]

In addition, it should be observed that the differentiation of highway- and transit-oriented metropolitan areas applies principally to journey to work transportation. By and large, usage of mass transportation during off-peak periods drops sharply compared to the peak hours, even in urban areas with relatively well developed public transportation systems. It has been estimated, for example, that the rapid transit facilities of San Francisco's BART system will handle only five percent of the area's total trips when it is completed. Most of the balance will continue to be made by auto.

All of this makes it obvious that considerable research remains to be done if the greatest possible effectiveness is to be achieved by federal commitments to technological advances in transportation.

Technological Responses to Growth

The last major factor to be dealt with in this section involves technological responses to growth. It relates directly to the projected growth of national population and the anticipated pattern of settlement which it will assume.

One study of the conterminous United States population in the year 2000 predicts that the total at that time will surpass 304 million.[13] It also estimates that twelve major urban regions of the country will account for approximately eighty-five percent of the entire net increase in population during this thirty-year period. In effect, although they will occupy only *one-tenth* of the conterminous United States land area, these regions would contain *seven-tenths* of the nation's population in the year 2000.

The dimensions of future urban growth stagger the imagination. Both the Los Angeles and New York Region are projected to have an urbanized area of 5,000 square miles each; Chicago and San Francisco Bay area about 2,000 square miles each; Detroit, Southeast Florida, and Washington from 1,200 to 1,700 square miles each. In addition, a number of other metropolitan areas are predicted to surpass sizes of 1,000 square miles each.[14]

The significance of these projected rates and concentrations of population growth to the dimensions of future federal influence on transportation technology is self-evident. What is not so evident are the specific strategies that should be adopted if the subsystems of national transportation, as presently conceived, are to survive and adapt to the enormity of the challenge that this growth represents. For it can be anticipated, even at this point, that transportation demand will not only grow strictly in terms of the numbers but also in intensified *per capita* demand for transportation. In this sense, the transportation needs of the future will assume geometric rather than arithmetic growth characteristics.[15]

Charles D. Baker, former Assistant Secretary for Policy and International Affairs of the Department of Transportation, has identified this problem as one of the most severe to be faced in planning future transportation facilities. He observed that, increasingly, sections of the nation, such as the Northeast Corridor, face problems that go beyond metropolitan commuter type congestion. The emerging problem is *absolute congestion*, a condition that imposes rigid constraints on the ability to move people and goods with even past rates of speed or levels of effectiveness. Complicating the enormity of this problem is the fact that the needs of urban transportation are enmeshed in the broader problems of urban development. The challenge is intensified by the competition for federal money generated by other pressing public needs. Baker noted that national transportation capacity cannot be doubled or tripled by the year 2000, as it must be, by building the same kind of things that have been done in the past. There is not the time, money, or, in many cases, even the space for this kind of policy response.[16]

These prospects raise a number of fundamental questions. Given this outlook, should federal policy be directed toward providing the technological basis for accommodating the use of 250 million or more autos in the year 2000, and a sharply increased number beyond that period? At what point, if any, should a *major* effort be made to develop new modes of high speed, high capacity passenger and freight service? How much of the leverage of federally sponsored technological progress should be used to encourage more efficient employment-residence patterns of transportation? What relative emphases should be placed on personal transportation and mass transportation? Should the federal government assume the primary responsibility for sponsoring and supporting technological research in all modes of transportation, as it has done for the aviation mode? In view of the tremendous magnitude of projected transportation needs within the next three decades, will sufficient pressure develop to create new mechanisms to achieve a more rational allocation of resources devoted to expanding national transportation capacity and efficiency?

These queries, of course, hardly cover the entire range of critical transportation policy issues which future patterns of growth will present. Nor do they deal with the longer-term consequences of decisions which will be made during the next thirty years. What this analysis does demonstrate, however, is that future federal policies, designed to influence and direct technological advances in transportation, will play a large part in determining whether future generations maintain or improve their mobility, or slowly sink to the level of mass immobility.

The Technological Future of Urban Ground Transportation

Few transportation problems have received as much publicity and generated as many expressions of official concern as has the problem of the technological future of urban ground transportation. Unfortunately, solid efforts to analyze the numerous dimensions of the challenge, develop alternative approaches to short-term and long-term solutions, and commit the required financial and technical resources to specific courses of action have not been forthcoming. In fact, the dominant tendency of federal transportation policy has been to move very cautiously and reluctantly into direct participation in, and support of, urban community efforts to deal with their knotty transportation problems.

On the other hand, it should be observed that increasing attention is being given to the technological facets of moving people in urban areas of varying densities. Studies are being made of the technical aspects of developing the transportation "hardware" that could be utilized in the urban environment. Attention is also being given to relating technologically advanced transport systems to the many other aspects of improving the "quality of life" in metropolitan areas. This section is devoted to an analysis of several of the proposals that have been advanced.

"Tomorrow's Transportation" – Report of the Department of Housing and Urban Development

As directed by the 1966 amendments to the Urban Mass Transportation Act of 1964, the Department of Housing and Urban Development undertook an eighteen-month study, utilizing seventeen contractors to examine the potential roles of new systems of urban transportation. The result of these evaluations, entitled *Tomorrow's Transportation – New Systems for the Urban Future,* was released just prior to the transfer of the Urban Transportation Administration from HUD to DOT.[17]

The report took a comprehensive approach to the problems of metropolitan transportation, including their relationships to many other aspects of urban planning and living. While the study predicted a continuation of urban growth, it expressed misgivings about the future quality of urban life. In particular, it defined eight primary problem areas:

1. Equality of access to urban opportunity.

   This problem concerns the non-driving portion of the population — the poor, the young, the old, and the handicapped. These categories of people might be termed the "transportation poor." Hamilton and Nance, for example, noted that one-half of all United States families with incomes of less than $4,000, one-half of all Negro households, and one-half of all households headed by persons over sixty-five own no automobile.[18]

2. Quality of urban transportation services.

3. Congestion.

4. Efficient use of equipment and facilities.

5. Efficient use of land.

6. Urban pollution.

7. Urban development options.

8. Institutional framework and implementation.

   Here the report noted that the blunt dichotomy of rail *versus* auto was an oversimplification. Instead, it recommended a pluralistic approach to the transportation needs of urban areas to achieve an efficient mix of services.

 Many of these problems were attributed directly or indirectly to the automobile. As an alternative to overwhelming reliance on private transportation, the report proposed a number of steps to introduce "balance" into future urban transportation planning.

Foremost among the recommendations made was one supporting a continuing research and development program in urban transportation to be conducted over a five- to ten-year period at a cost of $980 million. The report noted that only a small fraction of federal research and development expenditures had been devoted to a systematic attack upon urban transportation and related problems.

A second set of recommendations dealt with non-technical, "software" approaches such as training programs for transit operations, staggered working hours, and improved methodology in forecasting travel demands. Related to these were recommendations for creation of an Urban Transportation Information Center and an Urban Transportation Test Center.[19]

As might be expected in a comprehensive study of this type, the potential "hardware" improvements captured the greatest attention. In particular, the report described a number of promising technologies that could change the character of urban transportation. It concluded that present technological knowledge and anticipated advances would make it possible to introduce new concepts in transportation. Those considered most promising were:

Dial-A-Bus — a system of surface transportation employing telephone communication and central computerized control. The traveler would simply dial his destination and computer controls would continually route buses in optimum, individualized paths.

Personal Rapid Transit – envisages the use of small, one- or two-passenger vehicles automatically routed over exclusive rights-of-way. Guidance would be computer-controlled.

Dual-Mode Vehicle Systems – small vehicles which could be operator-controlled on urban roadways, and also utilize guideways for mainline transportation.

Automated Dual-Mode Bus – a vehicle carrying 20 passengers or so that would have the same operating characteristics as the Dual-Mode Vehicle.

Pallet or Ferry Systems – would be designed to carry various vehicles on high speed guideways.

Fast Intra-Urban Transit Links – automatic vehicles capable of operating independently or coupling into trains.

It should be added that the report made a number of interim recommendations for relieving present transportation congestion, such as improved bus service, use of exclusive bus lanes, and improved traffic controls.

Evaluation of the Report. Some participants in the study noted that their research demonstrated that possible strategies for improving urban transportation fall into two sharply different categories: the process of "gradualism" which would concentrate on building improvements in existing systems; "new technology" which in effect would provide new modes.[20]

Improvements of existing systems were found in the report to be inadequate for meeting future needs. This conclusion explains the emphasis given to new technology, as opposed to existing forms. But it still falls far short of a federal commitment to de-emphasize present forms in favor of such systems. In this regard, the HUD report, for good or ill, fell into the category of a "technical study" and, as such, carries more the overtone of information and guidance than a commitment to seek new modes and methods.

The report also contained much of the element of the gamble. If it is granted that the major proposals merit serious consideration, upon what basis do urban communities commit funds and other resources to the proposed courses of action? What are the specific technological bases for moving forward with any or all of the approaches proposed? What are the chances of success in implementing such systems? Should urban communities assume the risks of undertaking basic research which may or may not lead to improved urban transportation? The answers to these questions are far from clear-cut.

In reality, all of the varied proposals presented in the report share three common attributes: (1) all are aimed at solving the urban transportation problem, (2) all are very costly, even on a pilot basis, (3) there is no way of knowing whether they will work.[21] Thus, to some urban transportation administrators, the report offered suggestions and ideas for the future and little more. Its contents appear far removed from a plan for action.

Some have taken an even more critical view of the study, again reflecting the frustration of employing unproven, theoretical, long-range concepts in meeting urban transportation problems which cry for solutions *now*. In some quarters it is felt that this type of federal study fails to come to grips with the real problems of mass transit. Specifically, the advisability of ignoring existing subway and rail facilities has been questioned, as has the idea of imposing new intricate systems of urban transportation atop existing ones.[22] Again, this criticism reveals the growing conflict over the adequacy of existing modes of transportation in meeting the future requirements of urban transportation, versus the unknown and uncertain outcomes of research and development in "new technology."

Additional Proposals

Research on the development and application of "new technology" for urban transportation is continuing on a number of fronts both within and outside of the federal government, and is resulting in a number of additional proposals. Some of the results of these studies bear a strong similarity to the recommendations of the HUD report, while others introduce new ideas.

One of the most important has been "Project Transport," conducted under the direction of Assistant Dean William Seifert of Massachusetts Institute of Technology. This group favored use of 300 mph railcars riding on a cushion of air, after the fashion of the hovercraft.[23] Another approach employs the linear-induction motor for vehicle propulsion. In this system, the train moves on the track using the same electromagnetic forces that produce rotary motion inside an electric motor. As in the case of certain elements of the HUD proposal, such vehicles would be designed to operate on specially designed rights-of-way or guideways. Extremely high speeds, up to 500 mph, would be made possible by propelling the vehicles in evacuated underground tubes.

These technological innovations again raise some fundamental issues of public policy. One facet of the problem was addressed by Seifert when he noted:

We now have the technology or are within a step or two of having it, for a superb transportation network in this country. But it doesn't do any good to introduce an isolated technological improvement into this kind of mess.[24]

In general, the application of new technology does not lend itself to fragmented application. If such systems are to be developed they must have the characteristics of *systems,* i.e., complementary parts, overall consistency, planned interrrelationships.

Such high speed, high capacity transportation is applicable to both the functions of intracity and intercity transportation. But to be most effective, it would require the advantages of system-wide planning now accorded aviation.

Additional proposals for technologically advanced urban passenger transportation define the problem in terms of the distances to be traversed. For transportation under one mile, high volume conveyers with capacities of 36,000 passengers per hour have been proposed. For the range of one to nine miles, continuous underground trains, self-service taxicabs and automatic driving systems would be possibilities. Among the suggestions for longer distance intercity travel are those which would provide automatic highways with lane capacities of 10,000 cars per hour (five times the current capacity) traveling at speeds of 100-150 mph.[25] Other ideas which promise high speed, high capacity transportation are also apparently receiving some consideration.

Evaluation

These concepts, many of which are now being researched by the Department of Transportation, offer a wide range of possibilities for alleviating the difficulties of present and future urban transportation. But ideas by themselves do not solve problems. In fact, if it is conceded that metropolitan transportation has assumed the dimensions of a *national problem,* it follows that solutions to it will not be found without leadership by the federal government and substantially increased sums of federal money.

These needs exist in an environment which, historically, has relied heavily on fragmented, localized initiative and action. But as transportation problems become more complex and intensify, the inadequacy and undesirability of applying such outmoded approaches appears increasingly evident.

So that this point may be explored in greater detail, the next section is devoted to an analysis of the federal program of researching and developing high speed ground transportation.

The Federal Role in the Development of
High Speed Ground Transportation

The federal government has made a modest entry into the relatively unknown and unexplored area of high speed ground transportation research and development. In this section, these efforts will be reviewed in terms of their scope, emphasis, and accomplishments to date.

The High Speed Ground Transportation Act of 1965 provided the initial basis for direct participation by the federal government in advancing the state of ground transportation technology.[26] It authorized an expenditure of $90 million over a three-year period to establish programs of research and development in high speed ground transportation, demonstration projects to assess the contributions that such transportation could make to more efficient and economical intercity transportation, and a program to improve the scope and availability of transportation statistics. Subsequent extensions of the law authorized $16.2 million for 1969, $21.2 million for 1970, and $18 million in 1971. The 1972 budget request was for $29 million.

In March of 1972, the House authorized $315.2 million for fiscal years 1973-1975 for research and developments under the High Speed Ground Transportation Act. The bill provided railroad loan renewals, as well as funds for continuing the Metroliner and TurboTrain demonstration projects in the Northeast Corridor. Also extended was the project development of the tracked air cushion research vehicle.

Programs of the Office of High Speed
Ground Transportation (OHSGT)

In some ways, the programs of OHSGT reflect the conflicts which have attended definition of the evolving federal role in urban transportation. For the organization straddles the issue of "gradualism" versus "new technology." In administering the Northeast Corridor Transportation Project, for example, it is engaged in a demonstration program to determine what is the best passenger service that can be obtained, using the present "state of the art." But at the same time it is engaged in a number of programs exploring highly advanced technology. The goals of these programs are twofold: one is to find ways of transporting passengers that are competitive with air travel; the second is to design systems that do not impose heavy demands for space.

At the heart of OHSGT research and development efforts is the systems engineering approach. Its features include analyses of characteristics of alternative transportation systems, preparation of performance and cost estimates, and evaluation of subsystem alternatives.[27] One result has been the reduction of possible technological configurations, drawn from numerous concepts, to a handful of systems which now appear to be most promising. These include track-levitated vehicles (either tracked air-cushion vehicles [TACV] or electromagnetically supported); rolling support systems such as conventional rail or monorail; tube vehicle systems; multi-modal systems (roughly comparable to the HUD proposal of dual-mode vehicle systems and automated dual-mode bus); auto-train systems (comparable to the HUD proposal of pallet or ferry systems); automated highway systems; and continuous capacity systems (endless belts and conveyors).

Of these alternatives, the greatest attention is being given to the "hardware" characteristics of TACV. The brunt of the research and development effort is being borne by a number of aerospace firms and includes design and testing of propulsion systems, guideways, air cushion systems, vehicle suspension systems, and control systems. A special test site at which the combination of these new concepts can be tested is now being built.

The second choice, at least in terms of the current research and development effort being devoted to it, is the tube-type vehicle system. Although it offers the advantage of extremely high speed transportation (500 mph), it is less attractive than TACV at this point in time because of cost and the state of its technology.

In this case, there is a close relationship between the transportation technology involved and the status of tunneling technology. As a consequence, OHSGT has sponsored research on tunneling for the past five years in cooperation with the Bureau of Mines. Up to this point, however, there have been no major breakthroughs that would significantly lower present costs.

The other complicating factor is that tube vehicle aerodynamics is a technology which is only about four years old. Mastery of its problems, of course, will require a substantial technological "push" before it can be considered as a new mode suitable for passenger transportation. Numerous research and development contracts have already been awarded to attack the difficulties of tube drag, tube vehicle stability, use of a gravity vacuum, and tube vehicle propulsion and control. OHSGT is sponsoring a feasibility study of the linear induction motor for the propulsion drives systems of both TACV and tube vehicles.

It should also be added that studies are being made of the most important ingredients in these new systems – the passengers. These major problems include the phenomenon of "flicker," caused by a high speed vehicle passing trees, poles, and other objects that can result in disorientation for many and illness for some. Also of concern is the need for smooth stops and starts, particularly for old or physically handicapped people. And considerable doubt still surrounds the effects of pressure changes when a high speed vehicle enters tunnels.

The Department of Transportation also has another significant set of projects under way in the field of "new systems" for passenger transportation. These comprise the personal rapid transit systems (PRTs). One aspect of this effort was displayed at "Transpo '72" in Washington, D.C. In all, four different prototypes were demonstrated.

But, perhaps of greater importance in furthering PRT transportation is the full-scale system now under construction in Morgantown, West Virginia. The first phase will be available for testing late in 1972; the 2.5-mile guideway connects two of the campuses of West Virginia University, and will provide a unique test and demonstration of the feasibility of constructing and operating similar, fully automated systems in urban areas throughout the country.

The policy issue that surrounds this technological advance has much in common with the other systems already reviewed – the problem of cost. The cost of Morgantown PRT will probably exceed $30 million for a 2.5-mile system, in an area where right-of-way expenses hardly compare to densely populated metropolitan centers. Nor can the amount of revenue from ridership be overlooked. In Morgantown, the ridership is "captive" – largely students who, presumably, would use the system extensively throughout the day. But what of major metropolitan areas, with their typical peak periods occurring twice daily, five days a week? This raises a fundamental question: Can we look to new modes of transportation to be economically viable when even the use of commuter buses on "free" rights-of-way in metropolitan areas so frequently results in deficits?

The Northeast Corridor Transportation Project

The roots of the Northeast Corridor Transportation Project are deeply grounded in the national political process. For it was not a "technical" decision of the federal government to undertake this activity, but rather the mobilization of political pressure and interest in the project that finally led to its launching.

Highly instrumental in creating the program were Congressional hearings which examined the complex transportation problems of the Northeast and the publication of a book on the subject by Rhode Island Senator Claiborne Pell.[28] Both pointed to the rapidly deteriorating state of interurban transportation in the Corridor from Boston to Washington, and the dire need for federal action to assist in solving the problem. As a direct outgrowth of these pressures, President Kennedy and, subsequently, President Johnson, directed the Department of Commerce in the early 1960s to begin studies of the situation.[29] The immediate effect was the creation of an Executive Branch Task Force to examine the problem.

The work and conclusions of this group produced friction because its recommendations failed to deal with the *immediate* problems and solutions that were perceived by Senator Pell and others. Specifically, the Task Force concluded that the question of transportation in the Northeastern Megalopolis should not be confined to evaluation of the greater use and improvement of railroads in the Corridor, but the broader, long-term needs of the region.[30]

The sense of urgency felt by Senator Pell and others was completely lost. Thus the Task Force asked:

Does prospective demand warrant substantial outlay for more or better transport facilities in the region?

How could facilities be best provided?

What would be the probable impact of alternative courses of action?

The group concluded that what was needed was a detailed, comprehensive study. As a consequence, the first three years of the project were dominated by study design, and development of models and analytical techniques. Little was done to initiate any kind of action.

The scope of the study was defined in terms of eight broadly conceived reseach categories.

1. *Selection of Alternative Systems and Services* — the objective was to choose a small number of transportation systems and relate them to land use, location of economic activity, population distribution, economic growth, and

community structure. At the same time, the interaction between relevant policy objectives of federal, state and local governments, and the design of the various transportation systems was to be determined;

2. *Socio—Economic Forecasting and Impact Analysis* – was to utilize multi-sectoral econometric forecasting and regional impact models to measure the effects of alternative transportation systems. (As experience has since demonstrated, it takes considerable time for researchers to achieve the "grand circularity" envisioned when a project is initiated. This concept anticipated that system "feedback" could be used to conduct impact analysis through a series of simulations.);

3. *Demand Analysis and Forecasting* – to develop estimates of travel demand and modal split models;

4. *Network Simulation* – to use travel and demand data to subject various transportation systems to trial;

5. *Evaluation* – to apply techniques of benefit-cost measurement to the various possible transportation systems and their projected impacts on the region;

6. *Management and Finance Alternatives* – to examine the question of the mix of public and private enterprise activities that would produce the optimum system;

7. *Description of Means of Implementation;*

8. *Needs for Support Services.*

Although this program provided a theoretical framework for improvement of transportation in the Northeast, it offered no immediate, tangible benefits. This situation eventually led to pressure for the institution of "demonstration projects" to improve rail service between Boston, New York, and Washington. The capital costs for these projects were expected to exceed $80 million; however, only about $22 million was to be contributed by the federal government. The bulk of the investment was to be borne by the Penn-Central. In addition, it was anticipated that several million dollars will be returned to the federal government through revenue sharing.

The Boston—New York Demonstration Project. In January, 1966, OHSGT entered into a contract with United Aircraft Corporation to lease two TurboTrains which United had designed and built. These trains were to test the new train technology which this aerospace organization has developed, as well as potential market possibilities.

The TurboTrain was originally designed to be high speed, cutting one hour from the time of the conventional train run from Boston to New York. Specifications called for each TurboTrain to have a minimum top speed of 139 mph. In actual operation, performance at this speed has not been achieved, primarily due to the inadequate roadbed and curves on the line. As of this writing, the schedules of TurboTrain operation have been reduced to five round-trips weekly, with train capacity to increase to 240 passengers. For fiscal year 1972, DOT requested $3.6 million to continue this demonstration program.

TurboTrain is still coping with a multitude of malfunctions that, interestingly enough, are quite common to most conventional trains in the United States. Its experience indicates that even the aerospace industry is capable of producing highly sophisticated transportation vehicles that work less than perfectly!

The New York–Washington Demonstration Project. The OHSGT entered into an agreement with the Penn-Central Railroad early in 1966 for a two-year demonstration (since extended) of high speed rail passenger service between New York and Washington.

In contrast to the Boston-New York experiment, this program is cast along decidedly more conventional lines. The Budd Company was the major contractor for Penn-Central and was to provide fifty streamlined Metroliners for use in the service.

The Metroliner is based on existing railroad technology. Power is supplied by four 640 hp electric engines per car, which are to enable attainment of speeds of 125 mph in 120 seconds. The long-range goal was to make the New York-Washington run in under three hours, with a top speed capability of 160 mph.

Metroliners began service on January 16, 1969, after a delay of almost two years beyond the very optimistic target date. It now provides substantially all through-trains between Washington and New York, and Philadelphia and New York, including nine round trips on weekdays. Through 1971, DOT had contributed approximately $13 million and the railroad $55 million to the demonstration. For fiscal year 1972, DOT requested $5.4 million in additional funds for this program.[31]

Again, technical problems have been numerous, and anticipated speed of service has been disappointing. Substantial problems have been encountered in operation of car pantographs. In addition, the trains have experienced excessive vibration, surges of acceleration at high speeds, and difficulties in slowing and stopping. Many of these difficulties have been attributed to the severe constraints imposed by "making do" with existing conventional facilities. These facilities are being subjected to stresses beyond original design requirements – a fact made most apparent by the condition of the roadbed and the power supply systems.

But not all of the early problems of the Metroliner were technical. When service began, Penn-Central instituted service using cumbersome manual methods for making reservations. Although a computer-controlled system was later installed, this factor may have influenced the demand for the service (which has been high in spite of the problem), and may have initially distorted the data on the service which OHSGT was attempting to gather.

Project Data Collection and Analysis. As indicated earlier, the original concept of the Northeast Corridor Transportation Project was to conduct a comprehensive study involving extensive data collection and analysis. The study was to determine the ideal mix of transportation facilities to serve the region, and relate these to long-term "quality of life" considerations. Not surprisingly, public attention accorded this phase of the program has been usurped by the more immediate interest in the "hardware" aspects of the program.

Yet major progress has been made in moving toward a "grand design." Procedures were formulated for intermediate and long-run forecasts of passenger and freight volumes carried by all modes of transportation; a series of models for analyzing regional transport investments, forecasts of population, and income and economic activity in the corridor were developed; systems engineering and cost analysis work were accomplished.

Recommendations of the Northeast Corridor Transportation Project. The final report of the Northeast Corridor Transportation Project was released in September, 1971. Its basic recommendations urged action programs in terms of two time levels: one for the interim period of the 1970s, the second for the 1980s and beyond.

To provide necessary service in the 1970s, the conclusion that emerged from the Project was that the Corridor's huge investments in existing facilities ought to be tapped. Thus, the first recommendation called for improvement of high speed, high frequency rail service along the Washington to Boston "spine." The report looked to DOT to fund the effort, largely through loans and loan guarantees at a total estimated cost of $460 million.

Of course the other major existing transportation resource of the Corridor is its highway network. As the other phase of the program for the 1970s, the Project recommended institution of a "Real-time Highway Information System" that would allow intercity drivers to make informed decisions concerning alternate routes to their destinations. It was also suggested that intercity highway movements along the congested Washington-Boston spinal network be facilitated by improving the connectivity of the existing and planned networks. Estimated costs for providing additional short sections of freeway bypasses and interchanges were put at $50 million. In addition, the consolidation of existing highways into a new north-south route to bypass congested metropolitan areas was suggested.

For the 1980s, the Project presented a series of recommendations characterized by more innovation. The most important was its call for immediate planning of a new high speed, ground right-of-way along the spine of the Corridor that would be suitable for a tracked air cushion vehicle (TACV) system. A concomitant recommendation noted that possible institutional arrangements for operating such a system should be investigated. Closely tied to these recommendations was another; it underscored the need to expand and accelerate research and development of tracked air cushion vehicles, including particular emphasis on developing an *environmentally* acceptable system.

To provide sufficient highway capacity for the period of the 1980s and beyond, the study concluded that research and development on automated highways ought to be expanded to determine its feasibility. The potential benefits of this research were seen as possibly reaching fruition within the life of highways built during the next decade.

The other recommendation of major consequence made by the Project involved the future of major transportation investment decisions. Specifically, it was concluded that such decisions should be deferred until the outcomes of TACV, STOL and VTOL research and development programs are evaluated. The recommended "year of decision" is 1976.[32]

High Speed Ground Transportation in Retrospect

The work of exploring new vistas of transport technology and planning, and in furthering the progress of the Northeast Corridor Transportation Project, represents a unique facet of the federal role in meeting the challenges of urban transportation. At the same time, this involvement raises a number of important policy questions.

In the first place, high speed ground transportation, such as TACV, would constitute an entirely new mode of transportation — a net addition to existing capacity. As such, its full potential could not be tapped unless it were developed as a system.[33] Furthermore, the manner in which it would be integrated with existing modes has hardly been explored. Then, too, there is the question of the capital costs that would be involved.[34] In this regard, it is revealing to note that the Project report on the Corridor omitted placing a price tag on the TACV system recommended for the 1980s.

Secondly, there is the continuing question of how high speed, high capacity ground transportation, operating on fixed routes, would serve the megalopolitan areas of the future which are not only enlarging but *decentralizing* at the same time.[35] This characteristic would appear to limit the practicality of TACV and tube-type vehicles systems to very high-density areas.

Thirdly, an aura of considerable uncertainty surrounds the prospects for utilization of new modes of transportation. This doubt focuses not so much on the ultimate capacity of technology to overcome the problems now being encountered, but rather the manner in which future progress will be applied. Clearly, present programs have "seed money" overtones; there is no suggestion of federal assumption of responsibility for *operational* HSGT systems.

Fourthly, experience on the Corridor Project illustrates the popular political appeal of more immediate, tangible results in "hardware" development and employment. Certainly the TurboTrain and Metroliner, in spite of the over-optimism which characterized their operating features and the start of service, have helped to convey some impression of federal action on the problem of intercity transportation. In contrast, the long-range comprehensive studies projecting the transportation needs of the region into the 1980s and beyond, promise much less of an immediate political "pay-off" and identification. Not surprisingly, the appeal of comprehensive planning rationality is lost "when it takes too long."

Finally, the experience of the Department of Commerce, HUD, and DOT in dealing with technological advances in ground transportation illustrates the enormous complexity of relating public policy objectives, where they have been defined, to the mixed-enterprise characteristics of national transportation. It has become increasingly difficult to identify not only the points at which federal, state, and urban responsibilities begin and end, but — just as important — the line of demarcation between public responsibility and private interest.

Because of the importance of this subject to the evaluation of national transportation policy, the next chapter will continue to explore the impact of technology on the various modes and their relationships to the federal role.

Policy Issues and Technology

7

Policy Issues and Technology

This chapter considers further the impact of technological change on federal transportation policy. Particular attention is directed to a number of the complex issues involved in federal research and development activities. The development of the Supersonic Transport (SST) is examined in this context, particularly the unique commitments which the federal government made to its development.

For purposes of contrast and comparison, the nature of research and development expenditures affecting the other modes is also examined. Specific attention is given to developmental spending for urban mass transportation and high speed ground transportation. The analysis then turns to a review of policy issues involved in "coordinated" transportation, and their close relationship to technological advance. Finally, some of the more important barriers to innovation are considered, as are a number of strategies for overcoming them.

The Federal Government – Air Industry Relationship

As has been observed in previous chapters, the relationship of the federal government to aircraft manufacturers and air carriers is unique among all the modes of transportation. Aviation has benefited enormously from "protective" policies of economic regulation, federal assistance in airport development, and research and development on navigational aids and safety.

But even more, the industry has been the direct recipient of advantages accruing from the "spillover" effects of military aircraft development. As an illustration, the Boeing 707, one of the basic "workhorses" of the aviation industry, which contributed so much to making the transformation from piston engine to jet aircraft financially successful, is a modification of the military KC 135.[1]

But that is just one example. It is anticipated that Lockheed, if it survives its immediate financial crisis, would be in a position to offer for the civilian market a version of the C-5A, the world's largest cargo plane. Its commercial adaptation would carry 900 passengers, or 165 tons of cargo. It may be considered representative of projects in the jet age, since the costs of researching and producing it have made the aircraft another "billion-dollar project." As might be expected, controversy over the development of this aircraft has focused on the

153

enormous overrun in cost per unit. But, the direct benefit to private industry of its future sales as a civilian craft has been the subject of little discussion and almost no criticism as a matter of policy. In fact, the desirability of such applications is strongly supported by some members of Congress.

Such direct adaptation should not be interpreted as the primary means of providing federal support for the technological advances of aviation. The most valuable "spillovers," in fact, are indirect, as has been discussed earlier. For it is in the development of subsystems, with the interchangeable applications, and in the vast amount of general technological advances, that aircraft manufacturers have probably gained the most from their "working partnership" with the military. While these gains are sometimes referred to as "intangible benefits," in some respects that is a misnomer. The benefits are often very tangible; the difficulty lies in tracing them directly from source to application.

Another element deeply affecting technological advance within the aviation mode, and its relationship to the federal policy role, relates to rates of change and obsolescence. In turn, these have been influenced by a complex mixture of factors.

Foremost has been extremely rapid improvements in aircraft performance characteristics, underwritten by military research and development. Transferred to the civilian market, these advances have spurred intense competition among the airlines. Thus, carriers are constantly pushed to obtain faster, higher capacity aircraft. A second factor affecting the rate of change is cost. One of the great attractions of new aircraft, which are always on the horizon, is that they will increase revenues and reduce operating costs per mile flown. A third factor is passenger capacity. Aircraft capacities have been climbing steadily, and provide not only a means for increasing revenue but also to overcome, at least temporarily, the "squeeze" in airspace capacity and the congestion it causes. As they react together, these factors accelerate the pressure for and promise of change.

The rapid rate of technological change has become a "way of life" in aviation research and development; it has imposed the need for long-range planning on both private industry and government. Again, this need has served to continue the melding and interdependence of the federal government, manufacturers, and carriers.[2] The degree to which these relationships have evolved is illustrated by the SST project.

The SST Project

The evolution of the SST followed a tortuous path. Impetus for its development appeared in the late 1950s within the FAA. Contributing support to initiation of a major research and development effort for the aircraft were Department of Defense and manufacturers' pressures.

The project has seen a succession of special committees and commissions created by the President to either evaluate the merit of the program or to influence its direction. For example, Lyndon B. Johnson, as Vice-President, led a Cabinet level committee to determine whether the program should become a national commitment; later, as President, Johnson formed an Advisory Commission, headed by the Secretary of Defense, to evaluate the project.

Once the project passed its first trial — the consideration of whether it ought to be undertaken at all — it entered and completed a competitive design and study phase. The latter resulted in the selection of General Electric and Boeing as prime contractors for the engine development and airframe design, respectively. The selections resulted from an intensive evaluation by DOD, NASA, CAB, and FAA.[3]

Although funds were appropriated for the SST Project as early as 1961, it was in 1963 that President Kennedy announced a formal federal commitment to it. The most significant aspect of this decision was the concept of joint public-private development in which costs would be shared. Under this plan, the government was to be repaid eventually through profits from sales of the SST. At first the investment shares were to be seventy-five percent public and twenty-five percent private. But as expenses increased, so did the pressure for a larger share to be borne by the federal government. That share eventually rose to ninety percent.

The private sector contributions to the SST program were borne, in part, by nine domestic air carriers and one foreign air carrier. They paid $1 million for each delivery position they held. Their contract with the federal government provided that for each $1 million they invested, they would receive $1.5 million through royalties on SST sales. In all, this "risk" capital amounted to over $50 million, which was written off against the ninety percent federal share of the project.

Total cost of the prototype program to the federal government turned out to be much more substantial — $1.3 billion — most of which was spent on research and design. At the same time, it should be noted that the program was premised, in part, on the federal government recouping its entire SST investment with the anticipated sale of about 300 SSTs. The government was to continue to receive royalties after 300 craft were sold; FAA economic studies projected that the sale of 500 SSTs would generate $1 billion over the original investment.[4]

Certainly the "official" reports of federal executive agencies were considerably mory optimistic about the SST than were many members of Congress. This fact was reflected in the increasingly critical attitude of Congress in authorizing additional funds for the program. Nor was this attitude unsupported, for the costs of the project rose steadily, while the anticipated date of production drifted into the future.

Congress reached the point of balking in 1968. In that year, there was a Congressional recision of $30 million in the program. All 1969 budget requests were denied, and continuation of the program was made possible only by the use of funds that had been previously authorized. The situation was further aggravated when the Nixon Administration delayed its decision on whether, or how much, money should be requested for Fiscal Year 1970.

There were also second thoughts in other quarters. Some participating airlines, with their financial contribution to "risk capital" rising, began to reassess support for further SST federal budget commitments.[5] Their skepticism was strengthened when an *ad hoc* committee, appointed by President Nixon to restudy the merits of the SST project, concluded that the evidence was sufficient to support serious consideration of abandoning the project.[6]

SST Policy Issues

Several policy issues dominated the development of the SST. These included both positive and negative points of view.

Pros. The supporting arguments noted that the SST was a natural outgrowth of the technological advance that has characterized the growth of the aviation mode. In the eyes of some, not to undertake this "next step" would impede future progress in civilian aviation in the United States for the next three decades.

Development of the SST by the United States was also viewed by many as a necessity to the maintenance of national prestige and technological leadership in aviation. To abandon the field to the British and French Concorde, and the Russian SST, according to this view, would undermine the future of the United States role in international aviation.

Nor was the factor of vastly increased speed, and the aircraft utilization that would result, ignored. The upshot of this argument was that the SST, with its capacity of 250-300 passengers traveling at three times the speed of the Boeing 747, would do as much work as two 747s, or four and a half 707s.

Another argument noted that projected sales of SSTs would contribute to improvement of the balance of payments. It was anticipated that the sale of 500 SSTs would result in total sales of something in excess of $20 billion. Of this amount, about one-half would be sales to foreign airlines and thus would contribute to the balance of payments.

It was also maintained that the federal government has already made a big investment in the development of the SST, and to abandon it would be to waste $1 billion either spent or committed.

Another point asserted was that it would be difficult to suspend work in 1971, after having spent almost ten years on the effort. Over 20,000 people had been gathered in this period to work on the project; disbanding it would permanently damage any future effort to develop an SST. An associated argument related to the economic recession that the country found itself still in during 1971, and the reduction of worker income and jobs that project discontinuance would engender. As noted earlier, similar arguments have been used to support previous, major federal financial commitments in the field of transportation.

Cons. On the other hand, opponents of the SST contended that the cost of the project would be totally disproportional to the anticipated benefit. Federal investment through the prototype stage alone, they noted, would exceed $1.3 billion, and billions more will be required to produce 300 or more aircraft – if indeed there was a demand for them. In sum, such spending, for *one* aircraft at *one* point in time, reflected a misplacement of values and a misallocation of precious resources.

One of the most telling arguments mustered by the opposition concerned the potential damage to the environment that might be brought about by a fleet of SSTs. Criticism came from many fronts. It was contended that sideline noise of the SST on takeoffs and landings would be intolerable. Sonic boom became a primary issue. It was also noted that the plane would be able to fly at supersonic speed only over the oceans, because of the damage and annoyance that it would cause at ground level. Other environmental issues included the effect that exhaust vapor might have on the upper atmosphere, and the changes it might bring about in the ozone layer that protects the earth from ultraviolet radiation.

Critics also noted that purchase of SSTs by the airlines will represent a gamble of tremendous proportions. Each copy was estimated to cost about $40 million – almost double the cost of the giant Boeing 747. Associated with this problem was the matter of maintaining perspective in national spending priorities, in terms of the "public" served. Again, critics pointed out that SST service would be utilized largely by the most affluent, and those who comprise the "jet set." In other words, the real beneficiaries of this government sponsored undertaking made up a relatively insignificant proportion of the population.

It was argued, moreover, that the SST had a great many more technological problems than were generally acknowledged. Other problems of deep concern included the difficulties of accommodating movements of SSTs in the same flight control system with numerous, slower aircraft. Furthermore, it was noted that insufficient attention had been given to the ground servicing of such aircraft, particularly handling departures and arrivals of large numbers of international passengers at terminals already highly congested.

Finally, the whole matter of the SST's marketability came into question. Just how successful such sales could be was made highly uncertain by the late production date of the United States SST, compared to its foreign competitors.

Other SST Policy Issues. In many respects, the SST Project provides a prime example of the growing costs of revolutionary advances in transportation technology. Federal commitments to underwrite the costs of such advances, as this program demonstrates, can quickly "snowball" and devour billions. Such commitments, particularly in the light of other needs in the transportation sector, and in the economy as a whole, might well be challenged when the outcome appeared relatively certain. But it is open to even more serious question when this amount of funds is committed to a project still considered as "a gamble."

The magnitude of this commitment to the SST also appeared to shift the public-private industry relationship to the point of almost complete dependence on the federal government — akin in many respects to the historical relationship of the maritime industry and the government. If the SST Project were considered as portending the character of future major technological advances in aviation, no large scale developmental projects would be undertaken by private industry on its own. Spiraling costs would obviate the possibility.

In some respects, the difficulties of the SST also demonstrate the enormous challenges of planning for major transportation advances that must depend so heavily on extending technological frontiers. The planning problem is not limited to meeting huge technological challenges, for the "product" of the research must still be fitted into a framework filled with complex, non-technical considerations of values and economic, political, and social factors. Indeed, its technological complexity, overwhelming as it is, is but one part of a much larger framework for which planning must provide.

The SST Project also raises the policy question of the appropriateness of the federal role in aviation compared with other modes of transportation. Why limit application of national policy in other modes to "seed money" when in aviation, if the SST project is any indication, the federal government would be willing to underwrite so much of the harvest? What scale of values could be employed to justify this allocation of funds to the SST as opposed, for example, to HSGT, the improvement of existing metropolitan rapid transit systems, or the development of national maritime capacity?

Finally, the attitude of the federal government concerning the SST Project may be interpreted as another indication of its growing dominance of the aviation industry. But, one may ask, when federal policy provides the funds to underwrite the great bulk of high risk research and development undertaken by an important segment of private industry, who is dominating whom? Indeed, the demonstrated ability of the aviation industry to secure such a full measure of federal financial support reveals one of the most important dimensions of its political and economic power.

Early in 1971, Congress voted to cease funding of the SST Project in spite of strong pressure from the Nixon Administration. It also appears that the "risk" money invested by the airlines will be reimbursed, since the risk assumed involved possible technological failure, not a political turnabout.

For the moment those opposing the venture had secured a victory. Yet it is likely that the matter will continue to arise in the years ahead as a matter intertwined with evolving national transportation policy. During this time, no doubt, the pros and cons of the case will proliferate and intensify significantly.

Technological Change in Other Modes

The character of technological change in the long-established modes of transportation differs from that of HSGT and aviation. Several factors accounting for this difference have already been touched upon, including the peculiar aspects of historical development which surround each mode, the perception of and response to transportation "crises," and the regulatory and promotional policies of the federal government.

Of course there have been some direct, government sponsored efforts to promote technological advance in these modes. In ocean shipping, for example, the Maritime Administration sponsored construction of the nuclear powered cargo vessel, the *Savannah*. It was not anticipated that this ship would be economically competitive with conventional vessels. Rather, it was intended to explore the problems and possibilities of nuclear cargo craft. But its threat to maritime labor curtailed even these efforts.

Some members of Congress continue to press for the eventual development of a merchant marine which would be nuclear-propelled.[7] Again, the research and development foundation would presumably be underwritten by the federal government. In addition to this project, MARAD also sponsored development of the ninety-ton hydrofoil ship, *H.S. Dennison*. And, as an outgrowth of the relationship between maritime and defense policy, which has been discussed previously, substantial federal research and development assistance may be devoted to the future development of "fast deployment logistic ships."

In the remaining traditional modes and sub-modes, the influence of federal policy on technological advance has been far less direct, or non-existent. The nation's railroads have carried the burden of their own research and development — a fact which largely accounts for the limited efforts which have been made. Similarly, the inland water carriers have sponsored their own research and development, particularly in developing high powered diesel towboats.[8] And since World War II, the pipeline mode has assumed the responsibility for developing improved distribution systems and automated controls.

With the exception of the pipelines, most of the above carriers spend modest sums on research. And what is spent is intended for immediate application, not to secure broadly based knowledge, or to build a fund of information for future advances. Moreover, the accepted practice is for equipment and facility suppliers to conduct most of the research.

This approach to research and development has some advantages, but the drawbacks appear greater. Perhaps the most weighty handicap is the myopia which may result. Then, too, suppliers are interested in selling specific products, which may or may not relate to all the problems faced by the operator.

Suppliers, after all, are primarily interested in selling hardware at a profit.[a]

In sum, the weight of federal assistance in prompting or supporting research and development among the modes of transportation falls very unevenly. It runs the gamut from virtually complete support to nothing at all. Experience demonstrates that where technological progress has been most advanced, it can be related in substantial part to federal impetus and financial support. Likewise, there appears to be a close correlation between low federal research and development support and slow advance in technology.

"Coordinated" Transportation and Technological Advance

"Coordinated" transportation and technological advance have become the subjects of increasing attention in the consideration of transportation policy. In the broadest sense, "coordinated" transportation refers to fitting each form of transport into its proper place in the transport system. In a much narrower sense, the term pertains to the offering of joint services by two or more agencies of transportation.[10] Transportation developments involving both of these concepts will be analyzed here, beginning with the limited definition and working into the broader. In both cases, the significance of technological change will be reviewed and related to its impact on future policy directions.

"Piggyback" and Its Variations

The possibilities of achieving physical coordination among segments of the national transportaion systems, using "piggyback" and its variations, were recognized in the Interstate Commerce Act and were further emphasized by the Hepburn Act of 1906.[11] But in application, the old fear of monopoly arose again and this possibility for *inter-modal* cooperation was discouraged. In 1931, for example, the concept of "piggyback" was rejected by the ICC on the grounds that it would have disrupted existing rate structures.[12]

Another attempt to win ICC approval for such shipments was made in 1936, soon after passage of the Motor Carrier Act. The result was approval of movements of trucks on flatcars between Chicago and the Twin Cities. Later, the New Haven Railroad instituted a service in which carriers secured transportation business under which they reserved the right to substitute TOFC for the highway portion of the trip. From this small beginning, a complex group of specially designed services has developed. These received hesitating approval from the ICC

---

[a]It has been noted that General Motors undertook all of the background research, built, and demonstrated prototypes, and then conducted an aggressive sales campaign of the diesel locomotive for the railroads. This situation finds a parallel in the research and development conducted on rapid transit cars. Again, suppliers such as Budd and Pullman-Standard have been carrying the basic research load.

and have now resulted in the following major plans:

Table 7.1
Piggyback Plans

Plan	Originator	Supplies eqpt. and transfers	Delivers and picks up	Rate basis
I	Motor carrier	Motor carrier; rail carrier furnishes flatcars	Motor carrier	Motor carrier rates; blanket basis for all frieght.
II	Rail carrier	Rail carrier	Rail carrier	RR commodity rates
III	Shipper or forwarder	Shipper or forwarder furnishes trailers and RR transfers; RR supplies flatcar	Shipper or forwarder	Flat rate
IV	Shipper or forwarder	Shipper or forwarder furnishes flatcar and trailer	Shipper or forwarder	Flat rate
V	Motor carrier	Motor carrier	Motor carrier	Rail carrier tariff for joint motor-rail rates.

The growth of piggyback traffic has been little short of phenomenal, again indicating the extent to which technological change can influence traffic. In the period from 1955 to 1966 alone, rail piggyback loadings increased from 169,150 to 1,162,731, and accounted for over four percent of the total revenue of Class I railroads.[13] In considerable part, this traffic represented new tonnage for the railroads, since most of the shipments handled would have moved over-the-road otherwise. This fact has become of increasing concern to the trucking industry. In fact, both court and ICC proceedings reflect its view that the railroads are utilizing the new service, particularly Plan II, to carry freight that truckers have considered their prerogative.[14]

The use of coordinated transportation outside of railroad-truck coordination has proved of much less significance thus far. In large part, this lack of growth and enthusiasm reveals how deeply nontechnical considerations can affect the potential application of advanced technology. The possibilities of rail-water coordination, for example, appear in part to have fallen victim to outmoded tradition, unfriendliness, and the lack of an appreciation of the potential mutual benefits that might accrue.[15] But even more basic is the central issue of the competition of the railroads, which are completely regulated as common carriers, with the water carriers, much of whose tonnage is unregulated. In the view of some railroad representatives, this factor severely dampens the incentive for rail-water coordination.

National regulatory policies have also affected air-surface transportation coordination, i.e., "birdyback." This situation is complicated by the interplay of two major regulatory agencies – the ICC and CAB. For its part, the CAB has traditionally assumed that the basic intent of the Federal Aviation Act of 1958 was to keep the modes separate and distinct, and to foster modally-based competition. A second major hurdle to achieving a significant measure of coordination is that it would require the publication of more than 600 million joint rates under the cumbersome regulatory process![16]

Containerization

Containerization is a freight shipping practice which has undergone tremendous growth in the past few years. And, as in the case of piggyback growth, it was done initially without the benefit of large-scale *federal* initiative or sponsorship.

But this is not to say that this technological advance is devoid of implications for federal transportation policy. Indeed, its influence may require basic changes in traditional, modally-based policies, if the advantages of this facet of transportation technology are to be realized.

In its ideal form, containerization involves the shipment of freight in vans or boxes from origin to destination, as a unit. Since such shipments are not handled in the manner of less-than-carload freight, or general cargo, the greatest benefits of containerization are derived when the containers can be handled at both ends of the trip by specialized facilities, and can be transported on equipment designed for exactly that purpose. This technique holds the potential for drastically revamping freight transportation technology within virtually every transportation mode. Its primary impact involves interfaces among modes.

Thus far, the major effect of containerization has been felt in ocean shipping. Individual ports, largely through their own resources, now have hundreds of acres of upland area under development to accommodate container movements. At the same time, shipping lines and newly-formed consortiums, specifically organized for container operations, have made major commitments for the building of either partial or full containerships. Orders for ships in these categories now total more than fifty. And, this is in addition to shipping, which is already handling container cargo.

How broad will be the impact of the "containerization revolution?" Some analysts estimate that as much as fifty percent of future volumes of general cargo will move either aboard full containerships or in vans carried by combination break-bulk container vessels.[17]

The policy implications of these projections, without doubt, are far-reaching for all modes of freight transportaion. As far as the various shipping lines and port interests are concerned, they must contend with a number of "second level" development problems of containerization, including designing staging areas for container consolidation, improving containers, handling equipment, and developing the "major load center" concept. The latter involves the selection of key ports through which the bulk of traffic would move on regular schedules so as to assure frequent sailings and balanced movement of full containers from both ends of trade routes.

Impact on the Federal Role. As in the more limited case of piggyback traffic, these new adaptations of distribution hardware and organization will have an important impact on the federal role in freight transportation. If containerization is to reach its full potential, however, a flexible federal planning approach will be required.

One of the primary problem areas calling for federal leadership and coordination is the standardization of equipment. Such has not been achieved in handling piggyback freight, but, through the leadership of MARAD, may eventually be attained in much of containerization.

For example, agreement has been reached on international standards for the dimensions and corner fittings of containers.[18] Nevertheless, it will take sustained pressure to reduce the number of "non-standard" containers still being manufactured.

A second major problem is the question of inter-modal transfer. What is the ideal number of inland freight consolidation stations required for container handling ports? How should the need for these facilities, as well as their development, be measured? In some respects, this is a modern version of the "terminal problem," defined so well by the National Resources Planning Board in the 1940s. Nor is it easy to solve because national policy, dominated as it is by modally-based considerations, has not contended successfully with the interface problem.

A third problem area is similar to that already encountered in piggyback — the past inflexibility of federal regulatory and documentation policies and procedures, which undermines some of the enormous advantages of containerization. Here, some significant progress has been achieved in the development of a new inter-modal, international through-bill of lading. Federal research and development projects involving further improvements of documentation and procedures, commodity descriptions and coding, and high speed transmission of shipping and passenger data, among others, are now under way. They have been directed by DOT's Office of Facilitation.[19]

And, perhaps as important to the long-term future of containerization as it is for the United States maritime industry, is a fourth policy problem — the need to expand the ship construction subsidy program to include container purchases. This need is considered acute in view of the current state of finance in the national maritime industry. It has been estimated, for example, that a steamship operator might need 4,000 containers in one system. The cost of one small standard container is approximately $2,000. Total cost for one system would thus be $8 million.

Finally, there is the problem of information on containerization. Specifically, needs exist for data on origin and destination of freight, total distribution costs, modal splits of commodity movements, impact of labor policies on the future of containerization, and forecasts of future investments required for development of inter-modal systems.

Coordinated Movements of People

Although this analysis has focused thus far on the difficulties of achieving modal coordination in the transport of freight, perhaps more important is the matter of coordinated movement of people. If anything, the impact of technological change on federal policy in this field is even more extensive and unclear than it is in freight transportation.

"Balanced" transportation of people — the fitting together of the various uses of the transportation modes into their optimum roles — is an elusive concept. There is no agreement on which modes should be utilized as the "best" means for transporting people with increasingly diverse trip purposes, origins and destinations. Although substantial federal financial investments have already been made within the various modes, little has been done to consider the needs for modal interfaces and, more particularly, the federal role in planning for them.

Past policy failed to cope with the effects of modal barriers to coordination. Instead, it was characterized by a "segmental" approach, rather than one which took into account transportation needs from departure point to destination point. In the light of past performance, it is understandable why so many believe the fanfare surrounding "coordinated" or "balanced" transportation to be more mythical than real. Indeed, the "planning gaps" in transportation have been so numerous that they need scarcely be reviewed here.

Nevertheless, the need for conceptual change, particularly on the part of governmental policy, is at least being recognized.[20] This new perception accepts the premise that coordination includes more than just technological compatibility of equipment and facilities. Indeed, it recognizes that institutional and managerial considerations are a vital part of system planning, and that without them there can be no true system.

It is in this aspect of transportation that advancing technology is "forcing the hand" of the traditional national policy of preserving the "inherent" advantages of each mode. As carriers within the modes reach out for a larger volume of business and a greater share of the business of supplying transportation, they intensify their emphasis on technology.

This has produced what Hammond has called the "domino impact."[21] An example of this phenomenon is the reaction of Easter Airlines to the initial success of the Metroliner in the Northeast Corridor Transportation Project in drawing passenger traffic away from its air service. Eastern reacted by exploring the possibility of countering with STOL operations to recapture lost traffic and revenue.[22]

In retrospect, it is apparent that the physical distribution concepts of business have exerted some influence on approaches to maximize the gains of technological advance in transportation. This is opposed to approaches which would allow them to be vitiated by a "tunnel view" of transportation modes, which has been encouraged by traditional federal policies. These newer concepts are equally applicable to passenger movements. Essentially, they seek to view transportation in terms of portal-to-portal requirements. This might also be described as "thinking total transportation" – a systems approach.

The Transportation Company. One outgrowth of the approach to "total transportation" is the concept of the transportation company. This kind of organization would be an integrated company, combining the services of whatever modes were best suited to the geographic situation. Specific transport decisions would center about the combination of modal services most appropriate to the user in terms of service and cost. The forces of the marketplace would be relied upon to force transportation companies to use the modes as an integrated whole and to develop each in terms of its contribution to the whole. Likewise, the idea of the transportation company envisages the control of monopoly through competition with other companies, and anticipates that this would be more intense than present inter-modal competition.

When the concept of the transportation company was reviewed in the Doyle Report, it was looked upon as an interesting, theoretical possibility; however, it appeared to have little chance for practical application.[23] And even now the prospects for the idea appear dim. But several developments may, in time, culminate in more serious consideration. These include:

1. The rapid growth of technological change in transportation, which requires relatively free inter-modal movements in accommodating *total* needs of a trip;
2. Some indications that federal policy may shift from outright opposition to common ownership to a more favorably disposed point of view;[24]
3. The outcome of the railroad merger movement, leading as it is to competitive systems of "strong" railroads in most areas of the country, may provide the basis for transportation companies. Such could serve either regional or national territories on a competitive basis. Integrated companies would have some advantages over huge railroad systems *per se* in capitalizing on economies of scale and in eliminating waste and duplication;
4. The blurring of the "inherent" advantages of each of the modes – again primarily the result of technological advances – to the point where very little freight or passenger traffic can be considered "captive" to a single mode. This leads to the notion that various modes are different processes or methods of producing the same service – transportation;
5. The steady and growing inroads being made into common carriage traffic by private transportation. The transportation company would provide the flexibility and adaptability to meet increasing demands for specialized transportation services.[25]

The practical problems of implementing the transportation company concept are, of course, staggering. Motor carrier opposition is, and probably would remain, adamant. They criticize such companies on grounds that they would be dominated by rail facilities and that, to protect these investments, less reliance would be placed on other components than is supposed.

Protective labor practices and procedures also stand in the way. Encrusted statements of "national transportation policy" in the form of laws, regulations, and court opinions block consideration of specific proposals to form such companies.[26]

Yet the enormous pressures generated by technological advances cannot be dismissed lightly. For there is not only a growing quantity of change taking place, but also an increase in its revolutionary implications. In this sense, time will probably work in favor of new institutional approaches to transport such as the transportation company.

Other Barriers to Innovation

Other barriers to innovation exist. These extend beyond the constraints imposed by regulatory policy; the difficulties involved in introducing revolutionary changes in the midst of transportation systems dominated by more traditional hardware and managerial approaches; the complex process of integrating innovative developments with the *total* needs and plans of the areas to be served, particularly metropolitan areas; and the lack of reliable, reasonably complete information upon which to base transportation decision-making.

In this section, several of these constraints will be elaborated upon. In addition, the obstacles created by other politically- and economically-based conditions, particularly the problems of financing improvements in the transportation systems of urban areas, will be examined.

In new and undeveloped areas such as space exploration, only cost, ingenuity, and technological feasibility place limits on innovation. But innovation in civilian industry encounters a number of other barriers.[27]

This statement by Dael Wolfle has particular applicability to transportation, which extends its influence into so many other aspects of national life. While changes in transportation technology hold the promise of increasing the effectiveness of the system's operation, they also pose a number of threats. Foremost is their challenge to the existing systems, primarily in terms of the "sunk costs" that are involved and the amortization rates that may require usage of existing equipment over a considerable period of time if costs are to be recovered.

Another aspect of this problem of adjustment to technical advances reflects the organization of the respective roles of the regulatory agencies around the established methods of transportation. Here, precedent works to constrain quick response to a reshuffling of relationships.

But innovation in private industry transportation is frequently a product of the desire to participate in lucrative traffic. Such innovation may not depend on "pure" research, but rather on the result of shipper demand and carrier experimentation on an informal basis.

As Norton indicates, however, the record of the regulatory agencies is rather checkered in dealing with questions involving the impact of these technological changes. He cites the examples of the motor carriers' successful efforts to participate in the transportation of frozen orange juice concentrate, in spite of ICC reluctance, and the recapture of much of the market for transporting new autos that the railroads brought about through technological innovation. In the first case, the ICC discouraged innovation by its slow action. In the second, innovation was forced by the ICC because it denied rate cuts until the railroads had clearly demonstrated that new concepts in equipment (dual-level and tri-level cars) were to be employed.[28]

When it comes to applying innovative approaches and concepts to transportation problems of metropolitan areas, the barriers take a different, though no less self-interested, form. In this case, the fragmentation so evident in transportation is more than matched by the abundant political fragmentation of the metropolis and its surrounding communities. The myopia of individual modes finds its complement in the myopia of the component governments of metropolitan areas.

As Danielson points out, suburban areas practice their own brand of provincialism.[29] And because new federal transportation programs have just begun to affect selected suburban areas, this lack of desire to share costs or provide facilities jointly with central cities is likely to continue. Yet, if innovations in developing new modes of transportation or improving existing facilities are to be fostered, these institutional barriers must first be removed. Otherwise, prospective progress will be limited to services within the inner city and between cities. But the effects on regional transportation will be severely limited.

There have been a few signs that the barriers to cooperation, including financial participation, may be cracking in some parts of the country. Examples include the development of a rapid transit system to serve San Francisco and its environs (BART), and the multi-million dollar transportation bond issues passed in the States of New York and New Jersey. However, by and large, the picture is one of limited cooperation among units below the federal level.

Nor is this the total extent of the constraints on development and application of technological advances in transportation. Increasingly evident are the problems of analysis associated with the lack of information and statistics that pertain to the following relationships:

— the various transportation modes to each other;
— the modes to the economy as a whole, including its international component;
— the modes to various regional and industrial sections of the economy;
— transportation to the individual welfare and character of rural, suburban, and metropolitan life.[30]

Virtually every transportation study conducted in major metropolitan areas of the United States has found it necessary to develop its own data base. In freight transportation, data on vehicles not regulated by the ICC are sparse; little detailed information exists on the type of carriers used by shippers, the origins and destinations involved, and the commodities transported. Passenger information is even more limited. Particularly lacking are data on modes used, trip purposes, origins and destinations, routes used, and the like.

Financing – The Most Crucial Barrier

If any single barrier to innovation can be described as most crucial, it is the matter of financing.

One major aspect of this problem involves the financial status of existing transit operations in the United States. Obviously, shaky support and deficit conditions preclude the investment of funds in innovative approaches. In such circumstances, the fight for sheer survival leaves little or no money for research and development. Some indication of the magnitude of the problem is given by Tables 7.2 and 7.3.

What are the implications of these data? Clearly, the trend of operating income has been continuing sharply downward at a rapid rate. In fact, it is estimated that the 1971 deficit exceeded $332 million. Thus, transit operations

Table 7.2
Results of Transit Operations in the United States, 1964-1970
(in millions)

Year	Operating Revenue	Operating expenses (including depreciation)	Net Revenue	All Taxes	Operating Income
1964	$1,408.1	$1,342.6	$ 65.5	$ 77.9	$ −12.4
1965	1,443.8	1,373.8	70.0	80.6	−10.6
1966	1,478.5	1,423.8	54.7	91.8	−37.1
1967	1,556.0	1,530.9	25.1	91.7	−66.6
1968	1,578.3	1,609.8	−31.5	98.5	−130.0
1969	1,625.6	1,745.0	−119.4	101.2	−220.5
1970 (Prelim.)	1,707.4	1,891.7	−184.3	103.9	−288.5

Source: data extracted from *1970-1971 Transit Fact Book*, American Transit Association (Washington, D.C.: 1970), p. 4.

Table 7.3
Bonded Debt of 23 U.S. Cities

Transit System	Total Bonded Debt
Chicago Transit Authority (Illinois)	$ 73,278,000
A.C. Transit (Oakland, Calif.)	11,000,000
Columbus Transit Co. (Columbus, Ohio)	2,000,000
Indianapolis Transit (Indiana)	1,756,267
Massachusetts Bay Transportation Authority (Boston, Mass.)	230,764,632
Southern California Rapid Transit District (Los Angeles, Calif.)	31,385,000
Southeastern Pennsylvania Transportation Authority (Phila., Pa.)	79,500,000
Department of Street Railways (city of Detroit)	7,480,000
San Antonio Transit System (Texas)	1,660,000
Atlanta Transit (Georgia)	5,000,000
New York City Transit Authority (Brooklyn, N.Y.)	75,000,000
Milwaukee & Suburban Transport Corp. (Wisconsin)	3,649,658
New Orleans Public Service (Louisiana)	5,912,000
Memphis Transit Authority (Tennessee)	2,100,000
Cleveland Transit System (Ohio)	13,877,000
Bi-State Transit System (St. Louis, Mo.)	25,294,328
Port Authority of Allegheny County (Pittsburgh, Pa.)	50,000,000
Metro Dade County Transit Authority (Miami, Fla.)	6,252,653
Regional Transit Service (Rochester, N.Y.)	750,000
Akron Metro Transit (Ohio)	63,700
Dallas Transit System (Texas)	7,300,000
Fort Worth Transit (Texas)	208,700
Washington Metropolitan Area Transit Authority (Wash., D.C.)	880,000,000
Total	$1,514,231,938

Source: data developed by the American Transit Association and incorporated in the *Congressional Record*, 92d Cong., 2d Sess., (Senate) Vol. 118, No. 31 (Washington, D.C.: U.S. Government Printing Office, March 2, 1972), p. S 3109.

can be counted on to continue producing losses of increasing proportions, given the "ground rules" and economic conditions under which they function.

The Issue of Operating Subsidies. As has been discussed previously, existent mass transportation legislation is not only limited in its amount, but also in its coverage. At this point in time, the federal government provides no direct subsidies for operations of transit systems.

The year 1972 witnessed a growing tide of pressure for the federal government to begin making such assistance available. The vehicle for this consideration was the proposed Housing and Urban Development Act of 1972

(S. 3248). Most significant to federal transportation policy was Chapter 6, which would authorize the Department of Transportation to subsidize operating losses for urban mass transportation systems. In addition, the bill would increase the federal share of capital grants for mass transportation to ninety percent — equivalent to the federal share that prevails in the Interstate Highway Program.

An amendment introduced by Senator Jacob Javits of New York would provide $400 million annually for such purposes. Speaking on behalf of the amendment, Senator Javits noted that there were now 108 systems which are currently subsidized locally, and that the need for increased aid would most certainly continue. In addition, he cited data indicating that thirty-five additional cities were faced with the issue of initiating subsidies.[31]

Just how the Nixon Administration would react to these proposals was not clear. In the past, Secretary of Transportation Volpe had opposed federal financing for operating subsidies, possibly reflecting his past experiences as Governor of the State of Massachusetts, where state operating subsidies for Boston rapid transit have skyrocketed steadily over the past twenty years. But it should be expected that if operating subsidies become part of future federal transportation policy, they will most likely be tied to an incentive system that would emphasize improved service and more efficient operations — however those might be defined. Otherwise, the federal government might be put into a position of offering a "blank check" to cover uncontrolled mass transit deficits.

There is little question that the potential magnitude of federal funds that could be consumed by underwriting operating subsidies on a national scale would dwarf all previous assistance to mass transit. Undoubtedly, it is this long-term, almost permanent, "price tag" that has made successive administrations, Republican and Democrat, chary of any commitment to it.[32]

Another indication of the financing problem of mass transit is the number and magnitude of applications made for capital grant assistance to keep existing systems going or, in exceptional cases, to construct new facilities. As noted earlier, by April 15, 1971, the Urban Mass Transportation Administration had a backlog of eighty-nine applications requesting federal aid in excess of $2.6 billion.[33] And unofficial information available in mid-1972 indicated that the aid requested by the backlog of applications had swelled to over $4 billion. Thus, the number of pending requests exceeds by over six times the total of capital grants made since passage of the Urban Mass Transportation Act of 1964 — some $600 million for 149 projects.

Research and Development Expenditures. Federal policy reflected in *direct* expenditures on research and development in transportation represents another significant indicator of the magnitude of the financing barrier. Indeed, experience demonstrates that the amount and celerity of technological advance made within each of the modes is becoming increasingly dependent on federal support. For urban transportation in particular, the amount of federal money devoted to sponsoring research and development activities, and to underwriting most of the costs of selected demonstration projects and capital improvement programs, is becoming increasingly crucial.

This section evaluates selected aspects of federal financial support of research and development. It also examines proposed programs for financing future development of aviation and mass transportation systems. In both cases, the time period covered is limited to the life of the Department of Transportation.

Table 7.4

DOT's transportation research and development expenditures, 1967 – 1969, by Battelle Memorial Institute

Research and Development Expenditures

| | | Year-to-Year Changes | |
Organ. Unit	$ Millions	$ Millions	Percent
Federal Highway Administration			
1967	23.0		
1968	40.4	+17.4	+75.7
1969	45.5	+ 5.1	+12.6
Federal Aviation Administration			
1967	45.6		
1968	43.7	– 1.9	– 4.2
1969	39.8	– 3.9	– 8.9
Federal Railroad Administration			
1967	4.5		
1968	8.7	+ 4.2	+93.3
1969	12.4	+ 3.7	+42.5
Other R & D (DOT)			
1967	2.4		
1968	4.1	+ 1.7	+70.8
1969	6.5	+ 2.4	+58.5

Source: Based on Table VI-A-1, Leonard L. Lederman and Margaret L. Windus, *Report Number BMI NLVP-TR-69-1 (Part II) On An Analysis of the Allocation of Federal Budget Resources As An Indication of National Goals and Priorities to National Aeronautics and Space Administration Under Contract Number NASw-1146,* Battelle Memorial Institute, Columbus Laboratories, Columbus, Ohio, February 10, 1969.

Table 7.4 does not include research and development funds which have been devoted to mass transportation under the Urban Mass Transportation Act of 1964, as amended. It is estimated that the total amount of research and development funds expended under this program through the end of 1968 was about $4 million.

On the basis of the Battelle data, about forty-seven cents of every DOT research and development dollar in the three-year period were devoted to aviation, thirty-nine cents to highways, nine cents to the activities of the Railroad Administration, and five cents to other research and development purposes. While the rate of growth in aviation research and development has slackened, this could again be skewed by future reconsideration of the SST Project. And although total year-to-year changes in research and development expenditures has turned upward, it should be borne in mind that the starting base was negligible.

The Battelle data cover a very short time span and conclusions on major trends cannot be drawn from them alone. On the other hand, the general tendency is there to be seen. Research and development expenditures in aviation and highway development are clearly dominant.

As data in Table 7.5 indicate, *total* federal outlays for transportation in fiscal year 1971 further underscore both the immediate and long-range attention being given to the highway and aviation modes.

Table 7.5
Federal Outlays for Transportation
(in millions)

	Fiscal Year 1971				Fiscal Year 1972	
	Direct Appropriation	Trust Funds	Total	Percentage of Total Transport Dollars	Total	Percentage of Total Transport Dollars
Mass transit	$ 215	————————	$ 215	2.8	$ 327	3.9
Highways	166	$4,714	4,880	62.9	4,923	59.6
Aviation	1,250	370	1,620	20.9	1,834	22.2
Railroads	48	————————	48	.6	57	.7
Water	1,000	————————	1,000	12.8	1,123	13.6

Source: Based on data developed by the Urban Mass Transportation Administration, *Department of Transportation and Related Agencies Appropriations,* Senate Hearings Before the Committee on Appropriations, H.R. 9667, 92d Cong., 1st Sess., Fiscal Year 1972, p. 696.

New Financing Plans. As discussed in Chapter 4, the concept of imposing user taxes to enable movement toward the goal of great self-support in aviation was proposed by the Johnson Administration in 1968. It implied, but fell short of proposing an "Aviation Trust Fund," which would have been similar to the operation of the Highway Trust Fund. The proposal was not adopted.

In June of 1969, the Nixon Administration proposed, and saw adopted in 1970, its approach to the long-term improvement of airways and airport facilities. It bore striking similarities to the method of financing aviation advances proposed in 1968. Again, the stress was placed on providing *larger* amounts of money over the long-term for the technological and quantitative growth of aviation – but at a price. Thus, while significant funding is to be provided for airways, navigational improvements, and airport construction, the price has been the imposition of a much heavier scale of user taxes. The legislation passed also provided funds for research and development, including planning for the aviation needs of 1980 and the establishment of an "Aviation Trust Fund" to keep track of aviation income and expenditures.

Nevertheless, it appears that the advantages of this federal funding are not to be extended to assisting in the provision of airport facilities for inter-modal transfers and services. This reflects once again the "compartmentalization" of transportation policy considerations. As far as advances in inter-modal transportation are concerned, such decisions strengthen existing barriers to innovation and the integration of technological advance.

The limitations of this approach also mirror the quandary of national political leadership. For as was discussed in the analysis of the early evolution of transportation policy, decisions and proposals become enmeshed in the efforts to achieve other important goals. In this latest case, it would appear that the pressure to reduce federal expenditures and lessen inflation has limited several innovative paths that might have been followed to transcend modal barriers.

Without question, the problem of finance constitutes the most formidable barrier to innovation in urban mass transportation. As noted earlier, the Urban Mass Transportation Act of 1964, as amended, the High Speed Ground Transportation Act of 1965, as amended, and the Urban Mass Transportation Assistance Act of 1970 have been the primary vehicles for injecting federal funds into efforts to solve urban transportation problems.

The level of assistance rendered has been small indeed, in comparison to the magnitude of the problems. Moreover, the monies which have been parceled out largely represent efforts to "bail out" existing systems. In fact over eighty percent of *all* funds made available have gone into capital grants for operating systems. For the most part, these have played little part in encouraging technological advances of either the gradual or revolutionary type. Instead, the primary thrust has been to maintain existing services and equipment, or to augment the local financing of expanded systems.

Most grants have been made for the purchase of hundreds of railroad cars, rapid transit cars and buses; station modernizations; construction of ferry boats; tunnels and shop facilities; purchase of private bus systems; and the like. This is not to contend that such assistance is misguided. Rather, it is intended to demonstrate that current levels of support for innovation and intermodal research and development (as represented by the expenditures for demonstration projects and research and development) fall far short of a serious effort to explore alternative solutions to the many problems of urban mass transportation.

New proposals for federal participation in financing improvements in urban mass transportation may alleviate some of these problems. Early in 1969, for example, Senator Harrison A. Williams introduced a bill which would establish a "mass transportation trust fund" based on use of the auto excise tax for the period 1971-1974. Senator Williams estimated that the fund would provide a $1.8 billion for mass transportation over the four-year period.

During the same period, the idea of a "transportation trust fund" was reviewed by Secretary of Transportation John A. Volpe. The approach which was evaluated differed from the Williams proposal primarily in the financing term that was considered. But Secretary Volpe encountered strong opposition to the trust fund concept from both White House Staff and the Office of Management and Budget. Nevertheless, early in 1972, Secretary Volpe again expressed renewed support for the idea, and Congress took the matter under serious consideration. Opponents, of course, cite the disadvantages of "sheltered funds," principally their inflexibility.

Nor can the possibilities of federal revenue sharing be overlooked. If Nixon Administration proposals come to fruition, it is estimated that $2.8 billion yearly would become available to develop "balanced" transportation systems throughout the country. Under this program, states and local units of government would assume primary responsibility for allocation of almost all of these funds. Interestingly, though, it has been proposed that monies from the Highway Trust Fund and those to be made available under the Urban Mass Transportation Assistance Act of 1970 *not* be made available under revenue sharing. It may well develop that funds of the Aviation Trust Fund would also be withheld. That leaves the question of which funds of any real consequence will remain to be shared.

Also worthy of some attention are the common elements incorporated in the concepts of a "national transportation trust fund" and revenue sharing. Both would result in a pooling of essentially the same resources. Both would encourage the planning and development of transportation on a more integrated basis. However, the important differences relate to the relative strengths of federal versus state and local decision-making. Under the trust fund approach, primary control and initiatives would rest with the federal government, while under revenue sharing more prerogatives would be given to those areas in which transportation facilities are either planned or exist.

The brief history of mass transportation legislation and high speed ground transportation legislation have made plain the needs for large amounts of "new" money. But in spite of stirring rhetoric to the contrary, *actual* expenditures have been miniscule, particularly in comparison to those traditionally spent for highways and aviation. And the future requirements of mass transportation represent a long accummulation of un-met, pressing needs that have not disappeared because they were ignored.

In this regard, it has been estimated that at least $20 billion could be utilized in the next ten years, merely to implement *existing* plans for mass transportations. New, innovative, unconventional systems for the future would require expenditures of even greater magnitude. The question remains: Will federal policy depart from past trends sufficiently to recognize and deal with these matters of cost? Without the infusion of large scale federal expenditures, national transportation options for the future cannot help but decrease — and rapidly.

The Matter of Implementation. The final barrier to technological advance to be covered is the matter of implementation. It is a simple matter for business and government alike to so emphasize the hardware output of research and technology that the means for introducing them are ignored or underplayed.

The problem is more than organizational. It concerns the fact that for transportation innovation to be applied on a large scale, *total* system requirements must be taken into account. These include not only technical characteristics of proposals, but also the manner in which they would fit into existing political, economic, and social frameworks.

Where particular aspects of the existing structure do not appear totally appropriate, consideration of new arrangements and organizational structures may be called for. Indeed, it is apparent that if *institutional* barriers are not always interpreted as "givens," the possible applications and benefits of technological advances in transportation may be expanded well beyond present limitations.

Perspective on National
Transportation Policy

8

Perspective on National Transportation Policy

Up to this point, the formation of national transportation policy has been analyzed in terms of factors that have influenced its content and determined its directions and emphases. In this final chapter, highlights of this analysis will be reviewed and interpreted, particularly as they may affect future courses of policy formation. Where possible, these possibilities will be outlined not as a single future, but rather in terms of "alternative futures" that may result, depending on the mix of programs that are selected.

The Character of Transportation Policy

In spite of the analysis and study devoted to questions of national transportation policy formation, the concept remains an elusive one to characterize precisely. This difficulty is in large part explained by the fact that no single national policy has governed the evolution of national transportation development. In reality, the governing "policy" is a multitude of policies grounded in highly particular historical events; legislative, executive, administrative and court decisions; and a myriad of private-enterprise actions. At no point in national history has the development of transportation facilities and resources been directed from one source. And it is difficult to foresee a time when they will.

The absence of an *a priori* "grand design" for transportation policy formation, however, should not be interpreted as indicating that development of transportation facilities has therefore been completely chaotic or that no national transportation systems exist. For *systems* of transportation have been designed, albeit in a piecemeal, incremental manner. The character of this process may be described as a "growing together" which, in many respects, qualifies as a type of planning. Its principal weakness, of course, is that it suffers the drawbacks of limited coordination and the inefficiency, waste, and inconsistencies that frequently result from that condition. As has been discussed, this *ad hoc* pattern of national transportation policy formation may be attributed to several basic factors.

The Mixed Enterprise Characteristics of Transportation

Transportation policy formation in the United States has both benefited and

179

suffered from the fact that it is a product of mixed enterprise, i.e., designed to serve *both* public and private ends. In the early stages of its growth, the preponderance of initiative was exercised by private enterprise attempting to "go it alone," in linking isolated settlements and areas. The first goal was to survive and then, beyond that, to make business and trade profitable. This was followed by an important but somewhat confused period in which individual state governments participated directly on a highly competitive basis in these efforts. The failure of many of these activities necessitated the entry into transportation regulation and development by the federal government. At first, this entry was a reluctant one.

As the needs for greater federal participation in promoting the growth of transportation capacity became more apparent, the mutual dependence of public-private policies increased. This mutual dependence took different forms in each of the modes of transportation; in fact, it laid much of the basis for the array of modally-oriented policies and practices which gradually evolved.

The differentiation of federal policy applicable to the railroads from policies affecting other modes is accounted for in part by the character of its privately owned rights-of-way. Unlike other means of transportation, the railroads assumed the characteristic of a "natural monopoly." Thus, there appears to be no way in which railroad policy could be made completely commensurate with policy applicable to other modes of transportation, short of purchase of all rights-of-way by the federal government, or federalization of the nation's entire railroad system.

In retrospect, it has become apparent that federal policy has distinctly different roles to play in the development and regulation of each of the various modes. Those who would seek a "uniformity" of policy, and similar treatment "across the board," must contend with problems stemming from the individual character of each of the modes. Also to be dealt with are the continuous shifts of their individual capacities for growth and the complex interplay of political, economic, and social forces which have affected the rationale for federal support during particular periods, or in the face of unique circumstances.

The mixed-enterprise characteristic also obscures any clear definition of responsibility for the quality of national transportation. Who is responsible? In no case can private enterprise or government at any level be held completely accountable for the performance of either the entire national transportation network or its individual components. This situation is further complicated by the fact that transportation developments which call for explication of policy constantly require a redefinition of what is "public" and what is "private."

These factors have made it enormously difficult to evolve national transportation policies which would be most efficacious for the system considered as a whole. Thus, the fractionalized base of transportation policy-making must be accepted as a "given."

Another critical factor is that future national transportation policy will rarely be accorded the luxury of *de novo* planning. Only in the case of the development of new modes of transportation, such as HSGT, would this be possible. And even here the need for integrating new systems with the existing structure would still remain. There will be no "starting all over again."

The Role of Precedent and Tradition

Another aspect of national transportation development that has left deep, indelible marks on the character of policy affecting all modes of transportation is the role of precedent and tradition. Some analysts have discussed this influence exclusively in terms of the various regulatory policies which have evolved throughout history; most assuredly this is an important part of the transportation policy structure. But the influence of traditional action runs far deeper.

Precedent has not only provided the basis for attempts at the national level to apply patterns of policy cross-modally; more basically it has routinized the practice of developing policy on an *ad hoc* basis.

In a sense, the Executive Branch, Congress, the courts, and the regulatory agencies have confined themselves largely to an *operational* type of influence, rather than undertaking a strategic planning role which would seek to interpret and fulfill long-term needs. The result has been evolution of transportation policies which reveal the consequences of "hand-to-mouth" actions and reactions. Even though it may be granted that the nature of the possible federal role has been one of only partial responsibility, the circumstances have been few in which potentialities for comprehensive planning have been realized.

This pattern of formulating policy on an operational basis has also reinforced "compartmentalized" treatment of the individual modes and the consequent lack of emphasis which has been accorded coordinated planning. Again, the pattern is not confined to regulation; it permeates the promotional programs that have evolved as well.

The historical view of transportation policy development thus extends beyond providing a background against which present problems and needs can be better understood. In reality, it is part of the present and frequently serves as the justification for continuing or elaborating upon past policies.

Past actions also provide the legal foundation upon which future actions are based. Additions to this foundation have usually been changes at the margin or incremental adjustments. In this connection, it appears likely that periodic calls for "sweeping changes" in the structure of transportation policy are doomed to go unanswered because they ignore the cold realities of how the system evolved and the process through which it changes.

The promise of short-term gains also helps to explain the relatively strong emphasis that has been placed on achieving "cheap" transportation. As an explicit goal of early policy, the concept had considerable validity. Indeed, development and improvement of the modes of transportation resulted in enormous savings to producers, shippers, and, ultimately, consumers at a number of points in time. But in virtually all cases, the relative marginal efficiency of capital devoted to the *same kinds* of public investment has diminished. Yet the force of tradition has frequently served to justify continuance of many such investments.

As yet, little has been done in the transportation sphere to analyze comparative advantages of alternative investments. And as demonstrated in Chapter 4, moves to change the "rules of the game" regarding this kind of decision-making are bound to encounter stiff resistance from those who hold positions of power in the existing policy-making apparatus.

The Influence of "Crisis" on Policy

Significant changes in the directions or emphases of national transportation policy appear to be highly correlated with the perception of national "crisis." The entry of the federal government into the field of transportation regulation took place in a crisis atmosphere. Supplemental regulatory legislation was passed only after the mechanisms which had been created threatened to collapse.

World War I and World War II each provided crisis situations for imposing sweeping governmental influence on national transportation; the Transportation Acts of 1920, 1940, and 1958 were reactions to severe problems, particularly as they concerned the railroads. Likewise, the legislation that committed federal policy to expanded control over the merchant marine and aviation modes was stimulated by crises. Even the provision of federal funds for urban mass transportation may be interpreted as a reaction to a growing, if dimly perceived, transportation crisis.

Yet even the role of crisis in prompting changes in policy directions is influenced by precedent. In general terms, it appears that potential catastrophies, spectacular disasters, wartime emergencies and other extraordinary needs have provided many of the premises for differentiating the roles which the federal government has assumed regarding the various modes. By and large, these policies usually have exhibited a *modal* orientation. They have not been designed to redistribute federal financial support accorded to all of the modes of transportation.

This pattern of policy-making behavior provides an important lesson for practical application in the future. Put simply, it is this: long-range changes in the emphasis of federal policy, particularly promotion, are more likely to be achieved through programs which are *additive* rather than those which would seek to divert the resources devoted to existing programs to other programs. In retrospect, this thesis is borne out by the record of development of the highway and inland waterways programs and their success in resisting incursions that would lessen their importance in the interests of increasing alternative investments. Even the relatively small expenditures made thus far on urban mass transportation programs might not have been made at all if they represented diversions from highway spending.

Nor was this factor lacking in importance during the period which led to formation of the Department of Transportation. Indeed, part of the substantial resistance which developed to legislating the investment standards and criteria provision, as originally proposed, was the comparative allocation of funds which it promised and the trade-offs among programs which some feared would follow. Even though such procedures may occur to some degree under the legislation enacted, Congress has made clear its intent of making basic transportation policy in the traditional way – a highly political process unencumbered by the difficulties of making basic shifts in the direction and thrust of the federal effort.

Limited Efforts to Integrate Transportation Policy

By its very nature, the traditional approach to transportation policy formation has limited interest in efforts to integrate such policies. As noted earlier, the individualized treatment of the respective modes, each on their own terms, has played an extremely large part in prolonging this disinterest.

For the most part, the need for a more coordinated direction of policy has received only hesitating recognition. Outside of the crises that literally forced reconsideration of policy on that basis, the bulk of efforts have been concentrated on ineffectual studies and surveys. Although these activities have generated interest and have often produced sound cases for reorientation of policies, their impact has not been dramatic enough to effect fundamental change. In essence, the findings have comprised "good theory" but "bad politics."

Nor have broad statements of "national transportation policy" helped to clarify objectives and goals that could be made operational. As an example, a number of statements of "national transportation policy" contained in the Transportation Act of 1940 flatly contradict certain provisions of the Transportation Act of 1958. The former would preserve and encourage protection of the "inherent" advantages of the various modes of transportation; the latter would consider such a "balanced" approach as inappropriate in determining the future of competitive relationships. Experience demonstrates that transportation policy platitudes serve little purpose; they cloud the numerous practical issues which must be decided upon if transportation facilities are to adjust to the requirements of the time.

There is a lack of general enthusiasm on the part of Congress for coordinating transportation policy on a national basis. It is largely accounted for by the absence of a political base that would underpin such action. Beyond spasmodic internal Executive Branch pressures to progress toward this goal in the name of "efficiency and economy," and isolated Congressional actions in the same direction, the leverage to achieve such an end has been largely non-existent.

An exception to this traditional pattern of behavior was the successful drive to create a Department of Transportation. But even this effort wore the mask of "internal reorganization" designed to "pull together" the administrative agencies most directly concerned with the conduct of federal transportation activities and programs. Indeed, the concept was first presented in terms that would provide for an "umbrella" agency – not a new organization to alter the fundamental directions of national transportation policies. When it became clear that substantial disruptions of existing policies and power relationships might well result, Congress and private interest groups affecting it reacted with celerity to divest DOT, in advance, of much of the policy role that originally was intended. These actions amply demonstrated that administrative efficiency is looked upon as one thing, but power redistribution is quite another.

Future Transportation Policy – The "Agents of Change"

In spite of the inertia which is so characteristic of much of past and present federal policies in the transportation field, several "agents of change" have begun to exert some influence on the outlook for future transportation policies. Depending on the relative influence which these factors exert, the possible "futures" of federal policies may range from guiding concepts grounded in traditional practices to a pattern of highly integrated national transportation planning applying "rational-comprehensive" approaches to the full range of federal responsibilities in this area.

The Changing Character and Role of National Planning

Both the character and role of federal planning in American society have undergone marked changes since the end of World War II. And the need for a more pervasive federal role in national transportation development forms part of this emerging trend.

One factor that has been particularly crucial to the growth of this role is the view that the federal government ought to assume a greater role than heretofore in *guiding* certain basic aspects of societal growth. The general acceptance of an increasingly influential federal role in shaping national transportation resources of the future is part of a larger trend – one which looks to the potentialities of government, at all levels, as an initiator of policies that serve the "public interest" and the conglomeration of aims and goals that comprise it. Thus, the functions of federal promotion and investment in a broad range of programs now encounter fewer charges of being "socialistic" in origin. In fact, there appears to be a greater acceptance of the view that federal policy ought to work toward accomplishing goals on a *national scale,* rather than to react in the short range to individual pressures serving limited aims.

The record demonstrates that national leadership in transportation development has been dominated by narrowly conceived roles: mediator of conflicts, "emergency" repair-man for gaps and leaks in the system, promoter of distended development within highly selected areas. All of these functions have fallen short of the influence which might have been exerted. Increasingly, the gap between potential and actual performance has served to accentuate the shortcomings of past policy.

The degree to which the federal government may influence planning in general and transportation planning in particular in the future also has been accentuated by the steady growth of financial resources that it can bring to bear to solve transportation problems on a national scale. Clearly, the federal government holds claim to the purse strings that control the greatest concentration of money that can be devoted to this problem area.

There also appears to be growing recognition of the number of functions in transportation that call for federal action. In reality, these may have always justified a greater federal role. But the important point is that these needs now have been recognized as legitimate concerns of future federal transportation policy.

A primary example is the growing role of federal policy and funding within metropolitan areas. In the past, transportation policies affecting the cities were considered incidental to other purposes. In fact, these purposes often were designed to promote a particular brand of rural welfare.

While such a policy orientation still exists, it has grown less dominant. Even though the process has been slow, halting, and conservative, the crises of metropolitan transportation have qualified for attention as problems of *national* concern. The maintenance of essential commuter services in major metropolitan areas, for example, now qualifies as a need for which federal assistance can be justified. The effects of modern interstate highways on residences and businesses in urban areas are now receiving more serious consideration prior to approval of routes by the federal government. The development of urban-oriented modes of transportation has become an objective of federal policy.

These trends reflect a greater acceptance of a positive federal role in ordering some of the priorities which must be set, as both the number and complexity of policy problems increase.

Possibilities of "Catalytical" Planning

There is renewed interest in the possibilities of using transportation investment policies as one of the means for organizing policies and programs with broader objectives. The possibilities of employing transportation planning to shape configurations of population, industrial development, recreational outlets, and inter-regional relationships have always existed. But more often than not, the pressure to plan comprehensively in advance of growth has been applied only sporadically.

The more typical pattern of policy formation in federal transportation investment has been to await the generation of transportation demands before commiting funds for their satisfaction. Lacking have been strategies which would deal with the challenges of projecting alternate "futures" that might be attainable and selecting transport investments that appear best suited to achieve national goals.

Three relatively recent developments in transportation planning may signal some change in traditional approaches.

One is evidenced in legislation which mandates development of comprehensive plans prior to the approval of highway and urban transportation projects. This requirement is intended to reduce the scale of piecemeal planning and to integrate considerations of transportation policy with equally vital community concerns for housing, education, recreation, environment, commercial development, and cultural facilities. Certainly this device holds the prospect for increasing the long-term leverage of future federal transportation expenditures. It may also have the secondary effect of forging new types of permanent administrative and political mechanisms for making such planning efforts continuing and responsive rather than isolated and static.

The second development indicating a change in the course of traditional policy is the slowly growing technical capacity of planners to simulate the effects of alternate inputs in metropolitan, regional, and national transportation systems. As discussed in Chapters 4 and 5, modeling efforts still leave much to be desired. Particularly crucial are the needs to fill numerous informational gaps and to identify more explicitly the nature of important causal variables and their relationships to each other. But the outlook is for a steady growth in the capabilities of analytical tools, techniques, and data which would help make transportation planning more of a formative than reactionary process.

The third development that may establish the framework for speeding a major transition in transportation policy is the *1972 National Transportation Needs Study*. In many respects, this approach combines elements of the two changes noted above and adds a new ingredient. That ingredient is the participation, on a comprehensive scale, of all state and urban governments, as well as the federal government, in a massive effort to assess the present state of the nation's transportation system and its requirements through the year 1990. Another indicator of change in this approach is that the focus is *multi-modal;* the scope is more sweeping and ambitious than any evaluation undertaken to date.

The assessment also represents the first major project undertaken by the Department of Transportation to fulfill one of the primary missions envisioned when it was created. As a matter of fact, testimony given during the past year indicates that DOT plans to use the results of the study as the basis for framing a far-reaching statement of national transportation policy.

In shorter-range terms, the Study is designed to develop comprehensive data on the national system as a whole. In addition, it is hoped that it will provide the impetus for improving the quality of transportation planning at all levels of government.

Also of great importance is the emphasis of the Study on transportation as both a service and a force for shaping future national development. Furthermore, the Study should provide a firmer base for policy-making by including information and alternatives for the future in a relatively consistent manner. Hopefully, the Study also anticipates the stimulation of institution building involving government and industry that would "encourage more rational and intelligent decision making on the nation's transportation system."[1]

There are, of course, many other aspects of the Study that are worthy of mention, particularly as they may affect the basic course of future national transportation policy development. Of most interest, however, are the "ground rules" that have been employed for developing projections of transportation needs. These call for assessing needs in terms of alternative levels of federal funding that would apply to further implementation of existing legislation as well as to the loosening of present constraints to encompass public spending over a broader range of possibilities. Thus, assumptions concerning federal spending levels range from low to high and to possibilities beyond those now covered by existing laws. This approach moves beyond the "either or" choice problem and into the realm of decision-making that utilizes alternative futures and scenarios.

The recognition of the catalytical aspects of transportation planning is also likely to have other repercussions. As noted earlier, simple cause-and-effect assumptions have been utilized to make transportation development serve purposes ranging from nation-building to alleviating unemployment problems and inflation. In the future, it is likely that federal transportation investments will increase their potential for not only changing individual metropolitan areas, but of revamping the character of emerging megalopolitan regions as well.

Mobility holds the key to the viability of such urban concentrations. And if mobility can be provided through direct federal participation in developing and applying new transportation technologies on a more comprehensive scale than heretofore, it would supply a basic ingredient for "knitting together" the complex communities of the future.

In this regard, the primary, current possibility is the development of High Speed Ground Transportation. At present, this new mode holds the promise of facilitating intercity transportation and relieving the overloads which have resulted in the aviation mode. In the future, further refinements might well result in the facilitation of intra-megalopolitan transportation movements. In turn, these would affect locational decisions of both individuals and private enterprises.

Further transportation policy formation can also be expected to influence conditions that have worked to the disadvantage of minority groups within society. Past policies of highway development, for example, have often uprooted or isolated Blacks, Puerto Ricans, and other minorities in the name of overall transportation system efficiency. Moreover, transportation policies have at times served the purposes of racial segregation in their efforts to achieve economic integration. Human and aesthetic values have often taken second place to considerations of suburban convenience and "through-routing."

If transportation programs can be adjusted to meeting needs on short-term, narrow bases, they can also be utilized to serve as effective catalysts in solving difficult problems of access to employment and business opportunities for most members of expanding metropolitan communities. They can provide for linkages within densely developed areas and growth in living style options for all.

Effects of the "Service Society" on Transportation Policy

Future directions of transportation policy formation undoubtedly will be affected by other changes transforming post-industrial America into a "Service Society." Again, transportation will both affect and be affected by this fundamental change. There is already mounting evidence that the locational decisions of many of the "footloose" industries are becoming less dominated by straight-line computations of distances between points of production and distribution, availability of raw materials, and market size. More influential will be the changing composition of future employment. As the demand for a higher level of skills grows, it can be anticipated that greater importance will be attached to providing employees with new working environments characterized by multiple access.

The emphasis on transportation would extend well beyond considering the avoidance of congestion. Equally important, concern for positive advantages such as access to recreational opportunities, cultural activities, varieties of shopping facilities, and advanced educational institutions comprise several of the attributes that will become more important.

In many respects, these needs would require provision of a variety of transportation resources. In terms of personal transportation particularly, this may call for more intensive development of both private and public transportation. If such occurs, it could be expected that full capacity operations will not qualify as an objective of emergent systems at all, but rather comprise a condition to be avoided. Such a development would reflect a *change in values* in which greater importance, and hence potential public investment, is placed on the amenities of quality transportation – a system which would go beyond assuring speed, reliability and safety – and provide convenience, personal comfort and even enjoyment.

If the goals of the "Service Society" evolve to the point of decreasing the relative emphasis on goods and materials outputs, including the high value placed on attaining narrowly defined "economic efficiency" almost for its own sake, the impact on transportation policy would prove substantial. In fact, even broadening economically based goals to include social welfare functions would be consistent with the value now beginning to be placed on quality service.

Again, this would run counter to traditional policy which, in enunciating the principle of "inherent advantages of the various modes," finds itself closely allied with the "one best way" approach to problem solving. At this point, it appears that such traditional conceptions would prove inadequate in meeting the transportation needs of the future.

Intertwined with these changes in the nature of national transportation policy goals is the rising concern about the state of the environment. Transportation projects have had numerous effects on the environment – most of them deleterious. Up to the last five years or so, resultant damages were accepted as the "price of progress." However, the Transportation Act of 1966 charged DOT with responsibility for taking the environment into account before approving projects that planned acquisition of properties devoted to public purposes. Much more far-reaching and specific guidelines for all federal agencies were included in the National Environmental Policy Act of 1969 and the Environmental Quality Improvement Act of 1970. Further, the Urban Mass Transportation Assistance Act of 1970 stated that environmental preservation in developing transportation facilities was to be a matter of *national policy.*

This shift in emphasis provides another indication that national transportation policy is involved in a transitory phase. Federally supported transportation projects account for a large segment of all public works undertaken each year in the United States. The imposition of environmental planning constraints represents something new; projects have been brought to a halt where the threat to human and natural environment appeared acute. In view of the sustained public, and therefore political, interest in strengthening environmental protection, this change in the composition of national transportation policy is particularly significant. The consequence should be a distinct improvement in the character of transportation planning and a more informed policy perspective.

Technology – Influential Imperative for Policy Change

The potentialities of technological advance constitute one of the most influential imperatives for change in traditional transportation policy.

Most recent experience indicates that the federal role is becoming more influential in determining in which areas and to what degree such innovations will take place. The most important single factor affecting this role has been the magnitude of expenditures required to research and develop either new modes or advanced concepts in existing transportation *on a system-wide basis.*

To date, the principal beneficiaries of these modifications in the character of national transportation development have been the aviation and highway modes. Emerging as potentially greater beneficiaries in the future are the present systems of urban mass transportation and the nascent mode of High Speed Ground Transportation. The future may also see the exertion of similar influence on the next period of development in maritime capacity.

All of these developments have been deeply influenced by the merging concerns of public policy and private enterprise noted earlier. In the case of the aviation mode and, to a lesser degree, the maritime mode, it appears that research and development expenditures will continue to be heavily influenced by military spending. But it can also be anticipated that new, special projects similar in nature to that organized for development of the SST will be initiated.

Put simply, the costs of technological progress have become too enormous for private enterprise, even with its increased capacities for capital investment, to shoulder alone. Furthermore, the characteristics of the aviation mode have changed so markedly that development of advanced aircraft is but one element in a highly interrelated system for which there is little recourse but to intensify the role of planning at the federal level.

The conduct of research and development activities in High Speed Ground Transportation will present challenges of a somewhat unique nature. For, here, a firm federal commitment to underwrite the major portion of development costs is still lacking. And unlike the aviation mode, the problem is more difficult because no well-defined group of private enterprises now exists to research its possibilities and to provide both the "hardware" and "software" necessary for its support.

Such capacity would be created, of course, if demand were generated on a large enough scale. But perhaps more than any modal growth that has occurred to date, HSGT may require almost total federal direction of the necessary research and development, financing of much of the capital expenditures involved, and stimulation of specialization within private industry for its servicing.

Other Significant Issues

There are many significant issues that will affect the mix of possible "futures" that national transportation policy may assume. In this concluding section, five problem areas of general importance to national transportation considered as a whole will be reviewed. These include the relationships between national defense and transportation policies; the level of federal expenditures for transportation; the future needs for institutional change; the need to meet mounting crises both within modes and as a total system; and the degree of control that is to be imposed.

While national defense projects have increased their pervasive effects on a number of policy areas in national life, they have established a significant influence on national transportaion development over a long period of time. Examples of this close relationship include the enormous revamping of both equipment and facilities within modes during wartime crises, the development of highways justified in part on the basis of defense needs, and the "spillover" effects of military research and development efforts. As has been demonstrated, the "side effects" of such activities often have not appeared as ripples; on occasion they have formed the tidal waves that subsequently washed away old relationships.

Of all the problems produced by the intertwining of national defense and transportation policies, the most significant are those that affect the capacity of the total transportation system and the particular policies applicable to individual modes.

Such is particularly evident in wartime. One of the primary difficulties of maintaining transportation capacities for defense needs is that excess peacetime capabilities result. Planning for the extraordinary undermines policies designed for the ordinary. Where economic competition tends to remove excess capacity, defense planning promotes it. Where transportation policy attempts to equate user benefits and charges, facilities justified by defense policies obscure the bases of such policies. Where transportation policy might seek to balance the levels of government support and assistance given to the various modes, defense policy attunes such programs to achieve the greatest defense advantage.

In many respects, these policy conflicts will remain inevitable because of the different objectives pursued. But it does not necessarily follow that defense planning decisions must take precedence in all cases where conflicts arise. Neither does it mean that justifications for transportation development should give inordinate weight to projects presented in the guise of "defense needs."

Future levels of federal expenditures to be devoted to transportation support and promotion constitute another issue of general concern. In retrospect, federal planning to promote highway and air transportation has outstripped, by far, that invested in other modes. Each of these modes has been the beneficiary of a fragmented federal approach to transportation policy formation. Each has established a strong base of support for continuing high levels of expenditures.

But while prospects for continuation of this pattern appear likely, it is also evident that crucial decision points are being approached as they affect other modes, particularly ocean shipping and urban mass transportation. However, if extrapolations of past trends prove accurate, existing levels of expenditures made on the other modes would probably hold their current levels of increase. If such continues to be the "political reality" of the future, federal expenditures for new types of transportation would be in the form of *additions* to current levels. As noted earlier, significant cuts in funding devoted to existing programs are rare — as are major reallocations among the modes.

It has become apparent that the metropolitan transportation crisis is not lacking in recognition as a major problem area. But what is apparently feared is the *size* of the federal financial commitment required to make possible realistic solutions and to deal with the problem in comprehensive terms.

The prospect of steady growth in the level of federal spending for transportation is hardly startling in itself. But if the level of investment for urban mass transportation were to approach or to exceed that provided for the Interstate and Defense Highway System, the impact on federal fiscal planning would indeed be enormous. As noted earlier, existing plans for improving metropolitan transportation could easily consume at least $20 billion. Nor does this estimate include potential expenditures on HSGT.

Another significant aspect of future challenge to existing transportation precedents and policies concerns the institutions that develop, promulgate, and administer policy in one form or another. In the past few years, the most significant step taken to deal with this problem has been the creation of the Department of Transportation. The Department is now a reality; it provides the skeletal framework upon which the Executive Branch may structure a more integrated approach to transportation planning as a whole.

At the same time, however, it should be recognized that DOT is a part of a much larger "establishment" devoted to transportation policy formation. Its creation and operation guarantee nothing. In reality, great institutional problems remain within the federal establishment itself. Those involving the regulatory and legal systems of transportation, in particular, are intensifying.

Legalism is one of the formidable obstacles to basic changes in transportation policy orientation. As discussed earlier, it may effectively discourage technological innovation. In its extreme form, it may encourage continuation of the quagmire of commodity-by-commodity rate fights, case-by-case formulations of policy, and the like. Over time, its over-protective features can emasculate inter-modal competition.

In perhaps no other respect is national policy more entangled in the processes of its own design than in regulation. In the long run, this issue will have to be dealt with "full square." This would require little short of a massive revision of law – a complete redefinition of "new rules of conduct" superseding those now on the statute books.

Future requirements may also be expected to increase pressure for centralizing all regulatory functions in transportation in one agency – much as the administration of transportation programs has been placed in one agency. Without such a major reorientation, it is difficult to see how the advantages of flexibility and adaptability in regulation could be achieved. Such a need is most evident when multi-modal transportation is considered.

Technological innovation can also be expected to produce requirements for new institutional arrangments on other fronts – principally in coordinating transportation planning efforts at the metropolitan and megalopolitan levels. To attempt to replace existing units of government with institutions of a regional character would be politically unrealistic, at least for the foreseeable future. But this does not preclude the possibilities of using the leverage of federal support to encourage formalized, cooperative arrangements among existing governmental entities. And where it would be appropriate, institutional vehicles could also be created to broaden the base of transportation planning to include private enterprise.

Related to this issue is the future of federal transportation policy as it concerns the exercise of power and control. At this point, it is obvious that federal policy has inexorably moved toward securing a greater degree of domination over virtually all aspects of national transportation. Numerous examples of this growing control exist: detailed standards for improvement of inland waterways; control over virtually all standards of aircraft performance and maintenance, pilot training, schedules, fare structures, navigation; safety specifications and standards for federally assisted highway construction and for the manufacture of autos, trucks and buses; design and operational characteristics of shipping constructed with MARAD subsidies; detailed specifications for qualification for UMTA capital grants. These represent but a sampling of the totality of federal controls.

But in the long run even their influence may prove insufficient to meet the enormous transportation challenges of the future. We may be approaching the point at which national population growth and demand for greater transportation capacity will mandate control over the quantities of transportation conveyances produced and their usages. Such a possibility does not appear too remote when viewed against the background of a motor vehicle output growing at a much faster pace than the general population.

The present state of national transportation has also raised other disturbing "warning flags" concerning the future. Most important are the new transportation crises that have crossed the time horizon and, in some areas, have already reached the "emergency stage."

Most publicized is the concern for the future of air safety caused by the congested air space, less than adequate ground control equipment, and the exponential rate of growth in the demand for air travel during peak periods. Although this crisis may be temporarily eased by the "jumbo jets," the long-term outlook is for growing problems in developing and applying federal policies for the future. There is little doubt that extremely difficult political decisions lie ahead, particularly in accommodating the increasingly conflicting demands of general and commercial aviation. And even within the bounds of commercial aviation, the limitations of finite space, "spillover" effects of air pollution and aircraft noise, and congested ground facilities may force a reorientation of policy away from providing for unlimited demand and toward new policies governing the rationing and allocation of the limited commodity of space.

While the crisis of air safety has drawn a great amount of attention, other crises of even greater import continue to evolve. One concerns the safety of ground transportation, particularly by auto. The annual loss of life — 55,000 people — and the number of personal injuries — over 2,000,000 — are staggering.

Indeed, one may ask: If a "new" system of personal transportation were now being designed for the future, would a performance criterion forecasting such annual losses be acceptable? If the answer is negative, why, then, is the present toll so stoically tolerated? The influence of federal policies on reducing these losses, recent changes notwithstanding, remains negligible; the ultimate weight of federal leverage continues untested.

A number of crises cluster about the need for policies to deal with problems of congestion. In particular, the difficulties of movement on the ground in congested metropolitan areas during periods of journeys to and from work will force hard choices in federal policy. As discussed in Chapter 6, these will require choosing among alternatives in investments within the modes, as well as in inter-modal facilities.

This latter aspect of policy has received insufficient attention in both passenger and freight transportation. Yet the "terminal function" is generally conceded to be one of the most crucial of the problems faced in integrating national transportation facilities into a complete network of service. It is becoming more and more apparent that public transportation facilities will be severely hampered in overcoming "auto dominance" if the quality of transfer facilities continued to be an object of low priority in federal investment policy.

In many respects, this need to consider a broad range of policy choices underscores a related point. Specifically, there is a high rate of technological progress being made in many of the modes of transportation. These will intensify the need for greater coordination of federal policy, both in promotion and regulation. While the goal of coordination might appear desirable on its own merits, need for its achievement is no longer optional. Indeed, as pressures grow to accommodate travel demands with one or more modes versus others, the amount of leverage that could be exerted by federal influence in making such choices will continue to increase. And as has been discussed earlier, this influence will be most enhanced by the investment potential in the hands of the federal government.

In essence, the foci of future federal policies will have to extend beyond past and present emphases on various types of quality control. In the future, these policies will have to deal more concretely with the delicate and volatile questions of quantity control and the conscious selection and financial support of different types and modes of transportation for future development and promotion. Nothing short of positive, committed federal leadership will do.

Selected Publications on Transportation

Books and Pamphlets

American Association of State Highway Officials. *Road User Benefit Analysis for Highway Improvement,* 917 National Press Building, Washington, D.C. 1952.

Arthur D. Little, Inc. *Cost Effectiveness in Traffic Safety.* New York: Frederick A. Praeger, 1968.

Burch, Phillip H., Jr. *Highway Revenue and Expenditure Policy.* New Brunswick: Rutgers University Press, 1962.

Burkhardt, Robert. *The Federal Aviation Administration.* New York: Frederick A. Praeger, Inc., 1967.

Comprehensive Planning Office. *Metropolitan Transportation – 1980.* New York: The Port of New York Authority, 1963.

Danielson, Michael N. *Federal-Metropolitan Politics and the Commuter Crisis.* New York: Columbia University Press, 1964.

Davis, Grant Miller. *The Department of Transportation.* Lexington, Mass.: Heath Lexington Books, 1970.

Dearing, Charles L. *American Highway Policy.* Washington, D.C.: The Brookings Institution, 1941.

_____ and Owen, Wilfred. *National Transportation Policy.* Washington, D.C.: The Brookings Institution, 1949.

Dorfman, Robert (ed.). *Measuring Benefits of Government Investments.* Washington, D.C.: The Brookings Institution, 1965.

Drayton, Charles D. *Transportation Under Two Masters.* Washington, D.C.: National Law Book Company, 1946.

Farris, Martin T., and McElhiney, Paul T. (eds.). *Modern Transportation: Selected Readings.* Boston: Houghton-Mifflin Company, 1967.

Foster, C.D. *The Transport Problem.* London: Blackie and Son, Ltd., 1963.

Frederick, John H. *Improving National Transportation Policy.* Washington, D.C.: American Enterprise Association, 1959.

Fromm, Gary (ed.). *Transport Investment and Economic Development.* Washington, D.C.: The Brookings Institution, 1965.

Hobbs, F.D., and Richardson, B.D. *Traffic Engineering.* London: Pergamon Press, 1967.

Kuhn, Tillo E. *Public Enterprise Economics and Transport Problems.* Berkeley and Los Angeles, California: University of California Press, 1962.

Locklin, Philip D. *Economics of Transportation.* 6th Edition. Homewood, Illinois: Richard D. Irwin, Inc., 1966.

MacGill, Caroline E. *History of Transportation in the United States Before 1860.* Washington, D.C.: Carnegie Institution, 1917.

Meyer, J.R.; Kain, J.F.; and Wohl, M. *The Urban Transportation Problem.* Cambridge, Massachusetts: Harvard University Press, 1965.

Mishan, E.J. *The Costs of Economic Growth.* London: Staples Press, 1967.

Mohring, Herbert, and Harwitz, Mitchell. *Highway Benefits: An Analytical Framework.* The Transportation Center at Northwestern University: Northwestern University Press, 1962.

Mott, George Fox (ed.). *Transportation Century.* Baton Rouge, Louisiana: State University Press, 1966.

Moulton, Harold G. *The American Transportation Problem.* Washington, D.C.: The Brookings Institution, 1933.

Norton, Hugh S. *National Transportation Policy: Formulation and Implementation.* Berkeley, California: McCutchan Publishing Corporation, 1966.

Owen, Wilfred. *The Metropolitan Transportation Problem.* Rev. Edition. Garden City, New York: Doubleday and Company, Inc., 1966.

_____ . *Strategy for Mobility.* Washington, D.C.: The Brookings Institution, 1964.

Pegrum, Dudley F. *Transportation: Economics and Public Policy.* Rev. Edition. Homewood, Illinois: Richard D. Irwin, Inc., 1968.

Pell, Claiborne. *Megalopolis Unbound.* New York: Frederick A. Praeger, 1967.

Ringwalt, John L. *Development of Transportation Systems in the United States.* Philadelphia, Pennsylvania: Published by the Author, Railway World Office, 1888.

Ruppenthal, Karl M. (ed.). *Challenge to Transportation.* Stanford, California: Stanford University Graduate School of Business, 1961.

_____ . (ed.). *Transportation Progress.* Stanford, California: Graduate School of Business, Stanford University, 1964.

Sharp, Clifford. *The Problem of Transport.* London: Pergamon Press, 1965.

Thomas, Edwin N. and Schofer, Joseph L. (eds.). *Strategies for the Evaluation of Alternative Transportation Plans.* National Cooperative Highway Reasearch Program Report 96, Highway Research Board, Division of Engineering National Research Council, National Academy of Sciences — National Academy of Engineering, 1970.

Wilson, Ernest W. (ed.). *The Future of American Transportation.* The American Assembly. Englewood Cliffs, N.J.: Prentice-Hall, Inc., 1971.

Wilson, G. Lloyd (ed.)). "Transportation: War and Postwar." *The Annals of the American Academy of Political and Social Science,* Vol. CCXXX, November, 1943.

Winch, David M. *The Economics of Highway Planning.* The Netherlands: University of Toronto Press, 1963.

Winfrey, Robley. *Economic Analysis for Highways.* Scranton, Pennsylvania: International Textbook Company, 1969.

_____ , and Zellner, Carl (eds.). *Summary and Evaluation of Economic Consequences of Highway Improvements.* National Cooperative Highway Research Program Report 122, Highway Research Council, National Academy of Sciences – National Academy of Engineering, 1971.

Yoshpe, Harry B., and Brown, Fred R. *The Economics of National Security.* Washington, D.C.: Industrial College of the Armed Forces, 1961.

Articles and Periodicals

Arth, Maurice P. "Federal Transport Regulatory Policy." *American Economic Review,* Vol. LII, No. 2 (May, 1962), 416-21.

Barber, Richard J. "Technological Change in American Transportation: The Role of Government Action." *Virginia Law Review,* Vol. L (L964), 824-95.

Barsness, Richard W. "The Department of Transportation: Concept and Structure." *Western Political Quarterly,* Vol. 23, No. 3, September, 1970.

Barta, W.J. "Water-Rail Coordination." Speech Delivered at American Society of Traffic and Transportation, University of Indiana, Bloomington, Indiana, September 6, 1967. *Vital Speeches,* Vol. XXXIV, No. 1 (October 15, 1967), 5-6.

Beardsley, Peter T. "Integrated Ownership of Transportation Companies and the Public Interest." *George Washington Law Review,* Vol. XXXI (1962-63), 85-97.

Beesley, M.E. "The Value of Time Spent in Traveling: Some New Evidence." *Economica,* Vol. XXXII, No. 126 (May, 1965), 174-85.

Caputa, Vincent F. "The Year 2000." Speech Delivered Before the Transportation and Logistics Forum of the National Defense Transportation Association, New York Hilton Hotel, New York, September 23, 1964. *Vital Speeches,* Vol. XXXI, No. 1 (October 15, 1964), 11-15.

Dean, Alan L. Assistant Secretary for Administration, Department of Transportation. "The Making of a Department of Transportation." Conference on the Public Service, Washington, D.C., October 13-14, 1967.

_____ . "The Making of a Department of Transportation." *Good Government,* Vol. LXXXV, No. 3 (Fall, 1968), 15-20.

Doxiadis, C.A. "Man's Movement and His City." *Science,* Vol. CLXII (October 18, 1968), 326-34.

Duriez, Philip. "Rail-Motor Rate Competition – The T.O.F.C. Experience." *Transportation Journal* (Fall, 1967), 35-40.

Eastman, Joseph B. "Public Administration of Transportation Under War Conditions." *American Economic Review,* XXXIV, No. 1 (Supplement), Part 2 (March, 1944), 86-90.

Farris, Martin. "Transportation Cooperative and Coordinated Services." *Arizona Business Bulletin,* Vol. XV, No. 4 (April, 1968), 82-85.

Foster, C.D., and Beesley, M.E. "Estimating the Social Benefit of Constructing an Underground Railway in London." *Journal of the Royal Statistical Society,* Vol. CXXVI (1963), 46-78.

Garrison, W.L. "Urban Transportation Planning Models in 1975." *Journal of the American Institute of Planners,* Vol. 31, No. 2 (May, 1965), 156-58.

Gillilland, Whitney. "CAB Co-ordination of Unlike Modes of Transportation." *Public Utilities Fortnightly,* Vol. LXXVI, No. 5 (September 2, 1965), 15-26.

Hamilton, William F., II, and Nance, Dana K. "Systems Analysis of Urban Transportation." *Scientific American,* Vol. CCXXI, No. 1 (July, 1969), 19-27.

Hammond, Harold F. "The New Age of Transportation Coordination." *Traffic Quarterly,* Vol. XXI, No. 4 (October, 1967), 501-17.

Harris, Britton. "Introduction: New Tools for Planning." *Journal of the American Institute of Planners,* Vol. XXXI, No. 2 (May, 1965), 90-95.

Hendrix, Frank L. "Federal Transport Statistics: An Analysis." *Transportation Journal,* Vol. V, No. 1 (Fall, 1965), 6-10.

High Speed Ground Transportation Journal. Vol. II, No. 1 (January, 1968).

Hutchins, John G.B. "The Effect of the Civil War and the Two World Wars on American Transportation." *American Economic Review,* Vol. XLII, No. 2 (May, 1952), 626-38.

Knudsen, Semon E. "The Public Selects its Transportation." Speech Delivered at the Annual Banquet of the Society of Automotive Engineers, Detroit, Michigan, January 15, 1969. *Vital Speeches,* Vol. XXXV, No. 9 (February 15, 1969), 280-81.

Krutilla, John V. "Welfare Aspects of Benefit-Cost Analysis." *The Journal of Political Economy,* Vol. LXIX, No. 3 (June, 1961), 226-35.

Lebergott, Stanley. "United States Transport Advance and Externalities." *Journal of Economic History,* Vol. XXVI, No. 4 (December, 1966), 445-56.

Liipfert, Eugene T. "Consolidation and Competition in Transportation: The Need for an Effective and Consistent Policy." *George Washington Law Review,* Vol. XXXI (1962-63), 108-25.

Lowry, Ira S. "A Short Course in Model Design." *Journal of the American Institute of Planners,* Vol. XXXI, No. 2 (May, 1965), 158-65.

Maass, Arthur. "Benefit-Cost Analysis: Its Relevance to Public Investment Decisions." *Quarterly Journal of Economics,* Vol. LXXX, No. 2 (May, 1966), 208-226.

Melton, Lee J., Jr. "A Rational Approach to Highway Finance." *Land Economics,* Vol. XLII, No. 1 (February, 1966), 130-34.

——————. "Transport Coordination and Regulatory Philosophy." *Law and Contemporary Problems,* Vol. XXIV (1959), 622-41.

Mohring, Herbert. "Land Values and the Measurement of Highway Benefits." *The Journal of Political Economy,* Vol. LXIX, No. 3 (June, 1961), 236-49.

Moses, Leon N., and Williamson, Harold F., Jr. "Value of Time, Choice of Mode, and the Subsidy Issue in Urban Transportation." *The Journal of Political Economy,* Vol. LXXI, No. 3 (June, 1963), 247-64.

Moulton, Harold G. "Fundamentals of a National Transportation Policy." *The American Economic Review* (Supplement), Vol. XXIV, No. 1 (March, 1934), 33-44.

Murray, Gordon. "Balancing the Books on Transportation." Text of a Presentation by Gordon Murray, U.S. Bureau of the Budget, at the Annual National Transportation Institute, Chicago, Illinois, January 19, 1965.

Nelson, James C. "Highway Development, the Railroads, and National Transport Policy." *American Economic Review,* Vol. XLI, No. 2 (May, 1951), 495-505.

——————. "Policy Issues and Economic Effects of Public Aids to Domestic Transport." *Law and Contemporary Problems,* Vol. XXIV (1959), 553-56.

——————. "The Pricing of Highway, Waterway, and Airway Facilities." *American Economic Review,* Vol. LII, No. 2 (May, 1962), 426-35.

Norton, Hugh S. "The Department of Transportation – A Study of Organizational Futility." *Public Utilities Fortnightly,* LXXVIII, No. 13 (December 22, 1966), 19-24.

——————. "Influence of Innovation on Transport Competition: Two Cases." *Transportation Journal,* Vol. VI, No. 1 (Fall, 1966), 37-40.

——————. "A Modest Proposal to Improve Competition in Passenger Transportation." *Atlantic Economic Review,* Vol. XVIII, No. 5 (May, 1968), 17-19.

——————. "Survival of the Common Carrier: Is Integration a Solution?" *Public Utilities Fortnightly,* Vol. LXXVI, No. 5 (September 2, 1965), 29-41.

"Obstacles to Innovation." *International Science & Technology* (November, 1964), 45.

Owen, Wilfred. "Transportation and Technology." *American Economic Review,* Vol. LII, No. 2 (May, 1962), 405-15.

_____. "Transportation on Earth." Speech Presented at Opening Ceremonies of the Golden Jubilee Convention, Canadian Good Roads Association, Montreal, October 20, 1964. *Vital Speeches,* Vol. XXI, No. 10 (March 1, 1965), 293-96.

Pegrum, Dudley F. "Conflicts in Transport Policy." *Transportation Journal,* Vol. VI, No. 1 (Fall, 1966), 5-16.

Prest, A. R., and Turvey, R. "Cost-Benefit Analysis: A Survey." *The Economic Journal,* Vol LXXV (December, 1965), 683-735.

Reuss, Henry S. "Research is Needed to Develop New Modes of Urban Transport." *Transportation Journal,* Vol. V, No. 2 (Winter, 1965), 21-25.

Seifert, William W.; Breuning, Siegfried M.; and Kettaneh, Anthony. "Investing in the Future of Transportation." *Harvard Business Review,* Vol. XL, No. 4 (July-August, 1968), 4-12ff.

"Trucks, Trains, Planes, Boats, All in One Company?" *U.S. News & World Report,* Vol. LXIII, No. 13 (September 25, 1967), 118-20.

Tucker, William H. "Wanted: The Air-truck-rail-water-bus Company." *Columbia Journal of World Business,* Vol. II, No. 6 (November-December, 1967), 47-53.

Vickrey, William S. "Pricing in Urban and Suburban Transport." *American Economic Review,* Vol. LIII, No. 2 (May, 1963), 452-61.

Wilson, George W. "The Weeks Report Revisited." *American Economic Review,* Vol. XLIX, No. 1 (March, 1959), 130-32.

Public Documents

A Guide to the 1972 National Transportation Needs Study, Office of Systems Analysis and Information, Office of the Secretary of Transportation, Washington, D.C.: January 8, 1971.

Annual Reports. Fiscal Years 1967-71. Department of Transportation. Washington, D.C.: U.S. Government Printing Office.

Container Shipping: Full Ahead. A Forecast of How Containerization of Oceanborne Foreign Trade Will Develop by 1975, and Its Effect on the New York-New Jersey Port, The Port of New York Authority, May, 1967.

Creating a Department of Transportation. Hearings, Subcommittee on Government Operations, House of Representatives, 89th Cong., 2d Sess., Washington, D.C.: U.S. Government Printing Office, 1966.

Crumlish, Joseph D. *Notes on the State-of-the-Art of Benefit-Cost Analysis as Related to Transportation Systems.* U.S. Department of Commerce, National Bureau of Standards, Technical Note 294, Washington, D.C.: U.S. Government Printing Office, 1966.

Department of Transportation Act. House Report No. 1701, 89th Cong., 2d Sess., Washington, D.C.: U.S. Government Printing Office, 1966.

Establish a Department of Transportation. Hearings, Committee on Government Operations, United States Senate, 89th Cong., 2d Sess., Washington, D.C.: U.S. Government Printing Office, 1966.

Establishing a Department of Transportation, and For Other Purposes. United States Sentate, 89th Cong., 2d Sess., Calendar No. 1627, Report No. 1659, Washington, D.C.: U.S. Government Printing Office, 1966.

Federal Transportation Policy and Program. Washington, D.C.: U.S. Government Printing Office, March, 1960.

Final Report of the Highway Allocation Study. 87th Cong., 1st Sess., House Document 72, Washington, D.C.: U.S. Government Printing Office, 1961.

Fourth Report of the Federal Coordinator of Transportation on Transportation Legislation. H. Doc. No. 394, 74th Cong., 2d Sess., Washington, D.C.: U.S. Government Printing Office, 1936.

Interregional Highways. H. Doc. 379, 78th Cong., 2d Sess., Washington, D.C.: U.S. Government Printing Office, January 12, 1944.

Issues Involved in a Unified and Coordinated Federal Program for Transportation. Report to the President from the Secretary of Commerce, Washington, D.C.: U.S. Government Printing Office, December 1, 1949.

Modern Transport Policy. Documents Relating to the Report of the Presidential Advisory Committee on Transport Policy and Organization and Implementing Legislation, U.S. Department of Commerce, Washington, D.C.: U.S. Government Printing Office, June, 1956.

National Highway Program. H. Doc. No. 93, 84th Cong., 1st Sess., Washington, D.C.: U.S. Government Printing Office, 1955.

National Transportation Policy. Preliminary Draft of a Report to the Senate Committee on Interstate and Foreign Commerce, 87th Cong., 1st Sess., Washington, D.C.: U.S. Government Printing Office, 1961.

Needs of the National Highway System, 1955-84. H. Doc. No. 120, 84th Cong., 1st Sess., Washington, D.C.: U.S. Government Printing Office, 1955.

Ocean Freight Industry (Cellar Report). U.S. Congress, House of Representatives, Staff of Special Subcommittee No. 5, Committee on Judiciary, 87th Cong., 2d Sess., March 12, 1962, Washington, D.C.: U.S. Government Printing Office, 1962.

Problems of the Railroads. Report of Subcommittee on Surface Transportation, Committee on Interstate and Foreign Commerce, U.S. Senate, 85th Cong., 2d Sess., Washington, D.C.: U.S. Government Printing Office, April, 1958.

Proposed Department of Transportation. Message from the President of the United States, House of Representatives, 89th Cong., 2d Sess., Document No. 399, Washington, D.C.: U.S. Government Printing Office, 1966.

Public Aids to Transportation, Vols. I-IV. Federal Coordinator of Transportation. Washington, D.C.: U.S. Government Printing Office, 1938-40.

Recommendations for Northeast Corridor Transportation, U.S. Department of Transportation, Assistant Secretary for Policy and International Affairs, Office of Systems Analysis and Information, Strategic Planning Division, Vols. 1-3, September, 1971.

Regulation of Railroads. Sen. Doc. No. 119, 73rd Cong., 2d Sess., Washington, D.C.: U.S. Government Printing Office, 1934.

Regulation of Transportation Agencies. Sen. Doc. No. 152, 73rd Cong., 2d Sess., Washington, D.C.: U.S. Government Printing Office, 1934.

Report of the Federal Coordinator of Transportation. H. Doc. No. 89, 74th Cong., 1st Sess., Washington, D.C.: U.S. Government Printing Office, 1935.

Report of the Secretary of the Treasury, On the Subject of Public Roads and Canals. Made in Pursuance of a Resolution of Senate, of March 2, 1807, April 12, 1808, Washington, D.C.: Printed by R. C. Weightman, By Order of the Senate, April 12, 1808.

Revision of Federal Transportation Policy. Report of Presidential Advisory Committee on Transport Policy and Organization, Washington, D.C.: U.S. Government Printing Office, 1955.

Tomorrow's Transportation – New Systems for the Urban Future. U.S. Department of Housing and Urban Development, Office of Metropolitan Development, Urban Transportation Administration, Washington, D.C., 1968.

Transportation and National Policy. U.S. National Resources Planning Board, Advisory Committee for the Transportation Study. Washington, D.C.: U.S. Government Printing Office, May, 1942.

Transportation in the Northeastern Megalopolitan Corridor. U.S. Executive Office of the President, Task Force Report to an Executive Office Steering Committee, December 10, 1962.

The Transportation System of our Nation. Message from the President of the United States, House of Representatives, Document No. 284, 87th Cong., 2d Sess., April 5, 1962.

Notes

Chapter 1
The Evolution of National Transportation
Department (1780-1939)

1. Wilfred Owen, *Strategy for Mobility* (Washington, D.C.: The Brookings ✗
Institution, 1964), p. 192.

2. See John L. Ringwalt, *Development of Transportation Systems in the
United States* (Philadelphia, Pa.: Published by the author, Railway World Office,
1888), p. 149.

3. For a brief discussion of issues of "efficiency" in transportation versus
more broadly based goals, see George W. Wilson, "The Goals of Transportation
Policy," Ernest W. Williams, ed., *The Future of American Transportation,* The
American Assembly (Englewood Cliffs, N.J.: Prentice-Hall, Inc., 1971), pp.
10-14.

4. *Wabash, St. Louis and Pacific Railway Co. v. Illinois* (118 U.S.
557,1886).

5. Charles D. Drayton, *Transportation Under Two Masters* (Washington,
D.C.: National Law Book Company, 1946), "Introduction."

Chapter 2
Early Attempts to Integrate National
Transportation Policy

1. *Report of the Secretary of the Treasury, On the Subject of Public Roads
and Canals;* Made in Pursuance of a Resolution of Senate, of March 2, 1807,
April 12, 1808 (Washington, D.C.: Printed by R. C. Weightman, By Order of the
Senate, April 12, 1808).

2. John G. B. Hutchins, "The Effect of the Civil War and the Two World
Wars on American Transportation," *American Economic Review,* Vol. 42, No. 2
(May, 1952), p. 626.

3. Joseph L. White, G. Lloyd Wilson and James M. Curtin, "American
Transportation Facilities at the Outbreak of the War," Transportation: War and
Postwar, G. Lloyd Wilson, ed., *The Annals of the American Academy of Political
and Social Science,* Vol. 230 (November, 1943), p. 5.

4. Harry B. Yoshpe and Fred R. Brown, *The Economics of National
Security* (Washington: Industrial College of the Armed Forces, 1961), p. 5.

5. Joseph B. Eastman, "Public Administration of Transportation Under War
Conditions," *American Economic Review,* Vol. 34, No. 1 (Supplement), Part 2
(March, 1944), pp. 86-87. The author points out that the factor of the price

level has been often overlooked and in fact provided the rationale for a government take-over of telephone and telegraph as well. It was felt that rate increases imposed by government would be more palatable.

6. Dudley F. Pegrum, *Transportation: Economics and Public Policy,* Revised Edition (Homewood, Illinois: Richard D. Irwin, Inc., 1968), p. 310.

7. Hutchins, p. 632.

8. *Transportation and National Policy,* U.S. National Resources Planning Board, Advisory Committee for the Transportation Study (Washington, D.C.: U.S. Government Printing Office, May, 1942), pp. 146-47.

9. See Harold G. Moulton, *The American Transportation Problem* (Washington, D.C.: The Brookings Institution, 1933), pp. xv-xvi.

10. Ibid., p. 468.

11. Ibid., p. lxii.

12. Owen, p. 133.

13. *Transportation and National Policy,* pp. 268-69.

14. Charles L. Dearing and Wilfred Owen, *National Transportation Policy* (Washington, D.C.: The Brookings Institution, 1949), p. 444.

15. *Transportation and National Policy.* The study was requested by President Franklin D. Roosevelt on January 24, 1940 on the premise that " . . . . the building of a superior and more effective system is a basic essential to the fuller development of our national economy."

16. Ibid., p. 9.

17. Ibid., p. 275.

18. Ibid., p. 276.

19. Joseph B. Eastman described the situation as one in which the government entered "something like a partnership with the carriers." Principal reliance was placed on "leadership" and, only if necessary, "orders." See Joseph B. Eastman, "The Office of Defense Transportation," G. Lloyd Wilson, p. 1.

20. Yoshpe and Brown. p. 38.

21. *National Transportation Policy,* Preliminary Draft of a Report to the Senate Committee on Interstate and Foreign Commerce, 87th Congress, 1st Sess. (Washington, D.C.: U.S. Government Printing Office, 1961), p. 5 This report is hereafter referred to as the Doyle Report.

22. John J. Pelley, "American Railroads In and After the War," G. Lloyd Wilson, p. 25.

23. Wilfred Owen, *The Metropolitan Transportation Problem,* Revised Edition (Garden City, New York: Doubleday and Company, Inc., 1966), p. 75. See also Arthur M. Hill, "Intercity Bus Transportation," G. Lloyd Wilson, p. 72. Hill notes that in 1942, buses carried over one-half of the total intercity passenger traffic.

24. The report was entitled *Interregional Highways,* H. Doc. 379, 78th Congress, 2d Sess. (January 14, 1944).

25. Executive Order 9504, February 7, 1942.

Chapter 3
Modern Currents of Federal Transportation Policy

1. This point is discussed by Roscoe C. Martin in *The Cities and the Federal System* (New York: Atherton Press, 1965), p. 105.

2. Robert Burkhardt, *The Federal Aviation Administration* (New York: Frederick A. Praeger, Inc., 1967), pp. 155-56.

3. The significance of this legislation, particularly as it relates to innovation in financing transportation development and to integrated national planning, is reviewed further in Chapters 7 and 8.

4. For further discussion of these points, see *Department of Transportation and Related Agencies Appropriations for 1972,* Hearings Before a Subcommittee of the Committee on Appropriations, House of Representatives, 92d Cong., 1st Sess. (Part 2) (Washington, D.C.: U.S. Government Printing Office, 1971), pp. 480-485; (Part 3), pp. 1114-1117.

5. A summary of these activities is provided by the Annual Reports of the Department of Transportation.

6. Because of its significance to the emerging federal transportation policy and its relation to technology, this subject will be analyzed in Chapter 7.

7. *Ocean Freight Industry* (Celler Report), Staff of Special Subcommittee No. 5, Committee on Judiciary, U.S. House of Representatives, 87th Cong., 2d Sess., March 12, 1962 (Washington, D.C.: U.S. Government Printing Office, 1962), p. 382.

8. Public Law 91-469.

9. Pegrum (Rev. Ed.), p. 66. By the late 1960s, the oil pipelines accounted for over 20 billion ton-miles of freight — about 50 percent of the total freight carried by the nation's railroads.

10. Yoshpe and Brown, pp. 7-8.

11. These legislative enactments amended regulatory policy. The Railroad Modification Act of 1948 provided for greater flexibility in the repayment conditions of railroad securities. The Reed-Bullwinkle Act, also for 1948, legalized rate bureaus and placed them under ICC control. See D.P. Locklin, *Economics of Transportation* (6th ed.; Homewood, Ill.: Richard D. Irwin, Inc., 1966), pp. 253-54.

12. *Problems of the Railroads* (Smathers Report), Report of Subcommittee on Surface Transportation, Committee on Interstate and Foreign Commerce, U.S. Senate, 85th Cong., 2d Sess. (Washington, D.C.: U.S. Government Printing Office, April, 1958).

13. See Hugh S. Norton, *National Transportation Policy: Formulation and Implementation* (Berkeley, Calif.: McCutchan Publishing Corporation, 1966), p. 72.

14. *Department of Transportation and Related Agencies Appropriations for 1971*, Hearings Before a Subcommittee of the Committee on Appropriations, House of Representatives, 91st Cong., 2d Sess. (Washington, D.C.: U.S. Government Printing Office, 1970), p. 907.

15. Public Law 91-578.

16. The results of this study are outlined in *Needs of the National Highway System*, 1955-84, H. Doc. No. 120, 84th Cong., 1st Sess. (Washington, D.C.: U.S. Government Printing Office, 1955); *National Highway Program*, H. Doc. No. 93, 84th Cong., 1st Sess. (Washington, D.C.: U.S. Government Printing Office, 1955).

17. Michael N. Danielson, *Federal-Metropolitan Politics and the Commuter Crisis* (New York: Columbia University Press, 1964), pp. 125-26. Included were groups representing automobile users, truckers, manufacturers and suppliers, highway construction companies and various state and local road officials. Also see Phillip H. Burch, Jr., *Highway Revenue and Expenditure Policy* (New Brunswick: Rutgers University Press, 1962), p. 243.

18. *A Report to the Congress by the Commission on Organization of the Executive Branch of Government*, U.S. Department of Commerce (Washington, D.C.: U.S. Government Printing Office, March, 1949). The results of this transportation study are critically commented upon by Charles L. Dearing and Wilfred Owen in their book, *National Transportation Policy* (Washington, D.C.: The Brookings Institution, 1949).

19. *A Report to the Congress by the Commission on Organization of the Executive Branch of Government*, p. 15.

20. *Issues Involved in a Unified and Coordinated Federal Program for Transportation*, A Report to the President from the Secretary of Commerce (Washington, D.C.: U.S. Government Printing Office, December 1, 1949).

21. Ibid., p. 49.

22. *Revision of Federal Transportation Policy*, Report of Presidential Advisory Committee on Transport Policy and Organization (Washington, D.C.: U.S. Government Printing Office, 1955).

23. For an excellent discussion of these points, see George W. Wilson, "The Weeks Report Revisited," *American Economic Reviw*, Vol. 49, No. 1 (March, 1959), pp. 130-32.

24. *Federal Transportation Policy and Program*, U.S. Department of Commerce (Washington, D.C.: U.S. Government Printing Office, March, 1960).

25. *National Transportation Policy*, Preliminary Draft of A Report to the Senate Committee on Interstate and Foreign Commerce, 87th Cong., 1st Sess. (Washington, D.C.: U.S. Government Printing Office, 1961).

26. See *Modern Transport Policy,* Documents Relating to the Report of the Presidential Advisory Committee on Transport Policy and Organization and Implementing Legislation, U.S. Department of Commerce (Washington, D.C.: U.S. Government Printing Office, June, 1956), p. 116.

27. Public Law 87-70.

28. Public Law 91-190.

29. The Transportation System of our Nation, Message from the President of the United States, House of Representatives, Document No. 384, 87th Cong., 2d Sess., April 5, 1962.

30. Public Law 88-365.

31. Public Law 91-453.

32. Because of its close relationship to the development of transportation technology, the significance of this legislation will be discussed in Chapter 6.

Chapter 4
The Department of Transportation

1. "Intensive Lobbying Surrounds Death of Transport Bill," *Congressional Quarterly Weekly Report,* Vol. 22, No. 19 (May 8, 1964), p. 925.

2. See Alan L. Dean, Assistant Secretary for Administration, Department of Transportation, "The Making of a Department of Transportation," Conference on the Public Service, Washington, D.C., October 13-14, 1967, pp. 2-4.

3. Proposed Department of Transportation, Message from the President of the United States, House of Representatives, 89th Cong., 2d Sess., Document No. 399 (Washington, D.C.: U.S. Government Printing Office, 1966).

4. "What the President is Proposing," *Business Week* (January 22, 1966), p. 160.

5. "Shippers Would Limit Transport Department," *Railway Age,* Vol. 160, No. 8 (February 28, 1966), p. 50ff.

6. *Life,* Vol. 60, No. 11 (March 18, 1966), p. 4.

7. "Hearings Will Open on Proposal for New Department," *Congressional Quarterly Weekly Report,* Vol. 24, No. 12 (March 25, 1966), p. 614.

8. George C. Wilson, "Congress Fears Creation of Czar in Transportation Department Legislation," *Aviation Week & Space Technology,* Vol. 84, No. 15 (April 11, 1966), p. 43.

9. See *Establish a Department of Transportation,* Hearings Before the Committee on Government Operations, U.S. Senate, 89th Cong., 2d Sess., on S. 3010 (Washington, D.C.: U.S. Government Printing Office, 1966), pp. 79-82.

10. The author is indebted to David L. Glickman, Economist, Port of New York Authority, for the number of insights which he provided on the numerous considerations involved in the proposal to create a new Department of Transportation.

11. *Establish a Department of Transportation,* pp. 61-63.

12. Ibid., p. 116.

13. Ibid., p. 348.

14. *Creating a Department of Transportation,* Hearings Before the Subcommittee on Government Operations, House of Representatives, 89th Cong., 2d Sess. (Washington, D.C.: U.S. Government Printing Office, 1966), p. 114.

15. Ibid., pp. 233-36. The question of a power squabble over the proposed bill is discussed in "They All Want to Call the Shots," *Business Week* (May 28, 1966), p. 78ff.

16. *Department of Transportation Act,* House Report No. 1701, 89th Cong., 2d Sess. (Washington, D.C.: U.S. Government Printing Office, 1966).

17. *Establish a Department of Transportation,* p. 478.

18. *Wall Street Journal,* May 17, 1966.

19. *Creating a Department of Transportation,* p. 718. Also see *Newsweek* (September 12, 1966), p. 25.

20. See *Establish a Department of Transportation,* p. 88.

21. See *Establishing a Department of Transportation, And for Other Purposes,* U.S. Senate, 89th Cong., 2d Sess., Calendar No. 1627, Report No. 1659 (Washington, D.C.: U.S. Government Printing Office, 1966), p. 6.

22. See particularly the testimony and questioning of Charles M. Haar, Assistant Secretary for Metropolitan Development, HUD, in *Creating a Department of Transportation,* pp. 120-28.

23. *Department of Transportation Act,* pp. 88-89.

24. Ibid., p. 99.

25. See *Creating a Department of Transportation,* p. 599.

26. Public Law 89-670.

27. This general arrangement was confirmed when the President's Reorganization Plan No. 2 of 1968 became effective on July 1, 1968.

28. *Department of Transportation Appropriations for Fiscal Year 1969,* Hearings Before the Subcommittee of the Committee on Appropriations, United States Senate, H.R. 18188, 90th Cong., 2d Sess., (Washington, D.C.: U.S. Government Printing Office, 1968), pp. 36-41.

29. See the *Wall Street Journal,* July 11, 1967. For further background, see the issues of February 28, March 22, and May 2, 1967.

30. *Department of Transportation and Related Agencies Appropriations for 1971,* Hearings Before A Subcommittee of the Committee on Appropriations, House of Representatives, 91st Cong., 2d Sess., (Part 3), (Washington, D.C.: U.S. Government Printing Office, 1970), pp. 650, 922-24.

31. *Department of Transportation and Related Agencies Appropriations for 1972,* (Part 3), pp. 956-59.

32. "Federal Role in Mass Transit Growing Slowly," *Congressional Quarterly Weekly Report,* Vol. 26, No. 23 (June 7, 1968), p. 1399.

33. For a meaningful discussion of the issues involved, see the testimony of Milton Pikarsky, Commissioner of Public Works of the City of Chicago, before the House Appropriations Committee, *Department of Transportation and Related Agencies Appropriations for 1972*, (Part 3), pp. 1067-75.

34. See Grant Miller Davis, *The Department of Transportation*, (Lexington, Massachusetts: Heath Lexington Books, 1970), pp. 143-150.

35. Public Law 91-458.

36. *Department of Transportation and Related Agencies Appropriations*, Senate Hearings Before the Committee on Appropriations for Fiscal Year 1972, H.R. 9667, 92d Cong., 1st Sess. (Washington, D.C.: U.S. Government Printing Office, 1971), pp. 185-91.

37. Hugh S. Norton, "The Department of Transportation – A Study of Organizational Futility," *Public Utilities Fortnightly*, Vol. 78, No. 13 (December 22, 1966), p. 19.

38. See Richard Harwood, "The Sanctity of Pork," *The New Republic*, Vol. 155, No. 18, Issue 2710 (October 29, 1966), p. 7.

39. Richard W. Barsness, "The Department of Transportation: Concept and Structure," *Western Political Quarterly*, Vol. 23, No. 3, September, 1970, pp. 514-15.

40. *Department of Transportation and Related Agencies Appropriations*, Senate Hearings Before the Committee on Appropriations for Fiscal Year 1972, p. 845.

41. "The White House: New Traffic Center?" *Dun's Review and Modern Industry* (May, 1966), p. 231.

Chapter 5
Cost-Benefit Analysis – The Highway Models

1. Herbert Mohring and Mitchell Harwitz, *Highway Benefits: An Analytical Framework* (The Transportation Center, Northwestern University: Northwestern University Press, 1962), p. 3.

2. *Final Report of the Highway Allocation Study*, 87th Cong., 1st Sess., House Document 72 (Washington, D.C.: U.S. Government Printing Office, 1961).

3. Robley Winfrey, "Concepts and Applications of Engineering Economy in the Highway Field," *Highway Research Board Special Report 56*, Economic Analysis in Highway Programming, Location and Design, National Academy of Sciences, National Research Council, 1959, p. 25.

4. Eugene L. Grant, "Concepts and Applications of Engineering Economy," ibid., p. 8. The general theory, concepts and principles have been under development since the nineteenth century. Interestingly enough, these were first applied to problems of railroad development. See *Application of the Principles*

of Engineering Economy to Highway Improvements, Project on Engineering Economic Planning, Institute in Engineering Economic Systems, Stanford University, March, 1964, Foreword, p. iii.

5. Robley Winfrey, *Economic Analysis for Highways* (Scranton, Pennsylvania: International Textbook Company, 1969), pp. 20-21.

6. Charles W. Dale and Robley E. Winfrey, "Application of Highway Engineering Economy," *Highway Research Circular Number 29,* Transportation Economics, National Academy of Sciences, National Research Council, July, 1966.

7. For an excellent discussion of this point, see Eugene L. Grant, "Interest and the Rate of Return on Investments," *Highway Research Board Special Report 56,* pp. 8-9.

8. Ibid., p. 82. In this connection, Grant criticizes the zero interest rate which had been used by the State of California in highway cost-benefit analysis. The impact of this practice may explain in part the magnitude of highway expenditures that this state has made since the end of World War II.

9. American Association of State Highway Officials, *Road User Benefit Analysis for Highway Improvement,* 917 National Press Building, Washington, D.C., 1952.

10. D.W. Loutzenheiser, W.P. Walker and F.H. Green, "Resume of AASHO Report on Road User Benefit Analysis," *Highway Research Board Special Report 56,* p. 36.

11. G.P. St. Clair, T.R. Todd and Thurley A. Bostick, "The Measurement of Vehicular Benefits," *Highway Research Record Number 138,* Highway Finance and Benefits, National Academy of Sciences, National Research Council, 1966, pp. 1-17.

12. John V. Krutilla, "Welfare Aspects of Benefit-Cost Analysis," *Journal of Political Economy,* Vol. 69, No. 3 (June, 1961), p. 226.

13. Edward S. Quade, "Introduction and Overview," *Cost-Effectiveness Analysis,* Thomas A. Goldman, ed. (New York: Frederick A. Praeger, Inc., 1967), p. 18.

14. As Mohring indicates, this involves the question of the opportunity costs of the private passenger vehicle occupants and the interrelationships among volume, density, and travel time. These have seldom been studied systematically. See Herbert Mohring, "Urban Highway Investments," *Measuring Benefits of Government Investments,* Robert Dorfman, ed. (Washington, D.C.: The Brookings Institution, 1965), pp. 242-48. For a discussion of this question as it affects other modes of transportation, see Leon N. Moses and Harold F. Williamson, Jr., "Value of Time, Choice of Mode and the Subsidy Issue in Urban Transportation," *Journal of Political Economy,* Vol. 71, No. 3 (June, 1963), pp. 247-64.

15. Herbert Mohring, "Land Values and the Measurement of Highway Benefits," *Journal of Political Economy,* Vol. 69, No. 3 (June, 1961), p. 248. The approach used was based on empirical regression analysis.

211

16. Charles M. Hummel, "A Criterion Designed to Aid Highway Expenditure Programming," *Highway Research Board Bulletin 249,* Highway Needs and Programming Priorities, National Academy of Sciences, National Research Council, 1964, p. 52. The author concluded that all travel time is the equivalent of the "opportunity cost" of labor time.

17. Paul J. Claffey, "Motor Vehicle Operating and Accident Costs and Benefits Arising from Their Reduction Through Road Improvement," *Highway Research Board Special Report 56,* p. 112. For further discussion of this problem, see C. D. Foster, *The Transport Problem* (London: Blackie and Son, Ltd., 1963), pp. 209-12.

18. Claffey, p. 113.

19. See, for example, G.P. St. Clair and Nathan Lieder, "Evaluation of Unit Cost of Time and Strain and Discomfort Cost of Non-Uniform Driving," *Highway Research Board Special Report 56,* p. 117.

20. David A. Curry, "Use of Marginal Cost of Time in Highway Economy Studies," *Highway Research Record Number 77,* Engineering Economy, National Academy of Sciences, National Research Council, 1963, pp. 99-100.

21. Warren A. Pillsbury, "Economics of Highway Location: A Critique of Collateral Effect Analysis," *Highway Research Record Number 75,* Indirect and Sociological Effects of Highway Location and Improvement, National Academy of Sciences, National Research Council, 1965, p. 54. For a brief analysis of the major concepts underlying this approach, see Burton A. Weisbrod, "Concepts of Costs and Benefits," *Problems in Public Expenditure Analysis,* Samuel B. Chase, Jr., ed. (Washington, D.C.: The Brookings Institution, 1968), pp. 257-62. For a comprehensive review, see A.R. Prest and Ralph Turvey, "Cost-Benefit Analysis: A Survey," *Economic Journal,* Vol. 75 (December, 1965), pp. 683-735. For a recent, highly informative view of analysis recommended for application to non-user consequences, see, "Social and Economic Nonuser Consequences of Highway Improvements," *Summary and Evaluation of Economic Consequences of Highway Improvements,* Robley Winfrey and Carl Zellner, eds., National Cooperative Highway Research Program Report 122, Highway Research Board, Division of Engineering, National Research Council, National Academy of Sciences – National Academy of Engineering, 1971, pp. 109-24.

22. Robert G. Hennes, "Highways As An Instrument of Economic and Social Change," *Highway Research Board Special Report 56,* p. 134.

23. Robert H. Stroup and Louis A. Vargha, "Reflections on Concepts for Impact Research," *Highway Research Board Bulletin 311,* Impact and Implications of Highway Improvement, National Academy of Sciences, National Research Council, 1962, p. 1.

24. Weisbrod, pp. 258-59. As the author and other economists have noted, this distinction may be difficult to make, but it is nonetheless important.

25. For a discussion of these points as they concern urban transportation, see Alan K. Campbell and Jesse Burkhead, "Public Policy for Urban America,"

Issues in Urban Economics, Harvey S. Perloff and Lowdon Wingo, Jr., eds. (Baltimore: The Johns Hopkins Press, for Resources for the Future, Inc., 1968), pp. 603-06.

26. See *Summary and Evaluation of Economic Consequences of Highway Improvements,* pp. 116-17.

27. Edgar M. Horwood, "Community Consequences of Highway Improvement," *Highway Research Record Number 96,* Indirect Effects on Highway Locations and Improvements, National Academy of Sciences, National Research Council, 1965, pp. 1-2.

28. Mark C. Flaherty, "Commercial Highway Service Districts and the Interstate: Their Proper Relationship in an Urban Setting," ibid., p. 8.

29. Walter C. McKain, "Community Response to Highway Improvement," ibid., p. 19.

30. Sidney Goldstein, "Non-User Benefits From Highways," *Highway Research Record Number 20,* Highway Financing, National Academy of Sciences, National Research Council, 1963, p. 167.

31. Roger H. Ashley and William F. Berard, "Interchange Development Along 180 Miles of I-94," *Highway Research Record Number 96,* p. 57. In this survey, all major city interchanges developed high commercial values with service station sites selling from $75,000 to $170,000 and restaurant and motel sites selling for $12,000 per acre.

32. Arthur Maass, "Benefit-Cost Analysis: Its Relevance to Public Investment Decisions," *Quarterly Journal of Economics,* Vol. 80, No. 2 (May, 1966), pp. 208-09.

33. St. Clair, Todd and Bostick, p. 15.

34. E.J. Mishan, *The Costs of Economic Growth* (London: Staples Press, 1967), p. 88.

35. Robert Dorfman, "Introduction," *Measuring Benefits of Government Investments,* p. 2.

36. See *Strategies for the Evaluation of Alternative Transportation Plans,* Edwin N. Thomas and Joseph L. Schofer, eds., National Cooperative Highway Research Program Report 96, Highway Research Board, Division of Engineering, National Research Council, National Academy of Sciences - National Academy of Engineering, 1970, pp. 9-10, 39-40.

37. See ibid., particularly pp. 46-76.

38. See John R. Meyer, "Transportation in the Program Budget," *Program Budgeting,* David Novick, ed. (Washington, D.C.: U.S. Government Printing Office, 1964), p. 127.

39. W. L. Garrison, "Urban Transporting Planning Models in 1975," *Journal of the American Institute of Planners,* Vol. 31, No. 2 (May, 1965), p. 156. Information developed in the "second generation" of models is of course critical to making feasible a systems approach to cost-benefit analysis.

40. Crumlish, for example, observes that there is not complete agreement on whether current transport choices can significantly affect the path of further economic development of a highly developed region. See Joseph D. Crumlish, *Notes on the State-of-the-Art of Benefit-Cost Analysis as Related to Transportation Systems,* U.S. Department of Commerce, National Bureau of Standards, Technical Note 294 (Washington, D.C.: U.S. Government Printing Office, 1966), p. 3.

41. See Morris Hill, "A Goals Achievement Matrix for Evaluating Alternative Plans," *Journal of the American Institute of Planners,* Vol. 34, No. 1 (January, 1968), pp. 19-29.

42. For a brief evaluation of the problems of model building, see Ira S. Lowry, "A Short Course in Model Design," *Journal of the American Institute of Planners,* Vol. 31, No. 2 (May, 1965), pp. 158-65.

Chapter 6
The Policy Implications of Technological Change

1. For further examples, see Richard J. Barber, "Technological Change in American Transportation: The Role of Government Action," *Virginia Law Review,* Vol. 50 (1964), pp. 833-34. Also see Wilfred Owen, "Transport and Technology," *Transport Investment and Economic Development,* Gary Fromm, ed. (Washington, D.C.: The Brookings Institution, Transport Research Program, 1965), pp. 81-88.

2. Wilfred Owen, "Transportation and Technology," *American Economic Review,* Vol. 52, No. 2 (May, 1962), p. 407.

3. Wilfred Owen, Director, Transport Research Organization, The Brookings Institution, Washington, D.C. "Transportation on Earth." Speech Presented at Opening Ceremonies of the Golden Jubilee Convention, Canadian Good Roads Association, Montreal, October 20, 1964, *Vital Speeches,* Vol. 31, No. 10 (March 1, 1965), p. 293.

4. Dr. Paul W. Charington, former Assistant Secretary of Transportation for Policy and International Affairs, Department of Transportation, alluded to the difficulty of asserting federal leadership in making technological advances in highway transportation when the automobile is privately designed and privately produced. See his Remarks Before the Board of Directors, Transport Association of America, Washington, D.C., May 6, 1969.

5. For a discussion of this question as it pertains to urban transportation, see J. R. Meyer, J. F. Kain, and M. Wohl, *The Urban Transportation Problem* (Cambridge, Massachusetts: Harvard University Press, 1965), pp. 309-10.

6. Barber, p. 854.

7. For an excellent discussion of these points, see ibid., pp. 858-63.

8. Danielson, p. 4.

9. For a further analysis of this point, see "Balancing the Books on Transportation," Text of a Presentation by Gordon Murray, U.S. Bureau of the Budget, at the Annual National Transportation Institute, Chicago, Illinois, January 19, 1965.

10. See Semon E. Knudsen, "The Public Selects Its Transportation," Speech Delivered at the Annual Banquet of the Society of Automotive Engineers, Detroit, Michigan, January 15, 1969, *Vital Speeches,* Vol. 35, No. 6 (February 15, 1969), p. 280.

11. An imaginative, theoretical approach to these challenges is provided by C. A. Doxiadis. He stresses the need to determine city size in terms of the time required for movement from place to place and the preservation of all that is of value in our present settlements. See C.A. Doxiadis, "Man's Movement and His City," *Science,* Vol. 162 (October 18, 1968), pp. 326-34.

12. Meyer, Kain, and Wohl, p. 360.

13. *Trends and Projections of Future Population Growth in the United States, With Special Data on Large Urban Regions and Major Metropolitan Areas, For the Period 1970-2000,* Presented to the Ad Hoc Subcommittee on Urban Growth, Committee on Banking and Currency, U.S. House of Representatives, by Jerome P. Pickard, Office of Deputy Undersecretary, U.S. Department of Housing and Urban Development, Washington, D.C., July 22, 1969 (Technical Paper No. 4), p. 4.

14. Ibid., p. 20.

15. It has been estimated, for example, that for every dollar of GNP in the year 2000, there is likely to be 16 ton-miles of intercity freight generated — four times the rate of present freight generation. See Vincent F. Caputo, "The Year 2000," Speech Delivered Before the Transportation and Logistics Forum of the National Defense Transportation Association, New York Hilton Hotel, New York, September 23, 1964, *Vital Speeches,* Vol. 31, No. 1 (October 15, 1964), p. 12.

16. *Department of Transportation and Related Agencies Appropriations for 1972,* (Part 3), p. 772.

17. *Tomorrow's Transportation — New Systems for the Urban Future,* U.S. Department of Housing and Urban Development, Development, Urban Transportation Administration, Washington, D.C., 1968.

18. William F. Hamilton II and Dana K. Nance, "Systems Analysis of Urban Transportation," *Scientific American,* Vol. 221, No. 1 (July, 1969), p. 19. The authors were associated with one of the contractors in the study — General Research Corporation of Santa Barbara, California.

19. Ibid., pp. 28-30.

20. Ibid., pp. 20-22. This dilemma is discussed earlier in this chapter in terms of its influence on the federal role in advancing transportation technology generally.

21. "Proposed: Expensive Gambles," *Science News*, Vol. 93, No. 4 (January 27, 1968), pp. 89-90. Also see "Grasping the Nettle," *Science News*, Vol. 93, No. 26 (June 29, 1968), p. 616.

22. "Toying with Transportation," *Wall Street Journal*, June 21, 1968.

23. Nigel Calder, "Trains For the Seventies," *New Statesman*, Vol. 73, No. 1869 (January 6, 1967), p. 39. For a brief description of hovercraft, see "The Potential and Design of a Hovercar and Hovertrain: Perhaps the Next Important Vehicles to be Used for Long Distance Fast Travel," *Illustrated London News*, Vol. 241 (September 29, 1962), pp. 492-93.

24. Max Gunther, "The Transportation Mess. What's the Solution?" *Saturday Evening Post*, Vol. 241, No. 5 (December 14, 1968), p. 32.

25. "The Year 2000 . . . Rush Hour," *Atlas*, Vol. 15, No. 5 (May, 1968), pp. 42-44.

26. Public Law 89-220.

27. For a discussion of the technical aspects of the application of this approach to the Research and Development program of OHSGT, see Michael L. Yaffee, "Aerospace Technology Filling Major Role in High-Speed Ground Transport Programs," *Aviation Week & Space Technology*, Vol. 89, No. 14 (September 30, 1968), p. 50ff.

28. Claiborne Pell, *Magalopolis Unbound* (New York: Frederick A. Praeger, 1967).

29. *Northeast Corridor Transportation Project – Program Memorandum*, Fiscal Year 1969.

30. *Transportation in the Northeastern Megalopolitan Corridor*, U.S. Executive Office of the President, Task Force Report to an Executive Office Steering Committee, December 10, 1962.

31. *Department of Transportation and Related Agencies Appropriations for 1972*, (Part 3), pp. 505-06.

32. *Recommendations for Northeast Corridor Transportation*, U.S. Department of Transportation, Assistant Secretary for Policy and International Affairs, Office of Systems Analysis and Information, Strategic Planning Division, Vols. 1-3, September, 1971.

33. For an excellent discussion of this problem, see *Survey of Technology for High Speed Ground Transport*, Prepared for the United States Department of Commerce, Washington D.C. Under Contract C-85-65 by the Massachusetts Institute of Technology, Cambridge, Massachusetts, June 15, 1965.

34. The subject of research and development and capital costs for urban transit will be examined further in the next chapter.

35. See Edward N. Hall, "Central Elements of a National Transportation System," *High Speed Ground Transportation Journal*, Vol. II, No. 1 (January, 1968), p. 95. The author notes that the major characteristic of transportation systems of the future will be diffuse origins and destinations and trip lengths under 100 miles.

Policy Issues and Technology
Chapter 7

1. The KC 135 was developed for the Air Force as a jet tanker. The expense of its development was borne by the federal government as part of the military budget.

2. Near the height of their ascendancy in 1967, the 60 major aerospace companies of the nation had sales exceeding $25 billion, 80 percent of which were to the federal government.

3. *First Annual Report,* (Part II), Fiscal Year 1967, Department of Transportation (Washington, D.C.: U.S. Government Printing Office, 1968), p. 52.

4. *Department of Transportation and Related Agencies Appropriations for 1971,* Hearings Before a Subcommittee of the Committee on Appropriations, House of Representatives, 91st Cong., 2d Sess. (Part 2). (Washington, D.C.: U.S. Government Printing Office, 1970), pp. 550-51.

5. "Airlines Appear to be Diverging in Degrees of Support for SST," *Aviation Week & Space Technology,* Vol. 90, No. 7 (February 17, 1969), p. 25.

6. "SST Study Yields Negative View," *Aviation Week & Space Technology,* Vol. 90, No. 12 (March 24, 1969), p. 29; and "Pressure Grows to Delay SST Prototype," Vol. 90, No. 13 (March 31, 1969), p. 29.

7. Senator Warren G. Magnuson has been one of the chief advocates of this point of view. See *The New York Times,* May 21, 1968.

8. These efforts have led to development of towboats with 9,000 hp, which can handle 40 barges carrying 40,000 tons of freight. See Barber, pp. 842-43.

9. See ibid., pp. 847-49.

10. Locklin, pp. 830-31. Also see Martin Farris, "Transportation Cooperative and Coordinated Services," *Arizona Business Bulletin,* Vol. 15, No. 4 (April, 1968), pp. 82-85. More recently, the term "balanced" has come to replace "coordinated" to convey the broader concept.

11. Doyle Report, p. 653. "Piggyback" usually refers to the movement of highway trailers on railroad flatcars. A more traditional reference is "trailer on flatcar" (TOFC).

12. Ibid., p. 654.

13. Philip Duriez, "Rail-Motor Rate Competition — The T.O.F.C. Experience," *Transportation Journal* (Fall, 1967), p. 35.

14. For background on the issues which have evolved on this point over the last 25 years, see ibid., pp. 35-40; William J. Cunningham, "Correlation of Rail and Highway Transportation," *American Economic Review,* Vol. 24, No. 1 (March, 1934), pp. 45-52; "TOFC: A Coordinated Transportation Service," Martin T. Farris and Paul T. McElhiney, eds., *Modern Transportation: Selected Readings* (Boston: Houghton-Mifflin Company, 1967), pp. 356-61.

15. W. J. Barta, "Water-Rail Coordination," Speech Delivered at American Society of Traffic and Transportation, University of Indiana, Bloomington, Indiana, September 6, 1967, *Vital Speeches,* Vol. 34, No. 1 (October 15, 1967), pp. 5-6; Charles E. Walker, "Rail-Water Coordination," Speech Delivered to the Nebraska Transportation Institute, University of Nebraska, Lincoln, Nebraska, May 14, 1968, *Vital Speeches,* Vol. 35, No. 2 (November 1, 1968), pp. 63-64.

16. Whitney Gillilland, "CAB Co-ordination of Unlike Modes of Transportation," *Public Utilities Fortnightly,* Vol. 76, No. 5 (September 2, 1965), pp. 15-26.

17. *Container Shipping: Full Ahead,* A Forecast of How Containerization of Oceanborne Foreign Trade Will Develop by 1975, and Its Effect on the New York-New Jersey Port, The Port of New York Authority, May, 1967, p. 21. Also see "Containers: The Boom Begins," *Dun's Review and Modern Industry,* Vol. 87, No. 5 (May, 1966), pp. 113-14.

18. "Containers: The Boom Begins," p. 114. The size agreed upon is 8 ft. x 8 ft. x 20 ft.; 30 ft.; 40 ft.

19. *Department of Transportation and Related Agencies Appropriations for 1972,* (Part 3), pp. 993-1000.

20. Harold F. Hammond, "The New Age of Transportation Coordination," *Traffic Quarterly,* Vol. 21, No. 4 (October, 1967), p. 501.

21. Ibid., p. 515.

22. "Airlines Watch Metroliner Traffic," *Aviation Week & Space Technology,* Vol. 90, No. 13 (March 31, 1969), p. 26

23. Doyle Report, pp. 221-22. Also see "Trucks, Trains, Planes, Boats, All in One Company?", pp. 118-19.

24. William H. Tucker, pp. 47-53.

25. For a fuller discussion of these aspects of modally-based mergers versus integrated transportation companies, see Kent T. Healy, "The Merger Movement in Transportation," *American Economic Review* (May, 1962), pp. 436-44; Lee J. Melton, Jr., "Transport Coordination and Regulatory Philosophy," *Law and Contemporary Problems,* Vol. 24 (1959), pp. 622-41; Peter T. Beardsley; "Integrated Ownership of Transportation Companies and the Public Interest," *George Washington Law Review,* Vol. 31 (1962-63), pp. 85-97; Eugene T. Liipfert, "Consolidation and Competition in Transportation: The Need for an Effective and Consistent Policy," *George Washington Law Review,* Vol. 31 (1962-63), pp. 108-25; George W. Wilson, "The Goals of Transportation Policy," pp. 21-22.

26. George L. Buland and Frederick E. Fuhrman, "Integrated Ownership: The Case for Removing Existing Restrictions on Common Ownership of the Several Forms of Transportation," *George Washington Law Review,* Vol. 31 (1962-63), p. 184.

    27. Dael Wolfle, "Barriers to Innovations," *Science,* Vol. 150, No. 3694 (October 15, 1965), p. 295.

    28. Hugh S. Norton, "Influence of Innovation on Transport Competition: Two Cases," *Transportation Journal,* Vol. 6, No. 1 (Fall, 1966), p. 40.

    29. Danielson, p. 185.

    30. For a brief discussion of the dimensions of this problem, see Frank L. Hendrix, "Federal Transport Statistics: An Analysis," *Transport Journal,* Vol. 5, No. 1 (Fall, 1965), pp. 6-10.

    31. *Congressional Record,* 92d Cong., 2d Sess. (Senate), Vol. 118, No. 31 (Washington, D.C.: U.S. Government Printing Office, March 2, 1972), p. S 3104.

    32. For an excellent coverage of the pros and cons of the issue, see ibid., pp. S 3102-23.

    33. *Department of Transportation and Related Agencies Appropriations for 1972,* (Part 3), pp. 248-51.

Chapter 8
Perspective on National Transportation Policy

    1. *A Guide to the 1972 National Transportation Needs Study,* Office of Systems Analysis and Information, Office of the Secretary of Transportation (Washington, D.C.: January 8, 1971), pp. 1-2.

Index

About The Author

Herman Mertins, Jr. is Director of the Public Administration Program at West Virginia University and Associate Professor of Political Science. He earned his A.B. at Drew University in Madison, New Jersey and his master's degree and Ph.D. in public administration at the Maxwell Graduate School of Syracuse University.

Dr. Mertins' career includes thirteen years of experience with the Port of New York Authority, during which he held a number of positions, including that of Assistant to the Director of Planning and Development.

He has published a number of articles on the subjects of intergovernmental relations, public budgeting, and transportation policy. Most recently he coedited a book-length special symposium on "Changing Styles of Planning in Post-Industrial America" that made up the May/June, 1971 issue of the *Public Administration Review*. He is presently editor of a symposium that will appear in the *Review* in early 1973. It will be devoted to the significance of transportation planning to public administration.

205 — Drugs /